LOVE ONE ANOTHER

LOVE ONE ANOTHER

by

RAOUL FOLLEREAU

Translated by
BARBARA WALL

LONDON · BURNS & OATES
IN ASSOCIATION WITH
THE RAOUL FOLLEREAU FOUNDATION
FOR THE FIGHT AGAINST LEPROSY

BURNS & OATES LIMITED
25 Ashley Place, London S.W.1.

First published 1968

This is a translation of La seule vérité, c'est de s'aimer, 3 vols. (*Flammarion, Paris, 1966*).

Made and printed in Great Britain by
Billing & Sons Limited
Guildford and London

THESE RECOLLECTIONS AND TESTIMONIES
I DEDICATE TO YOU,
THE 1,500,000 YOUNG MEN AND WOMEN
FROM 105 COUNTRIES
WHO JOINED WITH ME IN ASKING FOR
A DAY OF WAR FOR PEACE,
IN FULL CONFIDENCE THAT ONE DAY
YOU WILL TAKE UP THE TORCH AGAIN.

CONTENTS

ILLUSTRATIONS

(Between pages 134 and 135)

ix

Part One

NO ONE HAS THE RIGHT TO BE HAPPY ALONE

I
EARLY YEARS

FORTY FIGHTING YEARS alone, or almost alone, at first. I've travelled two million kilometres, two-thirds of them by plane; visited two hundred countries; crossed and re-crossed frontiers a thousand times; and I've distributed two milliards of francs (i.e. old francs) to the victims of leprosy. That has been my life. So the time has now come to take stock and remember; and if I am to inspire other and younger people, so that when my heart stops beating other hearts may beat with the same rhythm, then I must take stock and remember out loud.

I think my earliest passion – and it was a proud and jealous one – was for freedom. And I've worn something that bears witness to this all my life, or rather, something that symbolizes it – a symbol often viewed as misplaced, if not arrogant. But after so many years it will surely be treated with indulgence, if only for the perseverance it displays.

I'm referring, of course, to my tie – the large floppy bow that I've sported for fifty years and which has seemed to flout public opinion. Originally it was a protest against one of the many servitudes to which we submit – the sartorial one.

One day Mussolini asked aggressively, "Why such a showy tie? It doesn't go down in Italy."

In no better mood than the Duce, I replied, "I've often asked myself that question, and you've just given me my answer. It's the most certain individual liberty that still remains to me."

He took this in good part, and laughed.

My dear old tie has often been laughed at, together with its wearer. It has made me ridiculous in the eyes of conformists. But consenting to be ridiculed over a period of fifty years has given me strength.

I acquired this taste for loyalty to an unusual fashion from a man whose memory is infinitely dear to me. He was a great poet with a noble heart – Edmond Rostand. It was during the 1914

3

war. The death of de Guynemer had "inspired" me to write a sonnet (?), and at the proud age of fourteen I'd had the impertinence to send it to him. The memory still horrifies me fifty years later – horrifies me and embarrasses me, for the poet paid me the outstanding compliment of replying.

A sonnet, as everyone knows, has fourteen lines. Mine had fourteen mistakes which Edmond Rostand pointed out, contriving meanwhile (such was the magic of his heart) to commend me for them. I was overcome. Today I am still more overcome. If he had rebuffed me perhaps my dawning vocation, frail and groping as it was, would have been extinguished, and I would have become I don't know what. I might even have become rich, and then Jean Mermoz would have said of me what I have heard him say of former companions-in-arms who have settled down and become fat and comfortable: "They have destroyed themselves."

I owe Edmond Rostand my respect for the young and my constant concern not to impair their ideal. Like everyone else, I had danced with joy for *Cyrano*, though it was *Chanticler* that I found the more fruitful, and my heart still quickens half a century later as it did when I read for the first time:

> *C'est la nuit qu'il est beau de croire à la lumière.*[1]

And this sublime yet humble profession of faith:

> . . . *Mais si je chante, exact, sonore, et si, sonore*
> *Exact, bien après moi, pendant longtemps encore,*
> *Chaque ferme a son Coq qui chante dans sa cour,*
> *Je crois qu'il n'y aura plus de nuit!*
>
> > *Quand!*
> >
> > > *Un jour!*[2]

Thus words became beacons for me.

*   *   *

Buenos Aires, Pacheco aerodrome. My wife and I were going to cross the Cordilleras of the Andes for the first time – a flight that would be our baptism of the air. We were both twenty-six. As a

---

[1] It's at night that it's so good to believe in light.

[2] . . . But if I sing, true, clear, and if long after me and for a long time each farm has its Cock which sings true and clear in its farmyard, then I think that there will be no more night! When? One day!

great favour the airmail service had agreed to give us places on this very light aircraft (a Potez 25, if I remember rightly), at that time trying to plot an ideal course in the sky above the Andes. Near the plane, which seemed to us so frail, so absurd, stood a tall young man with wavy wind-blown hair, and blue eyes that seemed to see beyond the horizon. This was Jean Mermoz.

The journey was to consist of two stages, the first – from Buenos Aires to Mendoza – being a simple flight over the Pampas. Yet Mermoz seemed uneasy, and I heard his calm voice giving orders: "Warn the emergency landing-grounds of Soler and Mercédès. Oh yes, and put a spotlight under the plane."

Whereupon I made the stupid and arrogant remark: "Why all these precautions? After all, we only die once."

Jean Mermoz turned his eyes towards me. He didn't look at me so much as scrutinize me, and he said in the same level voice: "It's not a question of dying, but of getting there."

I've never been so ashamed of myself. But I understood how grateful I should feel: he had taught me what was meant by duty; taught me too that for those who carry a message, or the mail, courage sometimes has to be daily heroism.

. . . Mermoz, too, sometimes wore a flowing tie, as if he also had some dream to conceal . . ..

*   *   *

My other "eccentricity", less unusual but to which I am just as attached, is my walking-stick.

It was given me by my mother on my twentieth birthday and was topped by a bear's head which she had had specially carved. This was a tender and witty reprimand, for ever since my youth I had been too taken up with social questions to interest myself in "good society", and this had earned me a reputation to which my cane knob bore eloquent if silent witness. For more than forty years this bear has never left me; nowhere or in any circumstances. The friction of my hand, repeated hundreds of thousands of times, has slowly worn down the ivory ears, and thus my fierce if jovial bear has, in growing older, become a dog. This is as it should be, for he has always displayed the best of the virtues, loyalty.

Shortly after he became Pope, John XXIII did me the honour of receiving me in private audience. He had already chaired my lectures five times, in Paris and Rheims (when he was Nuncio) and later as Cardinal in Venice, and he had always shown me great and radiant kindness.

I was kneeling when he entered the room. Without saying a word he placed himself in front of me and looked at me questioningly, while I waited in bewilderment. He was obviously worried because something was missing, and then, as I saw from his eyes, he realized what it was. "But where's your stick?" he asked. My tie he had noticed at once, against protocol as it perhaps was. But where was my cane and the bear turned dog?

"Over in the corner," I explained. "Your Holiness probably remembers that I can't get up without it."

"This time," said good Pope John, "I'll be the one to help you," and he held out his arms to me.

I have known four Popes.

Pius XI received me on the eve of my first visit to South America. He had a stern face, a soul of rock and a heart of fire. Pius XII I knew as Nuncio and then as Secretary of State; he always showed enlightened sympathy for my work and, when necessary, active friendship. John XXIII has now been taken to everyone's heart. Of Paul VI, to whom all hearts are opening and who, in his Bombay speech, resoundingly reinforced my United Nations appeal, "A Day of War for Peace", I shall have occasion to speak again.

*   *   *

And while I am calling up these delightful figures from the past, let me not forget the strangest of them all: Gabriele d'Annunzio. He seemed to me then, and still seems to me in retrospect, totally amazing.

I'd been told that he never answered his fan mail, either from men or women; that he locked these letters up in a room he called "the tomb", unread and often unopened. So by what chance did he open mine, read the poem it contained, and so discover how much I longed to meet him? It's a mystery which those near to him have assured me is insoluble. The fact remains that one day I received an invitation from him. As I was about to be married, my fiancée and I decided to make this visit – "pilgrimage" as I romantically called it to myself – our honeymoon.

He received me alone, while my wife sat serenely in front of the Vittoriale. A white-clad *carabiniere* in full uniform led me into this weird and whimsical palace – but my heart was beating too fast for me to take it in. I remember that I had to climb steps, cross great rooms, go along corridors. It all seemed huge and endless. Although it was the middle of the day, windows were shut and shutters closed, turning everything into mysterious twilight. Finally we arrived outside a door which opened. "Bend your head," whispered my guide, who then vanished. This wasn't a valedictory greeting but a warning, for the door was low.

The room to which it gave access was cluttered up with an amazing and exotic bric-à-brac, in the midst of which was a small man, balder and more clean-shaven than seemed possible, and with a slight *embonpoint*. He stood up, moved forward, opened his arms. "Kiss me," he said. That was my first encounter with Gabriele d'Annunzio.

Though the poet and hero, both then and later, left me with marvellous memories, it wasn't he who conquered me in the end but the region where he had chosen to situate his mysteriously-planned palace. Gardone, with its charm and beauty, its lake and cypresses, its olive-trees and rose-laurels, was to become for us the image of an earthly Paradise. We were fanatical devotees, and then habitués, of the place. Forty years later I had the joy of being made an honorary citizen of the town where I had cherished so many dreams and formed so many friendships. D'Annunzio had also been given this title. Thus as an older man I returned to the Vittoriale and rediscovered the faith and fervour of my youth – if they had ever left me . . . .

* * *

The good fairy who watched over my youthful hopes lived in a legendary château near Evian. She was known as "the good duchess" in the neighbourhood, though her real title was Royal Highness and she signed her name simply but proudly as "Henriette, Belgique-Vendôme". She was sister to the Belgian King Albert I. I can't remember by what good fortune I came to know her, but she watched over my youthful hopes and ambitions and became a friend and counsellor, infinitely patient, attentive and loving. I vividly remember my visits to Tourronde (the name of her château) and her chapel where she always made me kneel beside her ("It was King Albert's place," she whispered)

B

and the delightful hours at her table or in the garden. It was owing to her encouragement that I was able to begin my life-work at an age when usually you aren't yet taken seriously.

One day during the war we arrived at the château in a sort of carrier-tricycle that some helpful man had offered to drive for us. I described our means of conveyance to her and she came out on to the road to see it. She took hold of the handlebars and was about to mount it when her majordomo arrived on the scene, protesting, "Your Royal Highness! . . ." Whereupon she desisted as if caught out doing something naughty, then suddenly burst out laughing – a laugh as clear and pure as her soul.

Since this dear princess departed, we have often recalled her sweetness and kindness with King Leopold and Queen Marie-José; and more recently with that couple as noble and radiant as she was, King Baudouin and Queen Fabiola.

*   *   *

It was on 14 April 1928 that my poetry was first read at a Comédie-Française "poetry afternoon". I was inordinately pleased with myself, as can be imagined, as I was not yet twenty-five.

I owed this favour to another excellent friend, Madeleine Roch, the princess of poetry.

I and my companions, our ties flowing in the wind, had crowded into the box lent us by the Minister of Education, and it was with pounding hearts that we listened to the famous tragic actress recite – or rather, make her own – my first out-pourings towards Love.

> *Je sais qu'il nous faudra souffrir, combattre encore,*
> *Mais que se lève un jour où tout le genre humain*
> *Rebâtira l'autel de l'amour que j'adore,*
> *Je crois qu'une nouvelle aurore*
> *Se lèvera demain . . .*[1]

Afterwards we all went and dined in a café on the Place de la République. It cost 5 francs 50, and we had a lot for our money.

---

[1] *Le Livre d'Amour* (1922):
> I know that we must fight and suffer yet more,
> But may the day dawn when all the human race
> Shall rebuild the altar of love that I adore,
> I believe that a new dawn
> Shall rise tomorrow.

Then in a first-floor room reserved for meetings, Madeleine Roch recited poems till late at night – not only real poems, but also mine and my friends'. Now my twenty years have tripled, and also the prices at that little restaurant. And as I write these words about my great friend, now dead, I recall the miserable lines that she loved so much; perhaps she knew I was trying to express, though so falteringly, what was to become the golden rule of my life:

> *On doit avoir au coeur une force admirable*
> *Lorsqu'on est sûr du bien qu'on fait.*
>
> . . . . . .
>
> *On ne comprendra pas notre idéal? Qu'importe!*
> *Les quolibets pleuvront, lâches et dénigrants?*
> *Courage, amis! La lutte n'est jamais trop forte,*
> *Le rêve n'est jamais trop grand!*
>
> . . . . . .
>
> *Car la plus douce et la plus noble récompense*
> *Lorsqu'à se battre un contre cent on s'est usé*
> *C'est de relire au fond de notre coeur brisé*
> *Ces mots qu'en lettres d'or grava la conscience:*
> *"Je ne t'ai jamais méprisé."*[1]

When Madeleine Roch died, I was in Santiago, Chile.

Many years later another actor, as great in talent as he is noble in heart, in his turn leant the force and prestige of his remarkable voice to my dreams and aspirations. This was Pierre Fresnay. For when he had finished the film *St Vincent de Paul*, Pierre Fresnay laid aside the saint's external trappings but retained M. Vincent's

---

[1] We ought to have excellent strength in our hearts
When we are sure of the good we are doing.

. . . . . .

They won't understand our ideal? What does it matter!
Gibes will pour down, cowardly and insulting?
Courage, my friends! The struggle is never too bitter,
The dream never too great!

. . . . . .

For the sweetest and noblest recompense
When we are worn out fighting one against a hundred
Is to read in the depths of our broken heart
These words engraved in golden letters by the conscience:
"I have never despised you."

heart, which he puts every year at the service of our struggle with a devotion and generosity that dazzle me more and more as time goes by.

Early hopes and first steps

I was twenty when I wrote the lines that Madeleine Roch declaimed at the Théâtre Français, but they reflected a concern and voiced a hope that had existed much earlier. I was fifteen when I gave my first lecture in my native town, Nevers. It was organized for the benefit of the Little Sisters of the Poor and had as title: "God is Love". There is one quality that no one will deny me, and that's perseverance.

I have no intention of telling the story of my life. This has been excellently told already – by Elisée Servigne, my chief collaborator and friend, in *L'homme qui embrasse les lépreux*, and by Juliette Goublet, whose mind and heart are of the highest quality, in *Raoul Follereau, pourquoi?* All I want to do in evoking these memories is to prove to myself that I have been true to myself.

As far back as I can remember I nursed the desire to be able "to help others to live." At fifteen this desire made me seem naïve and rash, and even, perhaps, pretentious: witness my tie. While putting this book together I read the booklet I published in 1926 called *Du Soleil sur les roses* – a title that appealed to me at the time. In it, I gave orders to God (at twenty, that's normal enough!):

. . . . . .

> *Dites-nous: "je pardonne", afin qu'on puisse aimer,*
> *Criez-nous: "aimez-vous", afin qu'on puisse vivre.*[1]

In a poem dated 1924 I asserted myself vigorously . . . as a peacemaker:

> *Et si dans sa folie atroce et volontaire*
> *Un homme veut un jour, pour voir couler le sang,*
> *Mettre le feu aux quatre bornes de la terre,*
> *Tu te lèveras, menaçant,*

---

[1] Tell us: "I forgive," in order that we may love,
  Shout to us: "love each other", in order that we may live.

Pour étouffer la guerre,
O mon beau rêve blanc. . . .[1]

In *La lumière qui meurt* I proudly declared:

. . . *l'âme n'est pas à vendre,*
Je n'ai rien, mais je suis à moi seul, et mon coeur
Saura, le jour venu, succomber en vainqueur.[2]

These sentiments will perhaps seem naïve. So much the worse
for me. I feel no desire whatever to disown them.

My first poems were a clumsy expression of the ideal that would
inspire my whole life. In 1929 I published *Rédemption*:

Il n'y a pas de trop grands rêves:
Marche encore, ne t'arrête pas.
L'orgueil de vivre haut est la vertu suprême,
Et ton seul refuge est amour.[3]

Then in 1933 *Iles de Miséricorde*:

Pardonnez-moi, mon Dieu,
de n'avoir rien compris de cette vie,
parce que l'Amour m'a manqué.[4]

In his warm and generous book, Elisée Servigne recalls some
lines that I wrote when I was about twenty:

To those who have never suffered, we want to speak of those
who suffer. . . .

. . . The true criminals of life are these: those who say Me,
always Me.

. . . We must shout the truth to the world.

---

[1] And if in his atrocious and wilful folly
A man one day wants, so as to see blood flow,
To set fire to the four corners of the earth,
    You will rise up, threatening,
    To put a stop to the war
    O my lovely white dream . . .
[2]   . . . . the soul is not for sale,
I possess nothing, but I belong only to myself, and my heart
Shall be able, when the time comes, to succumb as conqueror.
[3] No hopes are too great:
March forward still, don't stop.
The pride of aiming high is the supreme virtue,
And your only refuge is love.
[4] Forgive me, my God,
for having understood nothing of this life,
because I have lacked Love.

. . . To live, is to enable to live. We must create other
happinesses in order to be happy.

Thirty years later, remarks Elisée Servigne, he (i.e. myself)
added the fruits of experience to his thought – the experience of
a man who had brought some small elements of his dream down
to earth – and revealed his finest secret in the phrase:

Happiness is the only thing that, having given it, one is sure
to possess.
The world is hungry for corn and love.
Let's work.

Talking, singing, crying, denouncing – all that is nothing, and
sometimes worse than nothing, if it's a pretext for not doing.

The League for Latin Union

It's because Christianity seemed to me the very incarnation of
my dreams of brotherhood that I founded the League for Latin
Union under the honorary presidency of the Duchess of Vendôme.
Its aim was defined thus: "to defend Christian civilization against
all paganisms and all barbarities". It will be seen that work was
not likely to be lacking.

When I started public speaking I did as everyone else: I wrote
my speeches out. I found this difficult but it gave me more confidence. However this practice didn't last long – to be exact it
lasted until 2 October 1930, when I had to make a speech in the
large amphitheatre of the Sorbonne. I was twenty-seven and it was
the first time I had entered this amphitheatre other than as a
member of the audience.

The meeting had been organized by the League for Latin Union
and Raymond Poincaré had agreed to take the chair. In fact he was
ill and had to stand down at the last moment, and his place was
taken by the president, André Tardieu. If I remember rightly, at
least two ministers were on the platform – Eugène Lautier and
Gaston Gérard – as well as a good part of the South American
diplomatic corps, as this was the continent concerned. All this was
a bit overwhelming for an "orator" of my age, and I had written,
re-written and re-written again a lyrical and forceful text satisfying
to my youthful vanity.

The dreaded hour arrived, and with my sheets of paper spread out in front of me, I began. I imagine I hesitated a bit at first, but soon gained confidence. And soon my confidence went too far, my voice became louder, my gestures more sweeping – in fact too sweeping, much too sweeping. For I wasn't watching the tumbler of water which, with a superb wave of my arm, I sent flying (and how much water it held!) over my sheets of paper which promptly became unreadable, and even over the trousers of my neighbour in the chair.

He didn't bat an eyelid, but merely whispered: "It doesn't matter; go on." Go on . . . and that was indeed what I had to do. I shut my eyes and plunged in – and all went well, a fact confirmed both by my neighbours and the audience. So ever since that day I have never written out a speech in advance (an unhoped for excuse for my laziness!).

With the aim of spreading our message, arousing consciences, and promoting affiliated or parallel action, I then undertook almost incessant journeys, either just with my wife or accompanied by a delegation of our first members.

Belgium, Italy, Spain, Portugal, Switzerland, Austria, Hungary, Bulgaria, Rumania, Czechoslovakia and Poland welcomed us and listened to us, as did the American countries of the West Indies, Brazil, Uruguay, the Argentine, Chile, Peru, Colombia and Bolivia. Indeed the youth of these countries was responding warmly to our call when the war overtook us while we were in Rio de Janeiro.

The return to France in a boat neither convoyed nor camouflaged, and which went at a very modest speed and had no defences, is a story in itself, and one that nearly finished as a tragedy as the ship's commander went mad in mid-ocean. On this astonishing and dramatic trip I acquired a friend who is still very dear to me: Pierre Blainville. We were drawn together by the hours we spent together and the dangers we shared. For the past twenty-five years he has been a member of our administrative council.

*　　*　　*

But before I close this first chapter of reminiscences so as to give place to the documents that will complete them, I ought in truth to write a few lines more.

My greatest good fortune

The greatest good fortune of my life has been my wife.

When we decided to marry our ages added up to thirty. Our parents were wise, and smiled. Nearly fifty years have passed, and now it's we who smile. I have never made a single journey without her. She has accompanied me to all the leper colonies of the world. She has always been my support and often my consolation.

I confess that I found it hard to control my annoyance when a good woman said to her, with a hint of ill-concealed envy: "All the same, you go on wonderful trips." My wife smiled, without replying.

Perhaps she was thinking of that night we spent in the heart of Bolivia in a hut that some Quichuas Indians had lent us. Suddenly she was struck with an attack of appendicitis, and we were a thousand kilometres from the nearest doctor. In the moonless night I could just see her, bent double, and I heard her groan, having nothing to protect her with but a jammed revolver the stub of a candle, and three matches. I had the strange and rather frightening impression, in that oppressive darkness, that my hair (I was thirty) was turning white.

Or perhaps she was thinking of the evening when the engine of our open boat stopped in the middle of the Amazon, and we tried (the sky was rent by lightning) to row to the shore with food-tins as oars. Finally we got bogged in the reeds quivering beneath the flight of mosquitoes and where huge caymans had established their dormitory.

Or of that other night that I had forgotten but of which I have just been reminded in glancing through my travel diaries. We were in a remote corner of Kasaï. My diary says: "Last night we both had high fevers. All night through we lay side by side, delirious. But our ravings were so different that we couldn't understand each other. 'What are you saying? I don't understand. Try . . .' And each of us withdrew again along our secret path, hostile, inaccessible. It was an appalling ordeal."

But the next day, in the morning, we set out again.

Two people together are invincible.

My greatest riches

My greatest riches have been my friends.

I shall never find adequate words to tell them what I think of them. In the course of nearly forty years they have never failed me, not once. Now that I am in all honesty taking stock of my life, it is to them that my thoughts turn, to their understanding, help and love.

My thoughts turn to that woman friend who doesn't want to be mentioned by name, who for more than a quarter of a century and with total self-abnegation and devotion has typed the best part of my letters, outside office hours, with no reward but having to put up with the uneven temper of an additional and exacting "boss".

To my secretary who, though ill and bowed down with work and cares, has for thirteen years travelled two hours in the train and two on the métro daily so as to be there; an example of loyalty and courage.

To that other woman friend who for years has addressed envelopes and wrappers at her house; and to the one who is in charge of the filing.

To my dear friend Alphonse Nockels, recently dead, who in 1965 celebrated his eightieth birthday and the thirty-third anniversary of his "commitment" to our struggle, to which he devoted his heart, his strength and his life in Luxembourg.

To my dear friend Major Angus-Jones whom I met shortly after the war at a conference at Sables-d'Olonne, and who thereafter and for years dedicated himself to our work in England and founded "The Order of Charity".

Without forgetting – how could I? – Amalia Filia, whom the lepers of Greece called "Mademoiselle Follereau", a "niece" by vocation, who in her own country pursues the battle against leprosy with a faith and self-abnegation so delightfully infectious that her husband, "Papa Nico", and all her friends were luckily "contaminated", pending the time when my three "great-nephews" will take up the cause.

And there are plenty of others.

Real tramps

Some months before the war I published a series of articles in our bulletin, *L'Oeuvre latine*, which were hardly of a kind to be generally pleasing. Their title was "Hitler, the face of Antichrist".

Not surprisingly, when the Nazis arrived in Paris they showed some interest. However, as I was under arms like everyone else,

I wasn't at home. Nor was my wife, who was trying to join me on the roads of the exodus.

There then started another period of travel. The distances were less great but considerably more difficult to traverse.

I found her in a village in the Creuse. She had managed to salvage a card-index containing the addresses of our best friends: her only treasure, but *what* treasure – for it enabled us to build up a battalion of the faithful, a battalion which quickly became a small army.

At first we found shelter and comfort with a herbalist in the rue du Grand-Moulin, Saint-Etienne. The herbalist was a poet with a generous heart and he kept us for months. For years Michel Ramaud and his wonderful silent wife looked after my correspondence in the unoccupied zone, while Léon Cordonnier, general-secretary of the League for Latin Union, spent the last weeks of his life keeping up contacts in Paris with a view to the tasks that lay ahead. Both these men are now dead, but they will always have a place in my heart.

After Saint-Etienne, we sought refuge in a little village in the Ardèche: Lamastre. It was from there in 1943 that I launched the appeal for the "Hour for the Poor". We had some months of relative peace at Lamastre, but when the situation became more difficult, then positively threatening, we had to move on.

Bourg-en-Bresse. Occupation, denunciation, powerlessness; for some, despair. At 4 rue Lalande, in the office of a young journalist, Raymond Guerrin, I used to draw up and launch my other appeals for hope and charity.

Every evening we set out in the car – General Desmazes, Raymond Guerrin, Louis Milot, my wife and I. Every evening we preached our brotherly crusade in some corner of the land, so as to sow confidence and kindle hope; in far-away villages, in icy rooms, and with the constant threat of having to move on. Every evening. The General spoke first, and this was a clarion-call to shake up consciences – he was simple, sober, but throbbing. A hundred people, sometimes two hundred, often less, applauded us. And then back we went to the Hôtel de la Poste where matchless friends were waiting for us.

In Raymond Guerrin I had found a brother; while at the Hôtel de la Poste, with Madame Alby and her daughters, we had found another family. And then one day – it hardly seemed possible – we had to separate, without ceasing to be united.

For me it was the dear Sisters of Our Lady of the Apostles in the suburbs of Lyons. It was a safe hiding-place – too soft. For General Desmazes it was Dachau. We then discovered that he was General Delestraint's adjutant. We understood why he had made certain journeys and the heroic part he had played in France's resurrection.

It was in this last refuge that I started – and it was to be a life-long commitment – the "Battle against Leprosy" about which I shall speak later. But before describing the circumstances, and recalling the first stages, I want to take stock of this period of my life. For it was during these years of exile and – to some extent – flight that I embarked on most of my life's enterprises. They were to constitute at first – and by the very dates of their successive births – so many messages of hope. I wrote about them in a small pamphlet which appeared in 1948 under the title of *La Charité sauvera le monde* (Charity will save the world). I shall quote from it later on, without changing a comma.

* * *

Appeals, projects, proposals – they were numerous and various. They were like the good seed spoken of in the parable (without comparing myself–please God–to the Sower!). Some flourished and brought forth fruit, such as the "Hour for the Poor." Others have found foster parents with more zeal than memory. What does it matter! Others again never saw the day; but are they dead for that?

If I mention them here it is because I am thinking of all you young people to whom I have dedicated these reminiscences. You are the 1,500,000 who signed my appeal to the U.N. Which of you will bring those causes back to life?

If I quote dates it isn't with a childish desire to play the prophet, but so as to give my appeals their exact context and significance.

In blood, lies and tragedy our dream of Latin Union had just collapsed (we are coming back to it today, but it's a bit late). Nothing remained of our hopes and efforts but bitterness and ruin. We had to build again; first in our own hearts, in secret, for ourselves. Rebuild a store of hope within ourselves, so as to prepare, in the great wilderness of horror that Europe then was, the future victory of man.

So it was from that little village in the Ardèche that I sent out my first appeal.

RE-CASTING MAN AS A HUMAN BEING

YESTERDAY the world was in flames and the hideous fire is still smouldering today. The world, having been martyred, terrorized and drenched in blood for five years, is at a loss to how to find its way again. It certainly wants peace. But everyone wants *his own peace*, peace as he conceives of it, as if any one nation were free in the world as it is today and able to dispose of its destiny single-handed. . . .

What is there for us to lean on? Progress? But we have seen that progress is an immense machine for slaughter. Human reason? But human reason has been debased, degraded, crushed underfoot. For five years man led mankind to suicide; the common grave has been the goal of his action; he has used his strength and his resources to kill and kill again, and to learn to dispense with pity.

Nevertheless men must now find each other again, recognize each other, join each other. Over and above the self-interested coalitions arranged by governments, those who want to live must learn to understand each other, to become aware of their common "humanity". Without sacrificing their justified national pride, nor the good and healthy love they feel for their homeland, men of all countries must rise to the rank of citizens of the world, must become "human".

Today all problems are universal. Only a universal spirit can encompass them, understand them, resolve them. But how is this spirit to be forged? How are men to be united? Lofty ideals have failed abominably, great dreams have been buried in hate.

Only Charity remains. It is by charity that the world will be united. Charity alone will save it. Because a man – whoever he is, wherever he lives, whatever he thinks – is distressed when he sees unjust misery, and if it is within his power to alleviate it he forthwith makes a "gesture". It is a natural reflex, it is his instinct as "human being" that demands it of him.

THUS TO THOSE WHO DON'T KNOW WHAT'S HAPPENING, JUST SAY:

Have you a house?

THERE ARE MILLIONS OF POOR PEOPLE WHO ARE COLD AND HOMELESS.

Have you eaten today?

THERE ARE MILLIONS OF HUMAN BEINGS WHO DIE OF HUNGER EVERY YEAR.

Are you ill? Has the doctor been?

THERE ARE 700 MILLION HUMAN BEINGS WHO HAVE NEVER SEEN A DOCTOR, AND 600 MILLION WHO HAVE NEVER BEEN VACCINATED.

Does a leper move you and horrify you?

THERE ARE MILLIONS OF LEPERS IN THE WORLD WHO DIE IN INDESCRIBABLE MISERY, WITHOUT CARE, WITHOUT HELP, WITHOUT LOVE.

And these figures are peace-time figures. They are the toll of a "civilized" century.

And how can we count the horrors born of our wars? How can we enumerate the multiple crimes that batten on the blood and the hope of the world? The task would certainly be beyond human capacity.

We won't do everything? Of course not, but we can at least dry a few tears, cure, teach, console. And by our example we can take with us the men who wield the power.

So let's try to promote a universal impulse towards charity. Let's start off by basing the universal reunion on the simple and holy grounds of human pity. By means of international committees, congresses and mass demonstrations, let's give the same rhythm of love to all hearts, that the same pity may possess them, the same impulse towards charity inspire them. This will certainly be the surest way of bringing them together, then of uniting them.

We must bring it home to people that in charity lies the shining secret of men's happiness. The selfish man is unhappy, the selfish man is lonely, the selfish man pretends to be gay – but at the very heart of his factitious gaiety he sees that his life is sad and absurd, because inhuman. For only charity can raise man above his mortal condition; charity is God's messenger, a spark of eternity.

A huge cry of distress rises from thousands of martyred hearts and bodies. Who can refuse to hear, if the cry reaches their ears? Charity doesn't deceive; charity cannot err; among so many errors and deceptions, it remains the radiant certainty. So let us hitch our destiny as men to its star. Charity will save the world!

The Hour for the Poor

It was in 1943 that I launched the Hour for the Poor.

I wrote at the time:

For people who think and love, the haunting spectre of the cruel things that follow in the wake of war and prolong its dire effects is now added to the tragedy of the hours through which we have lived: I mean poverty, ruin, failure, happiness cut short, hopes blighted. Who now is capable of rebuilding, consoling, loving?

The men who wrought this evil can hardly hope to play a part, but all human beings can do their share.

And it has occurred to us that if we devoted to mere peace, to the peaceful well-being of everyone, a fraction, a tiny fraction, of what men have squandered in blood, ingenuity, toil and money so as to kill and destroy each other, a big step would have been taken along the path of human redemption.

And thus we conceived the idea of "The Hour for the Poor."

In what does the Hour for the Poor consist?

The Hour for the Poor requires that every one of us should set aside AT LEAST ONE HOUR PER YEAR of his salary, income or profit to the relief of the poor.

It is a simple gesture, easy to make, within the reach of everyone, but it nevertheless has a moving significance. We are not speaking of the casual offering that we take absent-mindedly from our wallet so as to get rid of a tiresome beggar. If we devote one hour a year – or more – to the poor, we devote a moment of our life to them, we think about them, consecrate our toil to them. IT IS A WORK OF LOVE.

The Hour for the Poor is not a giving of alms but a BROTHERLY ACT in which the rich differ from the poor only in their power of doing more good in the same amount of time. But each man, however destitute he may be, CAN MAKE THE SAME GESTURE: offer an hour of his life for others in want. And his merit is the same as that of the more fortunate whose "brother in charity" he is. Thus all can know that sweetest and proudest of joys: of holding out the hand, not to take but to give. There is no purer happiness than that.

By the Hour for the Poor we hope to create AN IMMENSE CHAIN OF LOVE. We hope to make this blessed Hour resound through the world so that at every minute there will be someone on earth who has momentarily renounced selfishness, hatred and envy so as to work in joy to relieve, heal and bring comfort.

Vain attempts have been made to unite men round great ideas that were often no more than long words. By associating them equally in a work of common charity, perhaps they will rediscover THE PATH OF BROTHERLY LIFE.

THE HOUR FOR THE POOR is universal and missionary. It makes no distinction between men's beliefs. It is enough that they are in want and that we can help them.

In sending his Hour for the Poor everyone may indicate the work to which he wants it to be consecrated or the spirit in which he wants it to be used.

Millions of human beings, many of whom are our fellow countrymen and all of whom are our brothers, are in suffering and despair, and each of us can do his share, according to his means and ability, to heal them and bring them comfort and support.

One hour per year for the poor – to contribute to the building or maintaining, both in our own country and the world, of hospitals, dispensaries, crèches, schools, homes. . . . Who could refuse?

This is the work that we put before you, the work that you can accomplish with us, for the well-being that you will bring to others and the peace that this gesture will draw on yourself.

Happily for the poor . . .

An idea such as this at a time such as that seemed a utopian chimera.

And it was then that there entered into the fray those who always and everywhere have understood me better than anyone else, helped me more than anyone else and shown more love than anyone else: I mean the humble people, the poor, those for whom life is a daily struggle, but they are also the rich in the deepest sense, strong and blessed. How many times was I to repeat: Happily for the poor, there are the poor!

The poor! They flew to my help. We shall find them again in every good work, on every page. Listen to them:

From a poor old working man:

> Here is a humble, a very humble, offering. I'm rather ashamed to send so little. I'm 70 and not so strong as I was for work. But at least what I send is sent with all my heart.

From an ailing woman:

> I can't give much. I live alone and have been disabled for twenty years; I can't work and I live on the old age pension plus another 4000 francs. But I enclose 150 francs all the same.[1]

From another woman living alone:

> As I can't send money, as usual, will you accept these few children's books and two dolls? Perhaps you won't like them very much but they belonged to my daughter who was suddenly taken to heaven and it is painful for me to part with them. Up till now I've always kept her toys, but we have to make sacrifices for children in need.

From our little friend Annie:

> On my tenth birthday I send you a postal order for 500 francs that you will kindly distribute to our little poor children.

From a flower-maker:

> The other day I received a letter from a friend asking me to make her some flowers. She sent me 1000 francs. I only spent 300 on buying the paper, so send you the remainder — i.e. my work — for those who are poorer than me.

And here are other letters:

> Please accept 400 francs from someone with both legs amputated. And may God keep you long in this poor world where you are so precious.

> I'm not rich, as I'm only a labourer, but I AM SORRY FOR THE POOR OF THE WORLD. Here are 100 francs.

> This postal order represents the price of the wine that we have withdrawn from our table for the past three months.

> I own a small gold identity disc and also my mother's wedding ring. I was keeping the latter as a treasure as it's the only tangible souvenir of my dear departed that I possess. But in reading about such miseries I feel I can put the ring to no

---

[1] The sums indicated refer to old francs or new francs according to the date when they were sent.

better use than in giving it to the poor, as my mother, too, was poor. I'm sure she would approve.

I send you the modest sum of 100 francs which I deduct from my quarterly retired worker's pension: it is a widow's mite and I'm sorry it isn't more. I'm 72. I pray God to keep me in health. I give this small offering for those who are poor and old like myself.

We have received your appeal on behalf of the Hour for the Poor. Although we have very little money ourselves at the moment, as my husband has been ill for six months and may never be able to work again, we are sending you a small contribution. It isn't much, but it is sent with a full heart. All we ask in return is that you should remember us in your prayers; God won't abandon us for we have always given, however little, to those in greater need than us, and from our hearts.

And to end up with:

I send you 2000 francs. They are the savings of my son who starved to death in Dachau. Take them in memory of his father who was shot by the Nazis, and may they help you to heal and comfort.

Balance sheet

In the year of its birth the Hour for the Poor received, from more than 25,000 people, 497,000 francs which were distributed to 24 good works.

After ten years, thanks to this flying start and to the promoter's lectures, 250 million francs have been distributed to more than 500 organizations.

It was then that we took stock of the situation.

I've always thought that my task should consist of thinking up enterprises, expressing them in simple direct words capable of engraving themselves in the hearts of those listening to me, and then letting them take wing. And so it was with the Hour for the Poor. I had added to the manifesto printed above: "For ten years we shall be responsible for the collection and distribution of offerings for those who need this service. We want to teach our child to walk. Thereafter, strongly founded in a successful past, our child will offer itself for adoption by those who are willing."

When the ten-year period came to an end, we closed our experiment with a meeting in the large amphitheatre of the Sorbonne on 15 February 1953.

C

1946: THREE SHOES IN THE FIREPLACE[1]

CHARLES DE FOUCAULD wrote to his sister:

> Do you remember the Christmasses of our childhood? They are sweet memories that do us good all through our lives. Give your children a lovely Christmas and do all you can to make their Christmasses sweet so that they leave an ineffaceable memory of infinite loveliness.

On the thirteenth anniversary of the death of the man who liked to call himself the Universal Brother, I founded the "Père de Foucauld's Christmas" – a gesture of charity linked to the night on which the world received its greatest Message of Love.

By his life and work the "Desert Knight" had always seemed to me a lofty symbol of brotherly love, and it was so as to send forth this message that I had created the "Charles de Foucauld Fund" before the war. This fund, among other enterprises of faith and charity, ensured the completion of the church of El Goléa, near his tomb, and the building of two chapels at Adrar and Timimoum.

Our first appeal was drawn up thus:

> CHRISTMAS, NIGHT OF HOPE AND FEAST-DAY OF LOVE!
>
> WHEN THAT NIGHT COMES, WHO WILL YOU LIVE IT FOR?
>
> Just for yourself? You poor man!
>
> FOR YOUR NEAREST AND DEAREST, FOR YOUR CHILDREN? THAT'S BETTER, BUT IT ISN'T ENOUGH.

Christmas should be an act of universal love. Because of you, an old man won't be lonely on that day, and a child will laugh. . . .

BEFORE CHRISTMAS YOU, THE PARENTS,
while lovingly preparing the things that will give your children joy on this great feast-day, spare a thought for the poor children

---

[1] It is the custom in France for a child to put his shoes in the fireplace instead of hanging up a stocking.

24

who will receive nothing, for whom Christmas will be *a day like other days*,

a day when they will be hungry, cold and lonely.

Spare a thought, too, for the old who have no friends or relations and whose only visitor will be death, death so slow and long in coming. . . .

Let the immense warmth of Christmas throw out a spark of love for them, too.

On Christmas Eve,

You, the children, who will be happy in the sweet warmth of hearth and home, and filled with all good things by parents who love you, you must realize that there are thousands of children in the world who would like to laugh and be happy like you but who will have nothing on that day, who will be alone and in tears. When Little Jesus came into the world, he was poor. Would you not have wanted to share your happiness and toys with him? Little Jesus lives again in some sort in every poor child, and he is waiting for you to come to his help.

So this is what I propose to you: ask your father and mother on Christmas Eve if you can put *three shoes in the fireplace*. Two for yourself as usual, and the third for some unhappy child who, thanks to you, will forget his loneliness and suffering for a moment; thanks to you he will smile on the morning of the great children's feast-day.

In this way your joy will be greater because of the good you have done. And Père de Foucauld will protect and love you because you will have loved his little favourites.

* * *

This enterprise was a resounding success from the start. Parcels poured in from all over France so that we were immediately faced with a problem. Of the four smallish rooms which have been our home for thirty-three years (in rue Erlanger which became rue du Général-Delestraint after the war), two had already become offices and it was impossible for us to house the parcels that poured in. Thus we had to beg hospitality from a friend.

M. Hauguel, a member of our administrative Council as well as our printer, had hardly more room than we, but he stacked up the rolls of paper and boxes of envelopes so deftly that some precious square feet of floor-space were freed, and for years it was there that my mother, my wife, a few friends and myself spent the six weeks before Christmas.

Despite her advanced age my mother was the nimblest of us all. I shall always remember her struggling in the midst of the sea of parcels and exclaiming as each was opened, "Oh, Raoul, come and look!" and I went to share her joy; God knows how touching some of the parcels were! In the evening she was as exhausted as the rest of us, more exhausted probably, though she didn't let it show, and she used to say to the still-unopened parcels, "Till tomorrow!" Dear Mother – she performed the most modest tasks with a smile that remains like the sun in my heart.

One of us was detailed to bring up the sacks delivered ceaselessly by the postman; there were many of them and they were heavy. This was M. Marize, who worked in the press. At night, long after the rest of us had gone home, he went on carrying in the ammunition, a sack on his shoulder, a smile on his lips. When M. Hauguel, at my request, wanted to compensate him for so much overtime, he opened his eyes wide in bewilderment and turned to me as if he had done something wrong and we were punishing him. He finally managed to speak. "Pay me? But what for? Surely you're not going to stop me helping others too!" Dear Marize! I don't know what became of him in the end, but he always has a vivid place in my memories.

But we didn't receive parcels only. When we got home at night a huge mail was awaiting me which had to be answered. A mail heavy with love.

I wrote about this in an account of our Christmas of 1948. Here it is. My heart still quickens as I read it, after nearly twenty years.

What a day! Between answering the telephone and writing letters the hours have flown by without my noticing. There are still hundreds and hundreds of letters on my table to be opened, answered and the replies signed.

It's Christmas Eve, and I'm suddenly a bit tired. Disheartened? Certainly not. I shall never be disheartened. But tired, and perhaps a bit stunned by the huge success of our appeal. . . .

A ring at the bell. Not again! The bell has never stopped ringing all day. I open the door, a shade impatiently. There's a small boy outside, very pale, with huge eyes looking I know not where – obviously at something that grown-ups can't see. He hands me a letter and makes off. I recover from my surprise and try to run after him, but it's no good, he's already downstairs and the street has absorbed him.

I open the letter. There are twenty-five francs[1] and these few lines which I transcribe: "Monsieur. For the love of God please accept this modest contribution from a working-man in his sixth year of disability. The poorest must not be deprived of the joy of helping. I want to remain anonymous."

And I return slowly to my laden desk, this treasure in my hand. I take a blue file from my filing cabinet. It is full of oddments of paper covered with uneven handwriting displaying every possible spelling mistake. Yet it is worth more than all the treasures of the world. It is our Golden Book of Charity.

And I read:

"I send you 100 francs for your Christmas. I myself shall have fewer toys but that doesn't matter. I have plenty of fun on our farm so I can do without toys."

"I send you 100 francs that Mummy has given me. I'm seven. We aren't rich, but IT'S GOOD TO GIVE."

"Aleth and Marie-Françoise earned 3 francs every time they washed up or prepared the vegetables. They've bought a doll with this money and send it to a little girl who has no toys."

A hundred francs came with the following letter, written as well as she was able:

"I'm five, Mummy can't send you anything this year as she usually does, so my sister and I have taken this from our money-box so that on Christmas morning a child like us can smile at little Jesus to thank him."

And now for the old people:

"I am alone and have been crippled for the last twenty years. I'm 70 and live on my old-age pension. I can only send 150 francs."

"I am disabled and live on my disability pension and a little mending. But there are others poorer than me so I send you 30 francs."

Fifteen francs "with apologies" from someone who says:

"This sum represents two hours of my earnings and, for my daughter, an hour spent picking up sheaves."

And this woman who with heroic charity draws from her

---

[1] Old francs, needless to say!

suffering the desire to give, to protect the happiness that was taken from her:

"For the little orphans from my only daughter, Marie-Thérèse, who went to God on 30 October 1917 when she was seven. Her father had already gone 6 years before her."

Blessed are those that weep . . .

"In a day or two you will receive a parcel of clothes and toys, and also a child's bicycle, all of which belonged to our little boy who died a few weeks ago. May they bring joy to other children! I'm enclosing a p.o. to help you in your work. May God help you in your zeal to gladden the sweet faces of children."

Blessed are they that suffer persecution . . .

"It is in memory of my children interned like me for reasons of race, my daughter, my grand-daughter and my son-in-law deported in 1943, defenceless, without justice, martyred and killed, my wife dead of grief during the Occupation. All these memories turn one towards charity, and in their name I send you my contribution in a cheque for 100 francs."

And finally this letter which sums up all charity:

"The toys are from Michelle for children in want. The 100 francs are from the maid. The 200 are for an invalid from another invalid. Happy Christmas to everyone!"

I close the file, and suddenly I realize that I'm singing, though all alone.

For I know now that I shall never be disheartened, and that I shall never be tired, never again, and that I shall never lose patience, even at the end of an exhausting day and even if the doorbell rings a hundred times. For, in opening the door, I shall always hope to see the child, the pale little child with the huge eyes that look . . . I know what he's looking at now.

The little Christmas child who came to teach me Love.

* * *

In 1947 Père de Foucauld's Christmas had been crowned by the Académie française. In 1950 it brought help, gladness and joy to more than 80,000 old people and children. The habit of the "third shoe in the fireplace" had taken on.

The bird had strong wings. We let it fly under its own momentum.

OTHER SUCCESSFUL CAMPAIGNS

1. PÈRE PEYRIGUÈRE AND THE "BATTLE FOR QUININE"

IT IS TO Père de Foucauld that I am indebted for having known his double, his replica, his other self, Père Peyriguère. For I met him for the first time in the course of a lecture tour in Morocco. He gave me the royal gift of his friendship immediately, and it lasted till he died. For more than fifteen years an affectionate and trusting correspondence between us made him the witness and adviser of my struggles, and I in my turn sometimes had the joy and honour of being able to help him in his extraordinary apostolate.

Our old friends remember especially the "Battle for Quinine" which we launched in 1942.

On 24 September of that year I received a tragic S.O.S. from Père Peyriguère. An epidemic of pernicious malaria had just broken out in the mountain home of the Berbers, and there was no quinine. The war was on. France was occupied, rationed, anaemic. How could we hope to find the quinine so badly needed in Morocco in the so-called free zone of my country?

I didn't in fact think along these lines at first, and my first reaction, as always, was to appeal to my friends.

Going from pharmacy to pharmacy, pleading, persuading, convincing, we managed in a few hours to collect more than 12,000 doses which I dispatched to Kebbab by the most rapid channels. Fifty thousand doses were to follow – which arrived, thank God, after the battle was over. For, thanks to our lightning offensive, the malaria had withdrawn. The mountain breathed again. On 8 October Père Peyriguère sent me a telegram: "EPIDEMIC IN FULL REGRESSION THANKS TO YOU. THANK YOU."

However, he wanted to thank his benefactors in the person of the one (myself) who had mobilized them, so that on the occasion of another trip I made to Morocco in 1949 there was a big celebration at Kebbab in the traditional style of Berber festivals.

Though he treated himself so harshly, Père Peyriguère still remained lord and master to others, and it was on such occasions that this was apparent. Simple, smiling, happy, brotherly, he played his part, like everyone else, in the rejoicing. And I still see the old "Marabout" sitting on the ground, his legs crossed, clapping his hands in time to the dances of the girls who had come down from the mountains to honour his guests. Meanwhile the Berbers were singing odes composed by themselves to the glory of the Father: "O great tree in whose shadow the poor seek shelter. . . ."

Here are some revealing passages from his letters, many of which I have kept:

17 December 1950
I've received the splendid Christmas presents for my little Berbers. Though my words of thanks are simple, I assure you they are charged with emotion and true gratitude. They are also Christmas presents to me, for I suspect that the old missionary is perhaps happier to clothe these children than they are to be clothed. So in the name of the old missionary whose heart will be warm, and of my little Berber children whose bodies will be warm, a big thank you.

26 November 1951
You see, dear M. Follereau, I'd like to drown all that in a wave of French kindness, strike out mercilessly myself. I feel sort of possessed by a frenzy of kindness. Perhaps . . . perhaps they'll one day cease to mark up all these signs of love to my personal account – which they do to the point of overwhelming me – and mark them up also to the account of Christianity and that of France too.
. . . So, do you sense all that is contained in the "thank you" expressed by my poor clumsy wordiness – for helping me to fulfil these great duties?
Thank you for what you've sent: our little Berbers are naked – it's been a bad year, and their parents haven't been able to do anything – I clothe them. They come in an endless procession: it warms my heart so much to make them warm. And they're so charming in their total trust: it's too much human love for my old man's heart which had renounced everything and finds itself again beyond everything.

12 October 1954
I know you're just setting out on a long tour of kindness:

there's no need for me to tell you how my thoughts and prayers go with you.

As life draws to a close and one has got over many illusions, there's one thing that one doesn't get over: knowing that living is not worth while except insofar as one has been the person through whom a sufferer has ceased to suffer, or suffered less.

In heaven I shall have to tell God over and over again how much I owe to you for having enabled me to be that happy man!

Years have passed. Père Peyriguère is dead. But his letters continue to illumine my life.

2. "VOS SCHÉMAS"

It was round about the same time and with the same end in view – namely, to help missionaries in the pursuit of their charitable apostolate – that I asked Doctor Pierre Reynier to write *Vos schémas*, a clinical and therapeutic documentation of exotic pathology.

This work, which was clear, simple and comprehensive, provided and still does provide the greatest possible service to the cause of charity. And not content with having offered this priceless contribution to our work, Doctor Pierre Reynier insisted on paying the printing costs himself.

I want to take this opportunity of telling this friend – who has always been my doctor and has had to exercise considerable patience with this impossible "patient" ("When you allow yourself to be treated, I'll believe in miracles") – of the gratitude of the missionaries and their sick, and of the grateful affection I myself feel.

3. 1947 – THE GOOD FRIDAY STRIKE

In order to extend the influence of the Hour for the Poor and give it a spiritual significance for Christians, we put out the suggestion that Christians should make their offering on Good Friday. "A strike against selfishness!" we proclaimed. "Give charity in the Hour that Charity was born."

The text reproduced on p. 33 was offered free that year and every year to all charitable societies that wanted to make use of it, irrespective of their denomination, and hundreds of thousands of copies were distributed. "All you have to do," we told them, "is to fill the blank space left for the purpose with your address and any necessary information, so that offerings may be sent direct to you. Our aim is to bring about a huge convergence of charity at the most moving hour of the Christian year, so that at that moment a single love shall possess us all. . . . Is there a better means of drawing us together, then of uniting us?"

This initiative, however, earned me a severe, not to say malicious, article in a Paris weekly paper. As this paper claimed the backing of the Catholic hierarchy, I was somewhat put out and decided to appeal to Rome. The following is the reply I received:[1]

Dal Vaticano, il 17 dicembre 1949.

Segreteria di Stato di
  Sua Santita.
N. 216628

Monsieur,

At the time of the audience that the Sovereign Pontiff granted you some weeks ago, His Holiness deigned to interest himself personally in the opportune charitable enterprise which you are zealously developing under the name of "The Good Friday Hour for the Poor".

As it is not, alas, feasible for many Christians to recollect themselves in prayer at the anniversary hour of Our Lord's death, as they are occupied by their professional work, it seems at the least eminently desirable that this work should be offered to the suffering Christ in the person of the poor. That is the goal you are pursuing when you ask each one to make over to the most deserving good work the earnings of one hour of work on this day which is holy to us all.

How could the Holy Father not wish such a movement to develop! It is thus with a full heart that he calls down abundant graces on your action of genuine charity and bestows the Apostolic blessing on you yourself, on all the organizers of this venture, and on all those who will respond to your appeal.

I beg you to accept, Monsieur, the assurance of my religious devotion.

J. B. MONTINI.

The cause had been understood.

---

[1] It will be noted that this letter, written in the name of the Sovereign Pontiff, was signed by the man who was himself to become Pope fifteen years later.

Good Friday, 3 p.m.!

The Hour at which selfish and corrupt men put to death him who said:

> *Love each other!*

The Hour at which Christ's blood flowed so as to free man through Love.

Good Friday, 3 p.m.!

You cannot live this hour *selfishly, for yourself alone.*

> **Give to charity the hour
> in which Charity was born!**

HOW?

On Good Friday from 3 to 4 p.m., or during an hour as near to this one as possible, *you will work for the Poor,* you will give them the price of that hour's work, or that hour's income or revenue.

> Good Friday, 3 p.m.
> The Hour of Charity,
> may all be there!

Whom to give to?

> *To some local charitable society, which is in such great need of your help.*

IDEAS WHICH NEVER SAW THE DAY

THE SUCCESSFUL enterprises just described were set out in my pamphlet *Charity will save the World*. But I suggested others that either never saw the day (yet who knows what may happen in the future . . .) or were adopted by people who subsequently declared them to be "of unknown parentage".

Here they are as I proposed them nearly twenty years ago:

Against the religion of money

The evil of the century is money – less through the power it exercises than through the worship by which we surround it. The banknote has become the symbol of happiness itself, even when we have no illusions as to its real value. Any way of being happy, other than by trying to become rich, is now unknown to us. So we would like to show, by using similar signs and tokens, that there are other riches and another road to happiness, that we can aspire to the conquest of other treasure: strange treasure that "has no value" and yet is worth more than everything else in the world.

A "Charity Voucher" would be given to any person or society that has made a gift to some charitable work. This voucher would have no commercial value, thus couldn't be traded or exchanged; it would merely bear witness to the fact that a sum corresponding to the figure recorded on it had been dedicated to charity. The voucher thus wouldn't represent a power to be exercised indiscriminately for good or evil, but its value would show the sum that had been withdrawn from the vicious circle of money so as to be used for the good of men.

There would be no decline or fall in this voucher-fortune, and it would win respect. It would testify to an "amassing of riches" based solely on the happiness of others. What I have has not been taken from anyone. On the contrary, WHAT I HAVE IS WHAT I HAVE GIVEN AWAY.

34

These would be inaccessible and sacred riches, riches that know nothing of the fluctuations of the market; they couldn't be requisitioned or devalued; they would be immortal.

So each family would build up a patrimony different from its traditional and normal wealth, a patrimony more jealously guarded and one day more proudly bequeathed to posterity. "THE LEGACY I LEAVE YOU REPRESENTS THE GOOD I HAVE DONE."

The friend's house

If there is anything worse than poverty for the poor man, it is loneliness.

His misery creates a void around him so that he feels abandoned just when life alone has become too much for him.

Of course there is "public assistance" – the assistance he receives through filling up forms in front of unconcerned clerks. But important though this kind of help is, it can only postpone the collapse. What the poor man wants even more than alms is comfort, understanding and friendship. There are needs which money doesn't cure, which can't be alleviated by joining the queue at the pay-desk. And we have only to search our own hearts to remember that these needs are by no means the least distressing.

Now if poverty is a misfortune, often undeserved, it should never have to seem a fall from grace. And this is why we propose to set up "friends' houses". What is a "friend's house"? Neither a shelter nor an almshouse, but just an address, just a name on a front door, the name of a man or woman willing to welcome with intelligence and respect the hard-luck stories of whatever kind that may be confided to him.

This person would be called a "Director" because his role would be to direct or guide those who come to him towards the appropriate organizations, charitable societies or individual people that can give real and effective help.

Help involves understanding. The director must know how to listen. Charity often consists primarily of listening, listening patiently and open-heartedly to tales of woe: and long tales too, because the misfortunes have been so deeply felt.

The director should be constantly available, that is to say ready to put himself at any time at the service of each comer. Charity is a presence. He must not only give, he must give himself.

He must be in touch with all the charitable societies in his locality. He should have at hand an up-to-the-minute list of those people – doctors, lawyers, etc. – that a person in distress may need but would not have the courage or the means to approach of his own accord. The director must be unbiased and unprejudiced. He must receive whoever comes with the same esteem, and look on everyone equally. When someone comes to him, no one should be able to guess whether he has come to give or to receive. Thus the strong and jealous dignity of the poor man may be safeguarded – and this should be a constant care.

The director naturally has no prejudices as to race or religion. He should make Pasteur's phrase his own: "I'm not asking you about your opinions or religion, only about your pain."

The director's role is not to dole out help, and he would do this only in exceptional and urgent cases. He is there to receive, to understand and to put each comer on the way to regaining his peace and equilibrium. He is up to a point a doctor of souls; more than a benefactor, a friend.

His motto would be St Paul's saying: "Without love, almsgiving is nothing." He inscribes in his heart, if not on his door:

> Whoever you are, wherever you come from,
> O passer-by, stop here,
> For here your hope is born.

MAN COMES OF AGE

In the same pamphlet – published, let it be remembered, in 1948 – there were also these pages which seemed at the time very utopian and caused the shrugging of many official shoulders.
But since then . . .

HAVE YOU ever seen a frontier? It's a wooden fence or barrier with a policeman on either side. You come on it suddenly, lying in wait for you at the turn of the road. On the other side the trees and the sky are exactly the same. But not one's fate.

Sometimes the frontier impudently bars your way in the middle of a village. People talk to each other and shake hands across it . . . until the day comes when the men who govern them (why these rather than others?) dress them up, in blue on one side, in red on the other, and tell them to kill each other.

And they do kill each other. Because they are separated by a wooden fence with policemen on either side.

Here there is food; there there isn't. Why?

The problem isn't a recent one, but every day it assumes a graver significance, and its solution must not be delayed.

Man, having conquered speed, has narrowed down his earthly domain to an extraordinary degree. The small countries – those we can fly over in an hour – can no longer aspire to genuine autonomy; at most they can preserve an illusion of it. Nor can economic problems find a local solution now. The time is past when a rich country could live safely and for long next to a poor country. The upheavals, misfortunes and distresses of the one react on its neighbour and jeopardize its future. So we shall have to envisage a world-wide economy and a human distribution of wealth (in fact we envisage it already – the multiplicity of conferences proves it). This is an imperative of that brotherhood which should gather all men together so as to unite them.

This brotherhood would not exclude a single one of those

37

sacred sentiments that are part of man's being. I'm referring to man's feeling for his family and his homeland. Far from contradicting them, it crowns them.

When tribes first grouped themselves together so as to defend their pasture-lands and hunting-grounds, so that their members experienced their first notion of "national" territory, they didn't cease to love their families. And when they entered the national community, did the Burgundians cease to love Burgundy because they were learning to love France? Love of the homeland in no way impedes the posing and resolving of universal problems. There is no question of abandoning and disowning, but of completing the work and fulfilling man. There's no question of suppressing individual countries, but of uniting them for a destiny that will carry them further. The homeland is a sacred stage of man as he marches towards mankind; and those who love their country are better prepared than anyone else to reach the final stage.[1]

Love of one's country doesn't involve hatred of neighbouring countries any more than love of one's mother involves hatred of other mothers.

Love of one's family doesn't entail robbing, looting, killing one's neighbour. On the contrary, love of one's family not only implies but compels respect for other homes. No one admires the man who has rejected his parents. And it's the same with the homeland. The true patriot loves the idea of homeland in each man, and respects each man's homeland. It's not a question of internationalism but of a union of homelands as a way of arriving at man, so that he may become aware of his "humanity" and of the indestructible links that unite him with his kind.

Ten years later

Ten years later, in 1958, Pope Pius XII addressed the following message to the first international military pilgrimage to Lourdes:

[1] I had already put this idea forward at a congress held in Brussels in September 1936. I caused a motion to be adopted "that, faced with the rising anarchies, patriotism, a sentiment as natural as that of love of the family, should be cultivated, given pride of place and defended." And I took the theme up again in the chapter, "Allons, enfants de toutes les patries", in a booklet that came out round about the same period: *La Trahison de l'Intelligence* (*The Betrayal of the Intelligence*).

Great hope is born in our soul at this magnificent spectacle of Christian brotherhood between soldiers of different nations! It is surely a sign that the cause of peace is making headway in men's hearts despite such an accumulation of obstacles. Dear children, love your respective countries and serve them following your duty and your hearts' spontaneous impulses. But if your hearts are directed towards peace, then *this lawful devotion will become a source of richness for the whole world and not a pretext for rivalries and division.*

D

SOME PROPOSALS FOR "MAKING MAN A HUMAN BEING"

1. By teaching the child that he belongs to mankind

(*a*) Include in the school syllabus not only the history of the child's individual country but a history of mankind, of mankind's long and painful but beneficent achievements, such as the emancipation of women, the abolition of slavery, the decrease in infant mortality, a humane ordering of work, and so on. In this way the child will understand that he belongs to the home he is brought up in, to the town where he lives, to the country he loves, yes, but also to a human community towards which he also has duties.

(*b*) Intensify the study of languages called "foreign". Make this compulsory at a certain stage of the child's school career.

(*c*) Encourage exchanges between young people of different countries, for instance by the creation of holiday camps abroad. Let the child observe at an early age and through personal experience that the world doesn't stop at the frontiers of his country, but that "across the water" people live, suffer, love, are honourable and can even be happy.

2. By giving man a sense of his universal destiny

Develop opportunities for meetings, especially at the professional level. Organize international encounters and festivals in which the whole world can participate in one common emotion of admiration or gratitude. Thus there will be memories belonging to the common heritage of all men and these will become points of spiritual contact. In this way men will become aware of the links that bind them together and of the destiny that unites them.

The Good Friday Hour for the Poor can play this part with Christians, and indeed with everyone who recognizes the power for good in Christianity. It can constitute a sort of general strike of selfishness, in which all simultaneously stop thinking about themselves and working for themselves so as to reach out towards the needs of the world. And for children the Père de Foucauld Christmas is an illustration of what I have in mind.

3. Propose world-wide duties to men

By the creation of Social Service. Pending its abolition, military service should be partially replaced by a period of Social Service which every young man should be bound to do at the age of twenty. This will be carried out far away from the site of his usual occupations so that he may widen his horizons and his idea of mankind. This Social Service would consist in doing work dedicated exclusively to the common good. Naturally each man's aptitudes would be taken into account and also his wish to benefit by this opportunity so as to improve a skill he already has or learn another. As in the case of military service, young men would be dependent on the community and would receive a gratuity on being discharged.

By the creation of a fund for universal charity which would alleviate the severest misfortunes (famine, epidemics, etc.) and guarantee essential research, notably in the field of medicine. This fund could be based on proceeds from international services, for instance on the amount raised by postage stamps of the international administration and the telegraphic and telephonic takings that in the ordinary way form the object of international accountancy.[1]

By the creation of a voluntary tax called "The Hour for the Poor". As we have seen, this good work has been in existence since 1943.

*   *   *

In the course of my world tours I have often come across my cherished ideas to which I gave wings twenty years ago. These birds don't always sing exactly the same song. But they sing. And that's what matters.

---

[1] I was to take up this idea again sixteen years later when I proposed "A Day of War for Peace".

II
SOME REPERCUSSIONS OF THE FIGHT AGAINST SELFISHNESS

> The merciful are the profiteers' enemy.
> By demanding justice, by stirring up
> disinterested love, they are a nuisance.
> *Fr. L.-J. Lebret*

DEDICATION

I dedicate these observations, prompted by items of so-called sensational news accorded head-line status and often applauded by what are conventionally called the great information services, again to you, the young men and girls who answered my appeal, so that you may share my anger before partaking of my joy.

I wrote in 1947:

Come to the help of all human beings! Come to the help of man! Of man who himself brings about his misfortunes by his selfishness and hate. For the earth can provide enough to nourish all men of good will and make them happy. But men have set up between each other a demoniac mirage: wealth. They have constructed fortresses in which these over here live in comfort and abundance and watch dry-eyed those over there as they die for want of what the others have to excess.

No one has the right to be happy alone.

THE BLACK BOOK OF MONEY

1. SUPERFLUITY AMONG THE RICH

PLAIN STATISTICS:

In France during the year 1960,
27,200,000 lipsticks were sold for 8 milliard old francs;
11,226,000 boxes of face-powder for 5 milliard 600 million old francs;
10,110,000 bottles of nail varnish for 2 milliard old francs;
7,364,000 jars of cold cream for 13 milliard old francs;
2 milliard old francs were spent on anti-sunburn products.

48% of Frenchmen gamble 70 milliard old francs annually on the National Lottery.

Paris and the provinces bet to the tune of 180 milliards at the main race-meetings. In December 1962 2 milliards were placed on one horse alone.

At Christmas 20 milliards went on ski-ing; 70 milliards on food (3 milliards on *foie gras* and 15 milliards on oysters); 20 milliards on toys.

The French spend yearly: 400 milliard old francs on their tobacco; 20 milliards on their cinemas; 50 milliards on their alcohol.

Similar, or worse, statistics tell us the extent to which this evil has spread in the so-called civilized countries. Thus in an article in the American magazine *Time*, the accuracy of whose information we can hardly doubt, we read that:

It is estimated that in the U.S.A., during the year 1957, 4 milliard dollars were spent on BEAUTY CARE AND BEAUTY PREPARATIONS!

There are 110,000 beauty salons in the U.S.A.

In the Rubinstein beauty parlours in Manhattan 74,000 women per year are massaged and have their hair dressed. A woman who wants to spend a whole day in this salon can spend

43

up to 1,200 dollars on acquiring a more or less alluring complexion.

To give a leper a new complexion, to give him back his life, 10 new francs suffice.

TEN NEW FRANCS: one minute's time of a client in the Manhattan beauty parlour.

But these ten francs are not always forthcoming.

So while the thoughtless or the cynical are trying to recapture their fading beauty at 10 new francs a minute, millions of men are living without care, without help, without love.

St Augustine said: "The superfluity of the rich is the wealth of the poor."

2. A DANGEROUS PERSON

He's called Arthur Foster. He is twenty-seven. I suppose his description has been circulated to all the police forces of the world. And I'm sure I'm doing a public service and reassuring honest men by thus openly drawing attention to him.

Arthur Foster, having inherited a considerable sum of money, decided to distribute it among the poor. According to police reports he went from door to door in Baltimore asking people: "Are you poor? If I give you money will you put it to some useful purpose?" Then, depending on the answer, he gave 25 or 50 dollars to the astonished housewife. Sometimes the door was shut in his face. Then he waited a moment or two, knocked again and gave the money.

He was arrested, and interrogated at length by the police – whether he was manhandled we do not know – but nothing more could be got out of him.

No alcohol in the blood; no madness in the family. . . .

So what? So – and this is the important part – American legislation, though worked out in such detail, had not foreseen a case such as this! And he had to be released because (as the press agency reports – and I quote): "the police could find no law forbidding a citizen to give his money to others".

That's all. Indeed, what else could one add?

Happy good old days when St Vincent de Paul could serve "our Lords the poor" without fear of the police cells.

3. A POOR FELLOW

Certain newspapers which feed (there's no mistake about it!) on stories that wouldn't make a child laugh, tell us excitedly of this most recent exploit.

A millionaire – South American, I fancy – has come to France. Why? On business? as a tourist? for his health? just for a visit? to gather information? to admire? to criticize?

No. He has come to buy "chips" in the casinos. You know, those objects made of I don't know what that the leading lights of that very small world throw in handfuls on the green cloth of the gaming tables. Those "chips" that often represent small fortunes, that for poor people would bring happiness and often health, that perform an imbecile circle in front of jaded eyes and sagging breasts. . . .

Our millionaire doesn't buy on a small scale. The chips he purchases are worth 100,000 francs; not a cent less. And what does he want them for? So as to make a cigar-box.

What a stroke of genius to think of such a thing, and what good taste! And I gather that he is headline news in the infantile newspapers that the philistines who deal in society news produce for grown-ups!

Perhaps, his purchases made, he will return to his country – to his country where there are sometimes revolutions.

And if people who are hungry, and have been too hungry for too long, one day discover his cigar-box, they will hang our millionaire. Very amiably.

And the awful thing is that the poor man will die without having understood why.

4. WHEN ONE'S STOPPED LAUGHING . . .

Read this story that I found headlined in a paper – because it had nothing more important and doubtless nothing more moving to tell its readers that day:

Rich Widow, Aged 90, marries her Chauffeur

Adrianna N. . . . , a very rich widow aged 90, yesterday married her cook-chauffeur, Allen W. . . . , aged 28.

Madame N. . . , an invalid, had to be married in a wheel chair, before a coloured pastor, as three judges and a white pastor had successively refused to proceed with the nuptial ceremony.

And meanwhile thousands of children are dying of hunger, thousands of young men can't found the homes they long for, thousands of old people are alone in their destitution.

There, certainly, is one of the most repulsive aspects of barbarism.

5. HOW MAD CAN YOU GET . . .

Another important piece of news – to judge by its large type and its position on the page:

A cat cannot inherit . . .

. . . an item of information that will bring great cheer to the 800 million people who won't eat tonight.

To satisfy their appetite yet further, here are the details of this reassuring statement:

> In her will, Mrs A. McH . . . bequeathed a third of her fortune, namely 83,333 dollars 33 cents, to her black cat, Opal, "to ensure that it will live in luxury".
>
> The court has decided that a cat cannot inherit. Opal's share will thus be divided among the other legatees. The deceased's sister, Mrs M. F. . . . , has guaranteed to take care of Opal as long as she lives.

And some people actually deny the march of civilization!

As for Mrs M. F. . . . , she unquestionably deserves the Nobel Peace Prize.

6. REPUGNANT

A prospectus was lying on the hotel table. Automatically I flicked over its pages. And suddenly I was struck with a revelation.

It was dealing with India, where women are often thin (the author used the word svelte; I personally would call them skeletons).

I had thought, sentimental old thing that I am, that they never ate enough; I even recalled a horde of starving people that once besieged me in a large Asian town. But no, that's not the point; eating or not eating doesn't enter into it. A "scientist" has discovered their secret: they go in for massage.

They have gone in for massage "for centuries". What they use I don't know; obviously they use whatever the "scientist" is anxious to sell to the women of the West who eat three times a day. This industrious man has understood: the poor who are dying in the streets of Calcutta and Bombay have been over-massaged. That's all.

But when a little leper girl of twenty-two died before my eyes weighing three stone, I didn't find a massaging instrument by her body. Perhaps another dying girl, anxious to massage herself, had got hold of it.

One always thinks one has reached rock bottom where vileness is concerned.

And then one day . . .

7. THE CHARITY OF THE BONE THROWN TO THE DOG

"Madame, I've come to beg for the poor."

Madame answers from her bath. "Give them the master's old suit and the doll Marylène doesn't play with any more. Oh yes, and they could have her teddy-bear, you know the one, on the top shelf in the cupboard. It's broken, but they'll make do."

And while the tiresome man at the door is saying thank you, and the door bangs shut, Madame gets out of the bath with a soft, far-away look in her eyes as she thinks of "the good she has done."

And yet she has just done something very wicked.

No, Madame, it's not for the poor to "make do" with your leftovers. It's a base act to rid yourself on to the destitute and their children of belongings you'd otherwise have thrown into the dustbin. There's nothing for self-congratulation in that. You haven't understood that the poor are people, that poor children are the children of people, and that even if they accept your throw-outs out of bitter necessity, they don't really want what you have rejected.

Is that charity?

It's the charity of the bone thrown to the dog.

*   *   *

A woman, a very "well-born" one, sends me a crisp new ten-franc note accompanied by the following sensitive-sounding lines:

Please don't send me any more of those brochures with ghastly photographs of lepers. They've given me nightmares two nights running. Here are ten francs for them, but for the love

of God [where is the love of God going to find a home?] let
me hear no more about them!

I replied:

May God prolong your nightmares, Madame. It's the greatest
good I could wish for you. Until such time as the photos you
find so ghastly (oh, if only we could photograph souls!) no
longer provoke horror and still less a pity that you can only
express through a banknote, but shining and courageous love.

As you see, I'm returning your note because it was given
with such bad grace that I wouldn't know what to do with it.
You can give it to a beggar once you are able to open your
eyes to his misery and hold out your hand to him – at whatever
cost to your cosy insomnia.

You hoped to perform an act of charity, did you? In fact
what you hoped was that you'd get rid of us. Of us, and them.
Is that charity?
The charity of the bone thrown to the dog.

*   *   *

When Monsieur Vincent sent one of his first Daughters of
Charity to visit the hungry, he said to her, "Remember that you'll
need a lot of love if the poor are to forgive you for the bread that
you're taking them."

The first sign of love is justice. The fruit of justice is peace.

Charity isn't the condescending pity of the well-fed man, it
isn't a pleasure that one satisfies, but a compelling duty binding
on us all.

Love, and everything is possible.

May God give us all nightmares if these nightmares will draw
us to our brothers. May he give us the grace to be anguished by
the world's misery. So that we, such terribly happy people, may
forgive ourselves our happiness by learning to love.

8. TO THE UNFORTUNATE YOUNG LADY WHO WANTED
"TO LIE IN A BATH FULL OF JEWELS"

> My – unfortunately unattainable – dream
> is to lie in a bath full of jewels! (A main
> Paris newspaper, 29 June 1960.)

This paper has confided your dream to us in all its 500,000

copies. And also your despair at not being able to realize your
dream. Please accept our condolences.

It appears that you are eighteen years old. I can't believe it.
Young people of eighteen are usually thinking about love, about
spring, but you're thinking about a bath. . . .

The paper says that your father is the king of something or
other. But that hasn't made you a princess. Princesses don't put
their jewels in a bath. History tells us that they've sometimes sold
them to help the poor. But your ideal is to wallow in them. No,
yours is obviously a different aristocracy altogether.

Is it really true that you can't "lie in a bath full of jewels"?
What a shame. The idea was in such good taste!

The young working girls who would have seen the photographs
that you would certainly have had taken would have gaped in
ecstasy. Especially the ones who are really eighteen.

For they exist, you know, girls of eighteen. They are still to be
seen. Of course they have nothing in common with the little
plumed geese with whom you're accustomed to gaggle. No, they
are girls who like to wear their jewels – very artificial, no doubt –
over their blouses, not under their buttocks; girls for whom a
treat means going to the cinema on Saturday, or putting on their
"Sunday best" on Sunday, so as to make plans about the future
with some honest lad. Plans? That's another word that has no
meaning for you, for when one has everything one doesn't make
plans. One has caprices, that's all.

In fact you have nothing. Your joy is despicable; your jewels –
diamonds, pearls, solid gold – fit for throwing into the bath; and
your prince-charmings are phantoms, always between two
hangovers.

Perhaps you think I'm cross? Or even that I'm insulting you?
It's not so, my little one. I love you and I'm sorry for you. I'm
sorry for you because you have everything and yet you're missing
everything; and because you're a very little girl and you're totally
alone. One morning you'll wake up, and you'll understand. And
it will be terrible. Because it'll be too late.

I love you because I love the eighteen years that the civil
register gives you but which you've never had. No doubt you
are stifled beneath the hollow compliments made to your
beauty, your charm and, who knows? – the young men of your

world being so insincere – to your wit. And all sorts of grotesque hopes are cherished on your behalf.

Do you want to know what I hope for you? Then listen. I assure you that, given the state to which you have been reduced, there's no other way to be happy.

May your father stop being king of anything at all. Dethroned kings are quite the fashion nowadays. And if he no longer has anything, then certainly he'll no longer be anything. . . .

After that may you abandon high society and become a girl like other girls and, finally freed from money, may you marry an honest man, not a rich one, but one whom loves you truly for yourself. For that is where riches lie, as you yet have to discover.

And may he give you half a dozen children whom you will bring up with difficulty but with joy. On Thursdays and Sundays you will take your brood to play in the local playground. The grocer, the baker and the shoe-mender will nod to you as you go by and smile at the children when you go home again to prepare the evening meal, a sixth little one in the courtyard, and three pots of geraniums in the window.

And first and foremost, a shower. That's essential.

9. OPEN LETTER TO THE YOUNG LADY WHO HAS SUCH PRETTY TOES

I saw your photograph in a magazine in a waiting-room, the sort of magazine devoted to this sort of publicity. You struck me as being a very pretty girl – perhaps too conscious of the fact, but that has happened to others, and as it has passed with others it will pass with you. So it only remains for me to comment on the caption which was doubtless what earned you this display (together with sundry other obligations).

So your little heart has been "wounded" (no snapshot of that as yet, but it will come) and you want to go off and look after lepers. And at Lambaréné, at that. In Dr Schweitzer's hospital, no less. No one can say that you don't fly high!

So, one simple question.

Are you a doctor? a midwife? a nurse? Or are you merely – but it's wonderful – a missionary?

No, you're "broken-hearted". You're a poor little girl thirsting for publicity and your ambitions are only very dimly related to the well-being of our luckless friends. But you said to yourself, "What a marvellous opportunity to get myself talked about!" All right, then (and I shall be doing you a service by saying so), it won't catch on. Even backed up by large photographs your plan won't work. One of your illustrious predecessors tried this on, and her subterfuge foundered in ridicule. She didn't persist. At least follow her example in that.

You have many "natural gifts". Use them all, if you want to, to launch yourself – as many as you like and more besides. I couldn't care less. But don't use lepers; please stop at that. . . .

Some years ago I wrote on the occasion of a similar attempt at self-projection:

> We can never protest enough against the puerile view that people who go and look after lepers have to be heroes or saints. When one of these braggarts who "dares to touch a leper's hand" appears in the bush, the doctors and missionaries do no more than shrug their shoulders – patiently. But I don't. Because these "courageous acts" foster the myth of leprosy as a dangerous and damned disease. If it demands heroism to kiss a leper or even to shake his hand, then obviously leprosy can't be an illness like other illnesses; and obviously a man who has leprosy isn't like other men. It is precisely these attitudes (in which one perceives grotesque vanity) which still too often cause those ill with leprosy to remain lepers.

I'm sure you won't be unduly distressed by this outburst, for in fact you never really intended to go and look after lepers. The most you envisaged was a publicity trip to Lambaréné. A photo in front of Dr Schweitzer's hut surrounded by a dozen or so resigned lepers would provide a ready-made front page in one of the main organs of "information". And that's what's so shocking. Infinitely more shocking than you showing off your face, your profile . . . and other parts.

The magazine which has made itself your accomplice presents you in a costume which is not exactly that of a nurse: the legs are generously offered to the public, balancing a bunch of grapes that you're holding very skilfully between your toes. Very odd. But I'd seen it already at the circus.

It's true, Mademoiselle, that you have very pretty toes. And while I (like everyone else) was admiring them, I couldn't help being reminded of a letter I'd just received from a leper hospital on the Solomon Islands (even further away than Lambaréné):

The problem of the moment is the rats. We have six women with toes eaten by rats. As they have no sensation whatever in their feet the rats have had a fine feast. It's a pity. Naturally precautions have been taken, everyone is now on the alert and the rats are hard put to it to find uncovered toes. I admire them for they laugh at their bad luck; however, they're being very careful to hide their feet well so as to keep their toe-nails intact.

What do you think of that, Mademoiselle? There you have toes for which the grape harvest is over.

* * *

Come now, let's forget this nonsense. Each to his place.
And to each his leprosy.
I am fully aware that you are not infectious at the moment.
But our friends would not be much use at healing your "broken heart". Many of them have no hands. And the others disgust one so easily.
And the photograph in which you show off your nimble toes for our admiration – a display that is naïve rather than vicious and deserves a mere shrug of the shoulders, but that your false generosity makes it shocking – let that photograph go to its place, too. To the waste-paper basket, or, better, the dustbin.

10. CIVILIZATION

According to an official report, a major crime was committed every 11·3 seconds in the United States in 1958. And there was murder, manslaughter, rape or attempted murder every 3·9 minutes.

According to the federal police, juvenile crime increased between 1953 and 1958 two-and-a-half times more steeply than the increase in population.

During 1957, 47·2% of the arrests for major crimes were of young people under eighteen.

Statistics issued by the F.B.I. show a total of 2,796,400 major crimes in 1957, or 23·9% more than the average for the five preceding years.

Let it not be thought that these figures are exceptional or that they constitute some kind of record.

President Johnson, with a courageous frankness that does him credit, has recently declared that the crime rate, appalling though it already was, increased by 130% during the past year. In Nevada, California and Arizona the average is 13 crimes per 1,000 inhabitants; 37% of the criminals are under eighteen.

Is this what is called Progress?

11. DEATH TO THE POOR!

A certain Mr J. H. . . . (a millionaire, that goes without saying) has decided to found an "Institute" for the purpose of sterilizing poor women who are considered (by whom?) to have insufficient means for bringing up their children. "For humanity's sake," he assures us. We guessed as much. It seems that this gentleman declares himself a sociologist by profession. I would have guessed a grave-digger.

In his place I think I would have had another idea (a stupid one no doubt, as it didn't cross the mind of the sociologist-millionaire): the millions of dollars which in all humility Mr J. H. . . . says he'll devote to founding his "Institute" might possibly have allowed these poor women to be less poor, and hence to be able to remain women. . . .

St Augustine, who was neither a millionaire nor a sociologist, said, "It is good to help the hungry, but it would be better if no one was hungry." However, I don't think he had the above solution in mind. St Augustine was faithful to the Gospel. But who knows whether the sociologist-millionaire has ever heard of it?

In barbarian times a great war-chief won himself melancholy fame by his dictum: "*Vae Victis*" (woe to the defeated).

We have progressed since then. . . .

12. . . . AND TO THE SICK

We found an appalling news item in the official Bulletin of the Canadian Catholic Conference of 27 December 1964. It said that:

A Catholic organization of Alberta will ask the government of that province to put an end to the sterilization of its mentally sick.

The 150 members who attended the third annual reunion of the Catholic Welfare Association of Alberta unanimously supported the committee's resolution on sterilization.

Mr Frank Fleming, who presided over the annual meeting,

pointed out that the first legislation in Alberta on sterilization went back to 1928. This law allowed sterilization for people authorized to leave mental hospitals on condition that they gave their consent.

In 1942 the law was amended so as to include people defined as mentally abnormal and, in this case, *consent is not necessary.* The final amendment dates from 1955.

Mr Fleming pointed out that a similar law also exists in British Columbia and in several American States.

Three questions only:

Has the Government of Alberta ever heard of the Declaration of the Rights of Man?

Are there any Christians in the province of Alberta?

What does the U.N.O. think of these legalized crimes?

13. WHEN LOVE DESERTS THE WORLD (1)

Account sheet of a boxing match which, according to the papers, lasted . . . one minute:

	Dollars
Takings	201,000
Rights paid by television for live transmission	3,600,000
Radio rights and foreign rights	500,000
Total	4,301,000
Share of each boxer	700,000

Or 71,683 dollars a second – the income of a hundred Algerian peasants in ONE YEAR.

Three thousand "lucky ones" (!) had paid through the nose for the privilege of "living that minute"!

The winner (or the loser – I wouldn't know) declared modestly before the fight that he was the greatest, the strongest and the finest, that mankind was to be profoundly shaken, that he would become a legend – and he didn't raise a giggle from the audience.

When love deserts the world, cads are princes, and monsters kings.

WHEN LOVE DESERTS THE WORLD (2)

Some 2,000 inhabitants of the suburbs of Vienna (Austria) have bought for a sum of less than 50 francs a paper amulet bearing cabalistic signs and intended to provide effective protection against radiation resulting from atomic explosions.

Don't shrug your shoulders, don't laugh: the French, and Parisians in particular, are just as bad. Diviners, soothsayers, astrologers, fortune-tellers, clairvoyants of both sexes and every hue number nearly half a million in the country of Descartes and Pascal. And their business takings top the 250 milliard mark (old francs).

In Paris and the suburbs over 10,000 traders in delusion grow rich at the expense of 8 million superstitious citizens who call themselves sceptics and consider themselves advanced.

A wizard or a witch for every 800 inhabitants. Delphi with a vengeance!

Twice as many fortune-tellers from tea-leaves as doctors; five times as many priestesses of the tarot pack as priests of the Lord . . . which doesn't prevent their clients from claiming – and sometimes believing – that they have strong independent minds and are faithful apostles of each-man-for-himself, nor from chastising those pitiable retrograde people who still believe in God.

When love deserts the world, the reign of the sorcerers returns.

WHEN LOVE DESERTS THE WORLD (3)

Do you want a pair of pyjamas for a dog? It will cost you only 12 dollars. A nightdress for his girl-friend? Forty dollars. More expensive, yes, but it has the additional charm of a fur collar. There even exist, it seems, wigs for dogs.

Wall Street Journal – with a name like that, it must be serious – tells us that last year Americans spent 530 million dollars on *special* foods for their dogs, and 125 million dollars on the delicate stomachs of their cats.

MORE THAN ON THEIR CHILDREN.

England doesn't lag behind, nor does France. A paper of the serious type told us recently that "a holiday club for dogs" has been started near Paris. I quote:

> At an average price of 55 francs a week, four-footed holiday-makers will be able to frisk about in a large park, supervised by trained keepers, after having passed a qualifying medical examination. Moreover, a famous Paris veterinary surgeon has

E

drawn up a series of menus rich in calories which will be taken at fixed hours by groups of fifteen in a large refectory.

There's no mistake about it, those who make a profession of doing absurd things get rich. Thus a "famous painter" (I quote again) "takes a tiger-cat aged six months with him wherever he goes. While the 'Master' lives in one of the luxury hotels of the capital, the animal occupies an adjoining apartment in the same building. 'She's a remarkable creature,' the painter tells us, 'intelligent and very well-bred. She eats at the same hours as myself a special *paté* based on horse meat which I have sent from the United States.' "

Additional detail: the animal wears a necklace encrusted with jewels round its neck.

I love animals as I love all God's creatures. And it's because I love them that I'm ashamed. . . .

*   *   *

Heard on the radio: "*It's Christmas! Think of your dog.* . . . A shop has just created a bed with a canopy for him, a warm fur-lined coat, and also a cowboy suit on which the sheriff's star has not been forgotten. . . ."

When love deserts the world CHRISTMAS IS FOR DOGS!

14. HAVE PITY ON CHRISTMAS!

I was in the Douala-Paris plane. There was a magazine in the pocket of my seat. I picked it up automatically. On its chocolate-that-melts-in-the-mouth cover there was the picture of a girl. The standard female of the cinema – pretty, smiling. Worse than naked: undressed. In a pose that was titillative rather than artistic.

Just the usual in fact, as you'll have realized. What was less usual was the caption attached to this display: "Christmas Number."

No, not that! We're used to girls displaying their skin in mass-circulation magazines, and I'm told that young men nowadays yawn at strip-tease sessions. But not, please, under the sign of Christmas. Not on the cover of a publication which hopes to increase its sales by saying "Christmas Number".

Let those who see Christmas merely as a pretext for extra revelry or for staying in bed have the goodness to wait for New Year's Day. That's the day for those things. Not Christmas.

Let them leave Christmas with its message, its sweetness, the crib, the clay figures, the shepherds. And the children who go to sleep dreaming of the Child who will come to visit them, of the poor little Child who was born on that day and whose love was to shake the world.

Let them celebrate something else, anything, nothing, but not Christmas.

And although it's said that Christmas night is the night when the beasts talk, let them stay silent.

Christmas is the time for angels; not tarts.

15. AND THEY WANT PEACE TOO

We remember the scandal that flared up between the wars when we learnt that while coffee was a luxury in Austria it was being used as locomotive fuel in Brazil. But that was just a beginning.

Thus in 1934 – to quote only one year and one set of figures – while 2,400,000 people died of hunger, those having too much purposely destroyed:

> 200,000 trucks of coffee,
> 258,000 trucks of sugar,
> 26,000 tons of rice,
> 25,000 tons of meat.

But we've done better since then.

1957. *Le Courrier de l'UNESCO* (April) informed us that the American Chamber and Senate had passed a law the previous year whose aim was (we quote): ". . . to help farmers to withdraw part of their land from the production of foodstuffs of which at present there is a surplus."

The reductions in area hoped for by the American government were:

> 5 million hectares (*c.* 12 million acres) for wheat,
> 2 million hectares (*c.* 5 million acres) for maize,
> 1·2 million hectares (*c.* 3 million acres) for cotton.

(May we point out, for purposes of comparison, that the whole of France produces 4,500,000 hectares – about 11 million acres – of wheat, and 500,000 hectares – about $1\frac{1}{4}$ million acres – of maize.)

1959. A few lines in the corner of a paper; a few lines without a heading, hidden, almost ashamed. We shall see why.

The last wheat harvest in the United States was the most phenomenal in its history: 1,300 million bushels, compared with 500 million in 1953. The financing of the surplus costs the government as much as the army (i.e. 4,500 milliards). If the U.S.A. produced not a grain of wheat this year, it would still have 325 million bushels in 1960.

And meanwhile half the world has nothing to eat.

Today it's from a country of Black Africa, Ghana, that we get the following information:

In the presence of the Prime Minister and the Minister for Economics, the president of the Ghanaian committee of the International Commission for the control of coffee solemnly set fire to 500 tons of unroasted coffee of the 1964 harvest.

Similar ceremonies will be organized periodically until such time as Ghana has lowered by 5% her annual production of coffee in accordance with the world norms laid down by the International Commission.

And the news agency tells us that the ceremony took place "in the midst of an enthusiastic crowd".

*   *   *

While hundreds of millions of people are starving to death in Asia, China in her turn is gambling on the atom bomb.

India and Pakistan spend four times as much on armaments as on agriculture.

Hitler, who wanted to have guns instead of butter, was no more than a timid apprentice.

And they want Peace too!

THE BLESSED

Lord, hurt us with the sufferings of others

I WROTE in 1947:

A single cry should now rise from the world: Charity!
A single thought: Charity! A single command: Charity!
Neither you nor I will solve the problem of poverty. But if you and I do something, if we do all we can and even more than we can, then some of our brothers will be saved.

"There's so little I can do," people often say to me.
Are you sure?
Do you know that with the price of a packet of cigarettes you can buy two phials of vaccine that could immunize and perhaps save two human beings from typhus or cholera?
Do you know that the price of a cocktail is the price of five phials of quinine or biodure of mercury against malaria or syphilis?
Does a packet of cigarettes or a cocktail count with you as against lives saved and protected, as against the healing and relief of the sick?
That's what you can do with your "so little".

And now stop reading, and stand up. Look at your placid, well-fed face and clean clothes in the mirror. Then cast your eye round your comfortable room and the children who love you; observe your protected life.
And make up your mind.

1. MESSAGE FROM THE CHILDREN OF MILAN
TO ALL THE CHILDREN OF THE WORLD

When in 1964 the children of Milan sent me the marvellous and most moving result of all their small personal sacrifices, they also

sent this message which will go straight to the heart of the youth
of the world.

We, the children of today, are responsible for the world of the
year 2000
The grown-ups tell us to conquer;
but as for us, we want to love.
The grown-ups teach us to hoard;
but what we want is to give.
We've not been told about the existence of the hungry, of those
who suffer, not knowing why or till when.
We want to be of use to the poor people of the world.
We don't want to make war when we grow up.
We are well, we want for nothing, we eat when we're hungry
and sleep in our beds, whereas 400 million children in the
world live in great suffering.
We, children of today, we feel ourselves to be responsible for
the world in the year 2000.

Up till now we've been enthusiastic about victories in sport,
the conquest of space; but now we want to invite all the
children of the world to unite in a great enterprise, an
enterprise confined to the earth and whose goal is to make the
world a little happier, and above all:
a little less in pain,
a little less sick,
a little less hungry,
a little less divided.
And to begin this great action at once, we offer you, Monsieur
Follereau, the fruits of the sacrifices of lots of Milanese
children, so that you can help lots of other children less
happy than we are.
We thank you for having taught us that no one has the right
to be happy alone.

Milan, 9 March 1964.

2. HUMBLE YET DAZZLING CONQUERORS

The battle I've described in the foregoing pages (its early days,
that is), the battle I've waged for so many years and shall continue
to wage until I die – this battle would have been impossible
without all of you. I would have chucked it, given up, fled, if I
hadn't known that you were there, every day, in every post,
simple soldiers of the noblest cause, anonymous fighters, humble
yet dazzling conquerors.

Whether it was in giving your "Hour for the Poor", in encouraging your children to put "three shoes in the fireplace", in carrying out the "Good Friday strike against selfishness" – or whether, later, it was for Adzopé, for the lepers, for the World Day or for the Battle against Leprosy (which I shall describe in the following chapters) – you have always been with me, giving me support when the going was rough and often, without even realizing it, showing me the way.

If I've been able to wage these long and difficult battles, and wage them comparatively successfully, it is because you, the poor, humble, suffering workers (but you're the ones who are rich really), you whose names I do not even know, have been there, helping me, understanding me, loving me. I have been your ambassador to the poor; ambassador of the poor to the poor, that's what my life has been.

And my greatest glory and greatest treasure haven't been the honours I've sometimes received in the world, nor the joy of a victory often won at great cost, but the "blue file" where for over thirty years I've kept the evidence of your love.

If before remembering more things I open this file again, the reason is that nothing at all could have been achieved without all of you.

So all you unknown friends who are reading this book, I want you never again to doubt the goodness and compassion of this "Charity that will save the world". I want you to believe, and for ever, that man is marching towards his salvation despite his misfortunes, weaknesses and mistakes. And that the century of the atomic bomb can also be the century of Love.

Now read.

3. A GIRL GIVES UP HER ENGAGEMENT RING FOR ADZOPÉ

I enclose with this letter a money order for 10,000 francs for the building of Adzopé.

When I heard that you'd be coming here I wanted to try and organize some sacrifice for this work from among my friends. But it didn't turn out like that and the sum I enclose is the price of my fiancée's engagement ring. She wouldn't hear of anything else. So I'm happy twice over to be sending you this sum.

If you are able to give a name to one of the houses, as you suggested, call it Jacqueline and Pierre. Perhaps later on other

names will be recorded on the fronts of the Adzopé houses –
those of our children. . . .

I hope your French tour is arousing the same enthusiasm as
ever and that we won't be the only ones to show delight in
Adzopé.

Please believe in my great admiration, Monsieur, for the
mission you have taken on yourself.

How happy that home must be that is based on such radiant
charity.

4. A VISIT

She was a poor, humble woman, insignificant, almost destitute.
At the exit after one of my lectures in a Paris suburb she had
whispered to me: "I want to speak to you. But alone."

So she came to my office this morning and said:

It's years ago now since I first heard you lecture, but I've
been obsessed ever since with the idea of helping you win the
"Battle against Leprosy". I've only my old age pension to live
on – just enough to keep me alive. But I've still got some
strength left in my body and do a bit of char-ing, and I've put
aside the money I get for that for your lepers. In that way all
my working hours are dedicated to them, and I've brought you
the result.

And from an old leather bag she extracted a packet wrapped up
in old newspaper. I opened it in front of her. There were fifty
1000-franc notes.

Fifty thousand francs! For a char at that time that represented
something like 400 hours' work!

Thus for months this poor woman had sacrificed all but the
bare necessities of life (and sometimes no doubt a few of the
necessities) so as to help other unfortunates that she will never see.

5. THE TWO PETERS

He's called Peter. He's fifteen. We found him in 1957 in an
institution in the depths of the African bush.

He had been uprooted from school and dumped there. His
crime: leprosy. His sentence: to be a leper for life. I see him now,
his head obstinately bent, his eyes furtive, the look of a hunted
animal; and *in his despair he had lost almost completely the use of his*

tongue. You'd have to have seen it to believe it. It was only after we'd talked to him very gently and at great length and at last been able to kiss him that a smile lit up the terrible night of that little face.

He wrote to me some weeks later: "You are very kind to have decided to take me as your son. If only you could get me into some good place where I could continue my studies! My thoughts are set on that and my hopes are fixed on you. THANKS TO YOU, MY SOUL IS SINGING."

* * *

He's called Peter. He's fifteen. But, thanks be to God, he is well and lives in Paris.

He'd read the story of his unknown little friend in our bulletin and he badly wanted to do something for him. Only his parents were so poor, so very poor. . . .

So he set out one Sunday for the fields with a chum and spent all the afternoon picking flowers. And in the evening he sold them by the roadside . . . for his little leper.

He made 200 francs. But he thought it so little that he didn't dare send it to me. A friend did so for him.

And that's the story.

He's called Peter and he's fifteen, and he has no idea that he's done something deeply moving. And very important, too.

Because what he's done proves yet again that it isn't power or money that will carry the day, but love. Love, without which nothing is possible; but when it's there, everything is possible.

And our brightest victory is our little sick boy who feels his "soul is singing" because another boy held out flowers one Sunday evening on a French road.

6. A SUBLIME GESTURE

Bologna. The lecture over, I hobbled down the great steps of the Sala Bossi where once upon a time Rossini had taught and where a friendly crowd had just been listening to me.

The auxiliary bishop was playing the part of nurse with exquisite charity and supporting my faltering steps. Suddenly our way was barred by a young man whose body had been played havoc with by polio. The fact that he was walking at all seemed a miracle. We wouldn't have dared touch him for fear of sending him rolling down the immense steps.

Without saying a word he gathered his sticks into his left hand and with his right unclasped a little chain from round his neck. At the end of it hung a small gold medal, a souvenir of his first communion, no doubt. His most precious souvenir; perhaps his only treasure.

He put it in my hand then disappeared in the throng descending the steps.

Who was he? I've no idea. I shall never know, and I shall never see him again. But he will always remain in my memory and my heart.

7. A LETTER

Monsieur,

It is with tears that I beg you to accept these few franc notes for your lepers. These notes are relics. Our second son has just died in a mountaineering accident, buried under an avalanche. He was 18. He was found after eleven days with these few notes in his wallet, soiled and crumpled by their long sojourn in the snow. We wish in the name of our son that they may help you save the lives of a few lepers.

We would like to thank you for setting us the example in the fight for charity. And we beg you to believe in our feelings of deep admiration for your work.

8. LOVE IS STRONGER THAN HATE

From a parish priest in the suburbs of Rome:

I've spoken of your work in helping lepers to the children of my church; they have given their offerings and I send them to you herewith. It's not much – except a proof of brotherly love. We would like this offering to go to a leper colony in the ex-Belgian Congo so that it may carry the message of our brotherly forgiveness to the people who, on a dark day in November 1961, massacred in Kivu thirteen Italian airmen in the service of the Red Cross.

To this offering were added two small gold chains for the same cause and with these lines written by a child:

"May God in his goodness forgive everyone, as he has given us the grace to be able to forgive them."

9. THE STORY OF TWO WEDDING-RINGS

One day a young friend came to see me. He said: "I lost my mother and then, a year later, my father. Now I'm alone and I've nothing left. Nothing except their two wedding-rings, and I've brought them to you for your lepers." Then he hurried away so that I wouldn't see his tears. And I didn't try to stop him – so that he wouldn't see mine.

I've often shown people these wedding rings, symbols of the highest and most touching charity. Now I won't be showing them any more. I've given them away, following the wish of our friend.

It was in Tokyo that I gave them away, to the great and dear Mitsuda after he'd said to me: "You've convinced me." I'd just heard that a marriage had been celebrated at Nagashima between two lepers. For the first time they had been spared the ghastly and inhuman sterilization that made them "different from other men".

Father van Wesel, who had married them, put these rings on their mutilated fingers. And Mitsuda who wanted the putting-on of these humble wedding-rings to be photographed as an event – and an event it was! – Mitsuda whose heart had been won over, smiled at them, for now he is really their father.

And our friend who gave them will read this and smile too, with tears, yes, but they will be tears of joy.

10. THE MIRACLE OF THE SWEETS

She had been given a little bag of sweets as a reward for working well at school. Just a little one, but it delighted her as she wasn't used to getting presents.

First she took one for herself (fair enough, as they were hers), then she handed them round to her school-friends. When that was over she peered into the bag: there was only one left. Would she have it herself? The idea didn't even enter her head. Her little friends had only had one apiece, so why should she have two?

Then she had an idea, a very charming idea, such as only poor children have. She would give this sweet to the Madonna. The Blessed Virgin often received flowers at the altar dedicated to her in church, and sometimes she was surrounded by ugly marble plaques. But no one ever gave her sweets. So perhaps that would be nice for her. . . .

The curé reading his breviary at the back of the church saw the child approach the statue and hold out her hand towards it.

"What are you doing?" he asked.

"I'm giving a present to the Madonna," she said.

"What is it?"

"A sweet."

The old curé was moved but he didn't let it show.

"Our Lady is too grown-up to like sweets," he told her. "She thanks you and asks you to give it to the poorest child you know. The most abandoned child."

It was then that the little girl remembered the lepers.

"I'm going to send it to a leper child," she told her schoolmates.

And they said, "Why don't we all do that?" A collection was organized. They asked their parents, the grocer at the corner, their friends, people in the street, people who never thought about such things, everyone. "It's so as to send a sweet to a leper child," they explained.

As with the loaves and fishes blessed by Christ, the sweets increased and multiplied. Five thousand francs were collected to buy them with.

So that in a poor African village there was joy for a whole group of leper children.

Isn't it a story worthy of the Gospels?

II. NO, MUMMY

"Do you want some sweets?"

"No, Mummy."

"A chocolate? A lolly?"

"No, thank you, Mummy."

"Well, what *do* you want for your tea then?"

"Nothing, Mummy. Or rather, yes, something."

"What?"

"I'd like you to give me the money for my tea."

"Why?"

"To give to the lepers."

This conversation has taken place thousands and thousands of times in Austria – in Austria which is so poor and has been downtrodden for so long. Tens of thousands of children have gone without their cakes, biscuits, sweets or fruit so that lepers in some distant land, whom they will never know, may be helped, tended and healed.

The result of these sacrifices was handed over to me at an infinitely moving ceremony. The sum raised amounted to 2,200,000 francs. Think what that represents in terms of sweets and chocolates and goodies!

I shall never forget that day. I wanted to tell them about the great and beautiful thing they'd done, something infinitely surpassing the magnificent sum they'd collected. I wanted to say Thank you. But it was they who thanked me for having come.

I looked at the leaders. They were so happy. Nothing could have added to their happiness.

I said a few banal words, anything, so that they wouldn't see that I felt like crying – crying with joy.

12. ON ONE'S KNEES

A postal order for 100 francs with these words written on the back: "Collected for the lepers by a group of 35 cripples."

One should receive such an offering as that on one's knees.

13. AND MANY MORE . . .

Half my earnings

As I was happily able to do the grape-harvest in spite of my age, I'm sending you half my earnings, the other half goes to another good work, and rest assured that it's a great pleasure for me to be able to do it. (From a woman.)

Alone and almost completely disabled

3 francs. I'd like to be able to do much more, but I'm an invalid myself and have had to enter hospital. I'm alone and almost completely disabled, but I want to send you these few stamps – like that I save the price of a postal order. (From a woman.)

A rice day

200 francs. Instead of making a collection, which might have been unproductive as none of the boarders have any pocket-money, we had the idea of a communal economy. We took a

vote in all the classes as to the urgency of the measures to be taken, and what we decided on was "a rice day". Both the midday and evening meals were composed mainly of rice pudding which has enabled us to save 200 francs – which we send herewith.

My paralysed husband

100 francs. I don't know whether I shall be able to go on sending you my pittance, as my husband has been paralysed for the last six months and bedridden for a year. We have sold our house so as to live in a smaller one. But I want to mark this day by a contribution to your great work.

A mother's last note

As usual I send my contribution to your "Battle against Leprosy". This time I'm sending a 10 franc note (1000 old francs, but they're still valid). I want to send you this note and not a p.o. because it's the last of the ones that were in my beloved mother's purse when she died. I feel that by sending you this very note I'm including her with me as the giver.

One-and-a-half hours' housework a day

I enclose herewith 10,000 francs. I'm 74 and I pray that God will give me the strength to go on doing 1½ hours of housework a day so as to recoup this money. I live on my old age pension and this hour-and-a-half of housework gives me something over. I get 150 francs a day because they pay me according to my capacity for work (I do the washing-up).

You told us. . . .

250 new francs – on the occasion of my daughter's first communion.

You told us that "no one has the right to be happy alone."

To the end of our lives

My wife and I are seventy-five, I live on my workman's pension, and there are so many good works we are asked to contribute to – it's sometimes hard to turn a deaf ear. But to the end of our lives we shall remember the magnificent work that you have started with such outstanding devotion and, we are sure, at great personal sacrifice.

I sell oysters . . .

I sell oysters on a café *terrasse* in the rue de Flandre. On St Catherine's day the café proprietor gave a dance. I had the idea of doing a turn as a comic conjuror, and it was so successful that I asked at the end of my turn if I could make a collection for the lepers. I got 250 francs which I send herewith, asking you to acknowledge their receipt by return. I'm adding 50 francs on my own account.

A little mending . . .

I'm a cripple and live on an invalid's pension plus the little bit of mending that I do. But there are others poorer than me: here are 30 francs for your poor.

I'm a Communist

I've just heard your appeal on the radio for the poor lepers; I'm overwhelmed by the deep humanity of your appeal, and your parting shot is terribly true: "What have I done?" I can only answer, "What can I do?" Tell me, and I shall be happy to follow your advice.

Oh we aren't in perfect agreement as I'm a Communist, and proudly so, believe me. But our ideas meet precisely on this wonderful theme, of helping our brothers in distress.

I'm a free-mason

I'm only a simple artisan and free-mason, but I have a profound admiration for you as for all those who devote themselves to the good of Mankind without distinction of race or ideas. So whenever it's possible I'll send you my pittance, however small. Today I send 1500 francs.

If I need it . . .

Herewith a note for 5000 francs. Please God I won't need it! If I do, I'll bear the privation with joy for the sake of your dear lepers, who are dear to me too.

From a classroom

We apologise for sending so little, but we have all denied ourselves something to send this much. Some of us have taken money from our money-boxes for the lepers, others have gone without sweets. One of our classmates, Véronique, gave up ice cream during the hot weather though she saw her little sister eating it. She's given the money she saved to the lepers.

We hope that this sum will bring joy to your sick, and courage
to the man who is devoting himself to them.

Tram tickets

The enclosed is from my wife, to save a leper. It's money saved
franc by franc by putting aside the price of tram tickets for
so many journeys made on foot.

From prison

From the prisoners in the central block at C. . . .: 1000 francs.

No! to hate

Herewith 1000 N.F. Kindly accept, dear Monsieur Follereau,
part of a Victims of Nazism bonus – from a priest (33 months'
deportation) who offers you the ransom of suffering to tend
your poor lepers.

Paralytic

10 N.F. Gift from a paralytic to a leper.

Disseminated sclerosis

2000 F. from someone paralysed with disseminated sclerosis in
hospital at C. . . , with his very loving thoughts for all your
lepers.

Elephantiasis

For your dear lepers. I am myself seriously crippled as I am
stricken with elephantiasis and have only a small invalid's
pension to live on, but I am happy to send you my modest
contribution.

Sick and disabled

3000 F. from a small group of sick and disabled people in the
Hôtel-Dieu, for the 6th World Day for Lepers.

Victim of polio

500 francs. For your good work and for all your sick, please
accept this modest sum. As I am myself a victim of polio and
the father of two children, I know what illness and suffering
and need mean.

She regains her lucidity . . .

I send you 200 francs in stamps for "the Hour for the Poor",
for the lepers. It's sent by an old lady of 82, very poor and ill.

She has lost her memory and has every kind of affliction, but she always regains her lucidity when it's a matter of thinking of your fine work and remaining loyal to it.

Light in darkness

10 N.F. From someone confined in the psychiatric hospital of Villejuif (Seine). Here are her savings, earned by the work she does in hospital.

So that there may be less suffering in the world . . .

10,000 francs in memory of a sick woman who has suffered appallingly – so that there may be less suffering in the world.

Don't die! . . .

Yes, Monsieur Follereau, yes, please go on practising charity to those rejected by the world. How can one not be full of admiration for all that you are doing and getting done so as to improve their sad lot? Take care of your health and your morale, and . . . don't die! What would become of them then?

The offering of a life

Is this the last time I'll be writing to you? So be it! . . . I am at the moment following a course of injections, but, alas, it's chiefly to please the doc.

I've asked God for a "useless" miracle, to get me better, but it's preferable that men like you should have a long life for you have such great spiritual value and still have so much good work to do on earth, whereas I'm nothing but a typist with no future. . . . It's better like this. (From a man.)

Stronger than death

I send you this small p.o. for your dear lepers, with the hope that God will forgive me my cowardice; in face of an immense grief, I wanted to die. And then I thought of the physical and mental sufferings of your lepers and I decided to continue to struggle on, me too.

I'd like to have a heart big enough . . .

Herewith 100 francs. I apologise for sending so little, but I'm ill and on my own. . . . I'd like to have a heart big enough to enfold within it all the suffering of the world.

F

I shan't feel really poor . . .

Please accept these 20 francs. It's nothing, I know. But I'm on my beam-ends. However, I shan't feel really poor till the day comes when I shan't be able to send anything even by going without.

*   *   *

Humble and dazzling conquerors, it's you who have given me faith, strength and joy.

And it's you, tireless and undaunted as you are, who will give the same strength to the young people who will take my place and win the last battles, because they will also have taken my place in your hearts.

Part Two

FIFTEEN MILLION MEN

ADZOPÉ

As I EXPLAINED in Part One, it was during my war-period of "retreat" with the missionary Sisters of Our Lady of the Apostles that I made my decision to devote the rest of my life to lepers. This was not a leap in the dark, for I had known the Sisters of Our Lady of the Apostles for some time. As for lepers, I had already met them, too – as I described in a communication to the VIIth International Leprosy Congress held in Tokyo in 1958:

Our car had hardly left that African village when we had to stop near a stream so as to top up the radiator. Before long several frightened faces emerged from the bush, followed by skeletal bodies. I called to them to come nearer. Some did the reverse and ran away, while the braver ones stood rooted to the spot, gazing at me from sad staring eyes. I said to the guide:

"Who are these men?"

"Lepers," he answered.

"Why are they here?"

"They're lepers."

"Yes, so you said, but wouldn't they be better off in the village? What have they done to be cast out?"

"They're lepers," he repeated obstinately.

"Does anyone look after them?"

My guide shrugged his shoulders and walked away. And it was then that I realized that there existed an unforgivable crime, a crime deserving of any punishment, a crime without appeal or pardon: leprosy. And it was then that I made up my mind to plead one single cause for the rest of my life: that of the 12 to 15 million men whom our ignorance, selfishness and cowardice have made lepers.

So I owe it to car-trouble that I became involved in the "Fight against Leprosy". But also, and perhaps more, I owe it to my life-long admiration for missionaries and the immense gratitude that linked me for ever to the Sisters of Our Lady of the Apostles.

I came across them for the first time in 1935, when two shy, smiling, self-effacing nuns came to the door to invite my wife to their charity bazaar. One of them was the Superior-General of the Order: the other was later to travel all over France with me.

Thus started an acquaintance that soon ripened into a friendship that has remained steadfast for thirty years.

So that when I knocked at the door of their mother-house I was confident that I'd be received as a friend; in fact I was received as a brother.

Even then I knew the road well, for the nuns and I had already co-operated in a task – a bold one at the time, but a grandiose one – which was to play a crucial part in the "Fight against Leprosy", first as an example then as a symbol. I am referring to Adzopé.

But to tell the story of Adzopé we must go back a little.

1939. The Ivory Coast[1]

An island at the level of Abidjan. An island on the lagoon, an island no different from the other islands, with tall palm-trees and lush vegetation. An island that seems made for happiness, peace and repose, and with the gentle and attractive name of Desirée.

Yet this earthly paradise is really a hell. When canoes approach it, the rowers look away and make off again at top speed. For Desirée is an island inhabited by damned beings. Branded with the most horrible of all stigmas, they run away as you draw near, or hide themselves. Their dwelling-places? Wretched hovels built with their own poor mutilated hands. Their food? What they can find or what, on occasion, is thrown to them.

And this island, seemingly so full of promise and happiness, often re-echoes with cries of hate and despair. For it is the prison, the graveyard, of the lepers of the Ivory Coast.

It was near this island that Mother Eugénia's seaplane one day landed. She was then Superior-General of the Sisters of Our Lady of the Apostles. And so it was that these wretched people, the damned, saw the missionary of charity come down from the sky.

[1] Extract from the pamphlet *Le premier million d'Adzopé* (*The First million of Adzopé*) (out of print).

She was dressed all in white and she smiled and held out her arms. She talked to them and listened patiently to their heart-rending stories. They showed their sores, explained their plight. Mother Eugénia went on smiling, but her eyes were full of tears.

And it was then that she conceived her magnificent plan: to build a little town for the lepers. A little town where they wouldn't be cooped up like animals but treated like men, with the respect and dignity they deserved. A little town where they would have the illusion of freedom. No great walls blocking out the sky, hemming them in.

But how was she to reconcile this impression of freedom with the restrictions imposed by the health rules of the time? Our missionary found the answer: the town would be built in the middle of a virgin forest. Thus these unfortunates would be isolated more safely than by any wall, yet wouldn't feel cramped and confined. They'd be able to come and go at will in the town; they'd really have the impression of being free.

In this town which would be their own, Mother Eugénia wanted to gather them together in large numbers and give them a life as near as possible to the life of normal people. Each family would have its small house and its garden which the lepers themselves would cultivate – not only for what they could garner from it but so that they would have the beneficial illusion of "doing something", of living to a certain extent by their own work.

They would be taught a craft, a local artisanate would be created and possibilities for small trading. They would enjoy the recreations that progress has produced – the radio and the cinema. It would be like a little town anywhere. . . .

Nowadays all this seems simple enough. And natural – the "Fight against Leprosy" having effectively eradicated stupid prejudices and senseless fears. But in 1939 the project was revolutionary and, according to some, crazy. However, those who were scandalized at the idea were quick to reassure themselves: "It's just a utopian dream, chimerical, unrealizable. You can't build a town in a forest. She's a well-meaning woman, no doubt, but she just doesn't know what she's up against. Her charity has run away with her. The thing's out of the question."

The missionary Sisters, on the other hand, were convinced of the feasibility of their project and prepared to devote their lives

to it with enthusiasm and joy. But though conviction was necessary, it wasn't enough. They had to muster the material means
without which a dream does indeed remain a dream.

It was these that I volunteered to provide. When I look back on
those days after all these years my action astounds me, for, at the
time, the task I had undertaken was an almost superhuman one. I
can only assume that the nuns' charity was highly infectious!
And already had God's blessing on it. . . .

In order to obtain funds, I had one means only at that time:
the word. So I started talking about Adzopé. For ten years,
accompanied by two of the Sisters (of whom one, as I've said,
had come to our door in 1935) I was to travel all the roads of
France for this purpose. And after France, Belgium, Switzerland,
Algeria, Tunisia, Morocco and Canada.

If I remember rightly, my first lecture took place on 15 April
1943 in the municipal theatre of Annécy (the Occupation being in
full swing). But none of the towns of the southern zone was left
out. The opera houses of Lyons and Marseilles welcomed us, and
also the Capitol of Toulouse. At Vichy it was the Apostolic
Nuncio, Mgr Valerio Valeri, who chaired our meeting.

After the Liberation the Government offered us the Comédie-
Française to launch our campaign. Again it was the Apostolic
Nuncio who presided. But a new prelate had recently taken over
this post. He was called Mgr Roncalli. The whole world has
loved him since as Pope John XXIII, and today mourns him. My
friendship with him, based on mutual trust and affection, dated
from that day and never wavered during all the ups and downs
of our great project.

Meanwhile the collection taken by the Sisters every evening
after my lecture was sent to the mother-house. And every month
the money went from Vénisseux to the Ivory Coast and the work
went on. . . .

And what a work! It was only many years later, when I myself
went to Adzopé, that I realized what risks our enterprise had
entailed, what dangers, and what setbacks. . . .

* * *

Seven years have passed.[1]

[1] Extract from the pamphlet, *Adzopé, ville de la Charité* (Adzopé, town of Charity)
(out of print).

In the still splendour of the morning our little van sped briskly along the road. The weather was radiant; soon the air would be hot, and later torrid, so this moment was precious and we breathed in great lungfuls of the freshness that would pass so soon. The forest surrounding us, the cruel, treacherous forest with its deadly nocturnal beasts, was smiling and welcoming at this kind hour. We were bathed in peace and a joy newly minted. Our souls drank deep of it and revelled in it.

The lepers' town is 15 kilometres from Adzopé. It is reached by a road running through the forest – a road which the Sisters beat out yard by yard, then imposed on the forest. Yard by yard over 15 kilometres! They threw thirteen bridges over the marigots, or branch-channels, inhabited by somnolent caymans. Nothing, no one, can give the faintest idea of this gigantic task. But when I exclaimed in wonder, Mother Julia said in her calm voice, "Oh, it was nothing." And indeed it was nothing compared with what was to come.

It lies at the top of a slope. One comes on it suddenly. We had gone on and on through the oppressive forest, then suddenly there was light, space, life. A few months before, and that, too, had been forest. But the forest had retreated in front of charity.

It had been a terrible struggle. Huge great trees – baobabs, giant bombaxes – were supine on the ground, their burnt-out trunks bearing witness to it.

It was Mother Julia who told me the story, quite simply, as if describing an everyday occurrence.

Building the houses, that was nothing; but before doing that we had to reclaim the land, cut down the trees, clear the undergrowth, level the ground. Hundreds of workmen were required, but how were we to feed them? As you know, we're 15 kilometres from the nearest human beings, and that was why the business of building Adzopé meant first growing vegetables, making vegetable gardens so as to feed the workmen.

Then, who were the workmen to be? Who would consent to exile himself from his family for months or years so as to work in the middle of the bush?

Finally we got a small team together and they made the first assault on the forest. The small trees don't count, they come down by themselves, or almost. But the big ones are different. The wood of some of them is so hard that steel hasn't the slightest effect on them, while others have such vast trunks that it takes a team of five men three days to get one down. And there are hundreds and hundreds of this kind.

Building houses – that's nothing!

But the worst was to come. One day a false move brought a tree down on a group of workmen. Two of them were crushed and killed. So the rumour at once went round that the tree was a fetish, that the spirits of the forest were angry and would kill anyone who laid a sacrilegious hand on those venerated trunks.

The two hundred workmen so laboriously assembled took fright and made off. We chased them up, reasoned with them for days or weeks on end, but it made no difference; they wouldn't come back. Others had to be found – but where? We had to go right to the upper Ivory Coast to be sure of recruiting reliable men. Then it was the rainy season and we just had to twiddle our thumbs for a few months. That's just about how the work was done, at the heart of the virgin forest.

I shall never forget the first night I spent there. It was one of those stifling, oppressive nights when you get bogged down in a series of nightmares. . . . As soon as dawn broke resplendently on the horizon, I got up and went out in an attempt to rid myself of them. And it was then that I heard the sound of singing. I listened; I couldn't believe my ears. Someone was singing at the other end of the road – singing "Chez la Mère Michel, y a du bon café".

For a moment I thought I must still be dreaming. But no; I really was at Adzopé in the depths of the forest with the lepers. And I still heard the same refrain, "Chez la Mère Michel, y a du bon café."

So I went to investigate where the singing was coming from. It was coming from the dispensary. Sister Flora had already been at work for an hour, sleeves rolled up, blood on the bare fingers of her white hands – the blood of the leper she had just been tending.

And she was singing.

And the sick who were awaiting their turn joined in the refrain.

Thus this little new-born town was already radiant with hope – because it was a work of love.

*   *   *

That happened fifteen years ago in 1950, and yet I remember it as vividly as if it was yesterday.

So that's what Adzopé was like, Adzopé to which I joyfully consecrated the ten best years of my life (between 40 and 50). Nothing could have given me more delight than all those journeys that I made so as to build "the town of charity", exhausting as they often were, and sometimes disappointing, yet always exhilarating. And whenever I go to Vénisseux and visit my dear friends of such long-standing, I always want to say "Thank you" to them.

Adzopé has now become the Leprosy Institute of the Ivory Coast. In a speech delivered in 1961 on the occasion of the VIIIth World Leprosy Day, the Minister for Public Health of that country announced that 250 million French West-African francs (i.e. about £365,000) would be devoted to turning Adzopé into an institute for research and care with the most up-to-date equipment, and that an important social rehabilitation service would be established there.

250 million French West-African francs! In ten arduous years I had raised only a tenth of that sum! However, M. Houphouët-Boigny, president of the Republic, had the tactful thought of informing me of it himself and of bestowing on me with his own hands the tie of *commandeur dé l'Ordre national*.

It was thus that the wonderful story of Adzopé came to an end as far as I was concerned.

MY FIRST WORLD TOUR

BUT LEPROSY NOW had me in its grip. Not that I was infected by it, but I was its happy prisoner. I had seen too much pain, too much distress, too many faces eaten up by disease and shame; too many hopeless eyes had been turned towards me. . . .

And meanwhile the building of Adzopé had brought me an enormous correspondence, often tangential to the immediate purpose of the enterprise. Doctors, missionaries and the sick wrote to me from all corners of the world – letters that were often dramatic and sometimes violent. But whatever the tone, all could be summarized thus: "And how about us? Who's giving a thought to us? What are you going to do for us? No one thinks about us – or no one seems to. Our sick are outcasts, and we are intruders if not fanatics. How long is it going to go on? Will someone one day rise up and tell the happy people of the world about the appalling fate of the millions stricken with leprosy?"

"There are millions," someone wrote, "millions living without care, help or love." The figure seemed improbable, but one thing was certain: that the problem of the "leper" existed, and that it was a grievous, shocking and often discreditable one.[1]

In order to take my bearings and get the "Fight" going with full knowledge of the subject, there was only one course open to me: to go and see.

This was the purpose of my first world tour which took me notably to Molokai in the Hawaiian Islands where Father Damien had lived and died. Then, in the following year, I zigzagged across Asia, then Africa, and the islands of the Indian Ocean. In three

[1] In 1943, sensing the enormity of the task that lay ahead, and so as to avoid a dissipation and arbitrary distribution of effort, I had proposed the creation of a "World Leprosy Board" whose purpose would be to assemble as complete a documentation as possible on the number of victims, their geographical distribution, their social condition, and the type of aid that they could depend on. However, my proposal was inopportune at that time and had no follow-up. Twenty years later it seems to be coming into its own.

years I had travelled more than 200,000 kilometres, in the course of which my wife and I changed planes 91 times and I gave 296 talks in 35 countries. If my figures are so precise, it's because I kept a travel diary in which I noted them down.

It was during that time that I had my first encounter with Doctor Schweitzer. We arrived at Lambaréné on Good Friday. "We shall celebrate Our Lord's death together," he said, "you as a Catholic, I as a Protestant. I shall play Bach's Passion Chorals for our souls together. Would you like that?" And I shall always see him sitting at his modest instrument and playing with a sad gentle smile while the lepers made a silent circle around us. I often met Doctor Schweitzer after that – in France, and for the last time, shortly before his death, in Gaboon. He remains for me the epitome of all those admirable doctors who have dedicated their lives to the service of Africa, of those of whom the High Commissioner, M. Cornut-Gentile, said: "Has any other such tiny army achieved such a huge victory?" A brotherly army whence emerge venerated men of such stature as Jamot, Muraz, Richet. . . .

Tour du monde chez les lépreux (World Tour to the Lepers) was the book I wrote about these travels. It was published by Flammarion and is today out of print. In it I showed my anger:

> No, it can't go on! No, it's impossible! Or else don't tell me that we're in the twentieth century of Christianity, and chuck all that nonsense about liberty, fraternity and democracy. I'm ashamed, yes I'm ashamed!
>
> I'm ashamed to eat a hearty meal, I'm ashamed to sleep without nightmares, while millions of beings are dying or rotting away in the most appalling circumstances of solitude and filth.
>
> Lepers in madhouses, lepers in the desert, lepers in prison, lepers in graveyards – that's what I've seen on my travels.
>
> I shall say it because I must say it, without passion yet without reserve.
>
> And together we shall shout loud and long, as long and as loud as is necessary, so loud and so long that the world's conscience will be compelled to wake up from its sleep, and happy men will be forced to hear what we're saying.

PETITION TO THE UNO

BUT I DIDN'T only bring back a book from my travels; I also brought back the facts that enabled me to draw up a petition which I addressed to the United Nations Organization on 20 September 1952. I shall quote it in full because it forms the foundational document of the "Fight against Leprosy".

Monsieur le Président,

Article 13 of the Charter lays down that the General Assembly of the United Nations encourages study and makes recommendations with a view to "developing international co-operation in the fields . . . of public health, and facilitating for everyone, without distinction of race, sex, language or creed, the enjoyment of the rights of man and the basic freedoms."

The Dumbarton Oaks text is still more explicit. It says: "The United Nations will be responsible for *imposing* and maintaining . . . a *universal* respect for, and a *strict observation* of all men's rights and basic freedoms, without distinction of race, sex, language or creed."

It is in virtue of these declarations, and as an expression of their unanimous thought and will, that I make this appeal to the United Nations.

It concerns lepers.

In the year 1952, in the twentieth century of Christianity, when the words liberty and democracy are being used – if not understood – to the full, millions of beings are living in the world as outlaws, as victims of a sort of social excommunication, though having committed no crime other than being ill. . . .

Stricken with an affection less contagious than tuberculosis and less repugnant than syphilis, they are nevertheless banished by the rest of mankind.

If outstanding efforts have already been made on their behalf in several countries, and if the World Health Organization – thanks to men of feeling and talent – has already set effective action in motion, it remains true nonetheless that the leper normally remains condemned to leprosy in perpetuity

. . . often relegated to foul "ghettos" or abandoned to the evils of local superstition.

The indifference of civilized countries in face of this tragic problem is such that no country today would be able to provide even approximative statistics of the number of these victims, and no one currently knows to the nearest few millions the number of lepers that there are in the world.

Heiser and Sticker put the figure at 2 million.

Burnet, Rogers and Muir at 5 million.

Oberdoerffer at 7 million.

These statistics may differ, but they have one thing in common: they are all very much lower than the reality.

Having toured the world myself, having gathered information *on the spot*, and *myself* interrogated the best qualified people, I have come to the conclusion, to the conviction, that there are at least 12 million lepers in the world. That is to say:

1 leper for every 200 inhabitants;

1 leper for two tuberculosis victims.[1]

Why have investigations undertaken by equally qualified and equally sincere people led to such different conclusions?

Because in a number of countries leprosy is still a shameful disease. They hide their lepers; they cover them up, treat them as if they don't exist – in families as in nations.

Whether owing to ignorance or deliberate fiddling, the statistics are false.

The world of the future will be shocked at the callousness of our generation which leaves millions of human beings to rot in the world; it will find it hard to believe in our expressions of brotherhood so frequently voiced in speech, so seldom confirmed in practice.

And our cowardice and inertia have all the less excuse in that recent scientific discoveries allow us to believe that the great majority of lepers can today be effectively cured and rendered non-infectious.

The price of this treatment is paltry; its application extremely simple.

Without showing any exaggerated confidence whatever, it can be said that leprosy is now held in check. Within fifty years it could be conquered. It depends on nothing but our courage and good will.

But in order to free mankind of leprosy, men must first be

---

[1] Information gathered in the course of my travels since that time has led me to believe that the number of leprosy victims is over 15 millions.

wrested from the absurd horror in which they hold it, and lepers from the unjust and intolerable curse that dogs them. If as soon as their first symptoms appear, lepers too often flee, run to earth, hide themselves, this is because leprosy means the leper-colony, and these too often signify prison.

In a masterly work devoted to this disease, Dr Chaussinand, head of the Leprosy Service at the Pasteur Institute in Paris, puts it like this:

The internment of lepers has in our time taken on a harshness and severity unknown in the Middle Ages. . . . Today we speak of sequestration for life, and the leper-colonies are often situated on islands or in deserts so as to forestall any possible escape. At the time when convict prisons still existed, criminals were not always kept in such merciless captivity as lepers are today in some leper-colonies. This archaic notion of anti-leper prophylaxis displays a cruelty that one doesn't expect to find – at least in time of peace – in a world claiming to be civilized.

And the eminent leprologist adds:

These inhuman measures could just be excused if there was proof of their necessity. But it has now to be admitted that prevention of the disease based on the internment of the sick is not only illogical *and* ineffective *but* dangerous.

And he gives telling evidence for his statement.

Thus there is no reason whatsoever to condemn the victim *a priori* to isolation, less still to hound him from society.

The leper is sick as other men are sick. He should be cared for like other sick men – at home when his disease is taken early, is still benign and non-contagious, in isolation wings and even special hospitals or villages when the form of his leprosy constitutes a danger. But always with absolute respect for his person, his beliefs and his hopes, and without ever encroaching on that most sacred and precious of all men's goods: his freedom.

It is necessary, therefore, to promote a campaign of opinion in those countries where leprosy is rife so that the leper, having become an ordinary medical case – neither more nor less alarming than so many others – may be treated with human kindness by his neighbours. Once he is reassured and re-integrated into the human community whence ignorance and selfishness had banished him, he will be able to say, "I've got leprosy" without fear, and we shall be able to listen to him with no more emotion or hate than when we listen to someone saying, "I've got cancer," or "They've given me a pneumothorax." Without anyone thinking that he must be punished for it, as for some irredeemable crime.

The problem of leprosy is not exclusively medical today; it's also, and mainly, a human problem.

Do we, or do we not, consent to millions of people being banished from society because they are ill – being condemned to transportation and forced to die in misery and despair?

Silence can sometimes become complicity.

And that is why I have the honour, Monsieur le Président, to ask you to refer this appeal to the General Assembly of the United Nations and especially, in virtue of Article 62 of the Charter, to its Economic and Social Council so that it may initiate a census, honest and as complete as possible, of the populations affected with leprosy, and make immediate and detailed recommendations to the nations concerned "with a view to ensuring effective respect for the rights of man and the basic freedoms" which have been acknowledged as valid for everyone and thus are equally so for lepers. The United Nations Organization, in demanding this census and making itself the passionate and intransigent defender of "the saddest of the world's oppressed minorities" will give evidence of its effectiveness, which is the very condition of its difficult existence.

It would be desirable that in virtue of the same Article 62 the Council should publish a declaration, then prepare a plan for an international convention that shall draw up a statute for lepers to safeguard their dignity and protect their rights – which are the rights of all human beings.

The declaration could take the following form:

"The General Assembly of the United Nations Organization solemnly proclaims that the continued existence of leper-colonies as prisons, cemeteries or communal graves for the living is unworthy of nations that call themselves civilized and hope to be viewed as such.

"The General Assembly of the United Nations Organization, having been informed of the progress of the therapeutics of leprosy, recommends the closing of leper-colonies and their transformation into centres for treatment, into 'sanatoria for lepers' where the sick will come to be nursed, with the guarantee that once they have been rendered non-infectious and the security period has elapsed they may depart freely and go back to their jobs and their full social activity, without any discrimination.

G

"The General Assembly of the United Nations Organization recommends that all member States should:

—make a census of their lepers conscientiously and frankly, or enable this task to be performed by a mission delegated by the Assembly;
—solemnly proclaim that lepers are subject to the common laws and equally protected by them;
—undertake to guarantee their freedom as soon as responsible doctors have declared them to be non-infectious;
—grant them the same facilities, the same advantages, the same privileges as all other citizens, without exception."

I shall readily hold myself at the disposal of the Assembly to provide it with supplementary documents and testimonies should it desire to call on me and hear me in virtue of Articles 70 and 71.

FIRST REACTIONS

On 3 February 1953 I was received by M. Vincent Auriol, President of the Republic, and handed him the text of our petition. On 9 March I received a letter from M. Robert Schumann, Minister for Foreign Affairs.

Monsieur le Président,
The President of the Republic has transmitted to the Minister for Foreign Affairs the copy that you sent him of a letter addressed by yourself to the President of the 7th General Assembly of the United Nations concerning the problem of leper-colonies and your desire that this should be included in the agenda of the General Assembly of the United Nations.

Your petition has been the object of attentive study by the Department. The Ministers of Public Health, of France Overseas and of the Associated States, as well as the permanent French Delegation at the United Nations, have been consulted, and your proposal, which is in harmony with our own policy in the matter and with the conclusions of the Committee of leper specialists at the World Health Organization, has met with a favourable reception in these quarters. And they have indicated that the best course would be to submit the question to the World Health Organization.

The French Delegation on the Executive Committee of the World Health Organization, which has just been sitting in Geneva, has requested and obtained the inclusion of the Report of the Leprosy Committee on the agenda of the General Assembly of the World Health Organization next May. On that occasion the French Delegation will not fail to put forward the Government's views concerning this problem.

M. Maurice Schumann, Under-Secretary of State for Foreign Affairs, telegraphed us from New York: "I shall support M. Follereau's petition with all the means in my power."

And meanwhile M. Edouard Herriot, President of the National Assembly, wrote to me as follows:

Monsieur le Président,

You have very kindly sent me the moving petition that you are addressing to the UNO on behalf of the lepers of the world. I very much hope that your appeal in the name of justice and humanity may be heard by all men of good will, and that the fight against leprosy may be effectively organized and carried through.

With all my best wishes and faithful remembrances. . . .

On 22 April I had an audience with the Minister for Justice, and asked him if a text might be drawn up proclaiming solemnly and unreservedly:

—that the leper is a man like other men, subject to all the common laws and equally protected by them;

—that no one has the right to make an attempt on his freedom nor to curtail it in any way whatsoever, provided the patient has a non-infectious form of leprosy, or is carrying a medical certificate certifying that after treatment all risk of infection has disappeared.

However, if those in authority had been alerted and were prepared to act, public opinion still remained largely uninformed. The editor of an important Paris paper said to me, "Lepers are too depressing; they don't interest my readers."

. . . But I'm not a doctor

People "who didn't want to know" had a crushing argument against me, namely, that I wasn't a doctor. And they repeated endlessly, "Why can't he mind his own business. . . ."

I had to explain myself a hundred times over, starting from the beginning. And again recently, as in my pamphlet *Leur crime? Ils sont malades* (Their crime? They're ill):

. . . It's so as to prove that leprosy is a disease like other diseases, and to back my proof up by example, that I've travelled the world for thirty years holding out my arms to lepers and kissing them. I could call witnesses to this in all parts of the world, witnesses to the fact that I've kissed thousands of lepers and taken thousands of poor mutilated hands in mine, hands that were concealed, stowed away, and that sometimes I had to clasp almost by force.

I don't think people understood me at first. My behaviour was dictated neither by gallantry nor by any desire to defy public opinion. I simply had to prove the truth of what I was saying with all the strength of my conviction and sometimes, I must confess, with impatience and irritation when up against the prejudices of the healthy.

My evidence could be summarized thus: The proof that I believe leprosy to be minimally contagious is that I kiss lepers. Any lepers. And all – if they'll let me. With the same readiness. And that I've been doing so for 30 years. Look at me. I haven't caught leprosy. So . . .

In that way it became daily more difficult for people to maintain that I was either crazy or didn't know. . . .

Now, we all know . . .

Also I had to prove it to the lepers. To the lepers whom I often discovered cowering in forests, hiding in the depths of the bush. Why?

Because they too were frightened. Frightened that leprosy would mean the leper-colony. Frightened of being branded by the then ignominious stigma of: leper. Frightened of being condemned to "leprosy in perpetuity".

So they had to be reassured too. They had to be taught that henceforward they were men like other men.

But what proof was there to give them? *What proof?*

Not being a doctor, I couldn't tend them, but I could try to convince them.

I could do nothing for them except love them. So I gave them what I had. Plainly it didn't cure them, but it sometimes cured the healthy who saw me and who on occasion held the happiness of my poor friends in their hands.

Soon, moreover, science was to come to the help of love and bring decisive and definitive support to our campaign.

WORLD HEALTH ORGANIZATION
SPEAKING

IN SUCH A grave matter as this, it's vital that there should be no doubt or ambiguity of any kind whatsoever. So we'll now listen to what the highest international court has to say – the World Health Organization.

I shall quote from the minutes of the conferences about leprosy organized by the WHO since I launched this "Fight".

Much less contagious

(Leprosy is) ". . . much less contagious than tuberculosis and the majority of the other common illnesses" (WHO, second meeting of the Committee of leprosy specialists, August 1959.)

A husband does not transmit leprosy to his wife

"Conjugal leprosy is extremely rare" (WHO, Geneva, August 1959).

People can be immune to leprosy

But this goes one better. During that same meeting the experts revealed that "there exists a very definite predisposition to leprosy. Whereas people placed even in close contact with a victim are themselves not liable to contract the disease."

So let's be done with all the stuff and nonsense that's been talked about leprosy, with all the pious tear-jerkers that have for long lined the pockets of serial-story-writers with easy money.

Perfectly curable

". . . the Conference emphasizes that leprosy is a curable disease and that the presence of various irreversible after-effects in some cases does not mean that these cases are infectious or that they are not cured" (WHO, Tokyo Conference, November 1958).

Speaking on Lausanne radio on 30 June 1961 in the series of

broadcasts entitled, *"La Chaine internationale du Bonheur"* (the international chain of happiness), Professor Gay-Prieto, the then director of the Leprosy Service at the WHO, said:

"Of the two and a half million leprosy victims currently under treatment, more than half may be considered as being already cured."

And the children?

Leprosy, as we know, is not hereditary. The children of lepers are sound when they come into the world.

What should then be done?

This is the answer of the WHO:

". . . Children, who constitute the most vulnerable age-group, very often do not contract the disease from their parents" (Geneva, 1959).

"It appears to be dangerous to take children from leprous mothers at birth, so as to place them in special institutions, in view of the high infantile mortality rate that results from this practice and the disastrous psychological effects produced on those that survive. . . . In any case it is essential not to curtail maternal breast-feeding" (WHO, Brazzaville Conference, 1959).

". . . The separation of children from their families should not be envisaged except in cases where the family cannot ensure their upbringing and education (very poor families, parents in hospital). In this case children should be placed, if possible, in healthy families or in orphanages or children's homes" (WHO, Istanbul Conference, 1961).

At school?

"Children sent away from boarding-schools owing to having leprosy should be taken into special establishments where they can pursue their studies normally. Day-boarders can continue to attend their schools on condition that they are regularly treated. In such cases health instruction should be given to their fellow-pupils and their families" (WHO, Brazzaville, April 1959).

Down with leper-prisons!

The WHO Conference held in Tokyo in November 1958 ". . . unanimously repudiates compulsory segregation."

It declares:

"Leper-colonies should be transformed into institutions capable of treating very infectious cases who need hospitalization and especially at reaction time, and of serving as a centre for surgical rehabilitation and professional reorientation. These institutions are also necessary for research and for the training of personnel required for the furtherance of the campaign. . . . In the general hospitals cases at the acute reaction stage or with intercurrent disorders should be admitted – measures which could avoid the unnecessary expense of new buildings and help to root out prejudice."

The cause has now been won.

Leprosy is a disease like other diseases, that must be treated, and can be cured.

Those stricken with it are patients like other patients. And once cured they should become men like other men.

Men like other men (*Des hommes comme les autres*) was the title of my second book published by Flammarion in 1956 and now out of print in its French edition. This is how it concluded:

A leper in perpetuity

Over a period of thirty years I've seen them, and on a route that has taken me thirty times round the world.[1] I've seen them cowering, hidden away, desolate. Oh what terrible memories!

I remember vainly trying to persuade a young girl, only just infected, to come out of her filthy hovel. "I can't," she said, "they'd throw stones at me. Besides, I'm ashamed. . . ."

I remember the woman whose despair had sent her mad and she insisted on crawling round and round her hut on all fours. And that other woman riveted to the ground by her appalling elephantiasis, opposite her son who with his fingerless hands was tirelessly shaking her foot which hung down like some monstrous pendulum. There they both were, half crazed, and waiting.

What were they waiting for? Nothing. They were just waiting. And when we offered them some help of which we were ashamed, they had the charity to say "thank you".

And others – so many others. . . .

That poor girl, for instance, whom we found in the country alone except for an old cat which was licking her wounds – her

[1] Forty times now (1966).

wounds which she quickly covered up with leaves if anyone passed. And that child whom we found half eaten by rats, although her family – who had isolated her – was well off and, as they say, "well-born". And that blind one, blind and solitary, lurching along in her twofold night. And that other one who is not only a leper, but hungry, and has four children who are hungry too, clutching on to her rags. And that leper-girl (let women who gorge and stuff themselves throw the first stone) who becomes a prostitute at night so as to eat.

And so many others. . . .

*   *   *

"But I know this place, I've been here before," said Dr Montestruc one day when we were visiting a leper in her hovel.

Above the one filthy room there was a sort of loft reached by a staircase that defied all the laws of equilibrium. The director of the Pasteur Institute went on:

"It was in 1940. While I was visiting this woman I heard plaintive little cries, like a kitten. The woman explained, 'Yes, there's a baby up there. The father's been called up, the mother's just died in hospital, and the baby's been forgotten. I can't go and fetch it myself because I haven't any feet.' " The doctor bounded up, reached the garret, then the miserable cot. The child was buried beneath an unspeakable swarm of ants which had already half devoured it. The doctor wrapped it round in a blanket and took it away, but two days later it was dead.

*   *   *

So now you understand.

You understand that it isn't a question of vaguely drying a tear when someone talks to you about lepers, nor of casually producing a note from your wallet. It's a matter of stopping being a coward.

No one today should be condemned to leprosy in perpetuity. But it depends on us. On us, the healthy ones, the sound ones, the happy ones, the too-happy ones.

How does it help if science has now got the better of leprosy if in spite of everything the victim remains a "leper"? If we still impose on him this absurd, mad and criminal form of "social excommunication"? If we think we've discharged our debt to him by gulping down a cocktail or kicking a cha-cha-cha "in aid" of

him? While all the time we refuse to hold out our hand to him,
help him, love him. . . .
    For then, Lord,
    You who are God,
    must tell us, in Your heart, who are the *real* lepers?

AT THE NATIONAL ASSEMBLY

I FELT THAT the moment had now come to ask Parliament to enlist itself in the "Fight against Leprosy" by giving its support with as large a vote as possible to the petition I had put before the UNO – the petition which had been adopted, as we have seen, by the French Government. So I initiated an assault on my country's National Assembly. The first thing I did was to find a friend there. This was Abbé Gau who at that time represented the department of the Aude in the Chamber, and was to become a warm and zealous advocate of our hopes.

We began by winning over influential deputies, or simply those capable of being moved and of infecting others with their emotion. We tracked them down, whether centre, right-wing or left-wing, everywhere and anywhere.

Every Wednesday Abbé Gau and I met for lunch in the restaurant of the Chamber. The food wasn't good, but one hardly had time to notice that. The members whom we had won over were enthusiastic. When one of them cautiously said, "I shall talk to my party about it," Abbé Gau parried with, "When it's a matter of saving men's lives, there's no question of party but of conscience."

I then realized how sterile, absurd and often harmful party labels are, that there are honest, good-hearted men everywhere, and that decency and goodwill are not the preserve of any one party. And I am still convinced of this today.

*　　*　　*

We had hoped for a large majority. But it was with *unanimity* that on 25 May 1954 the National Assembly voted for the resolution that had been tabled on 9 March by a delegate of each of the political parties represented in Parliament. Its text ran as follows:

PROPOSED RESOLUTION

whose aim is to invite the Government to act so that the
drawing up of an international statute for lepers should
be put on the agenda of the next session of the United
Nations Organization

tabled

by MM. Gau, Aujoulat, Jacques Bardoux, Baylet, de Chambrun,
Eugène Claudius-Petit, Edouard Depreux, Jean-Michel
Flandin, Mme Gabriel-Peri, MM. Jarrosson, Guy Petit,
de Sesmaisons and de Villeneuve, deputies.

STATEMENT OF GROUNDS

Ladies and Gentlemen,

Among the many scourges that afflict humanity, the fate
reserved for lepers in vast areas of the world remains one of
the most cruel and least known.

A Frenchman, M. Raoul Follereau, has devoted himself to
this terrible problem for many years. With exemplary faith and
self-abnegation for which the whole world pays him homage
he has visited nearly all the leper-colonies however remote and
well defended. He has visited tribes affected by this appalling
disease in Asia, Africa and Oceania. And those who have read
him or heard him on his return from these haunting expeditions
have been shocked to learn that so many horrors and betrayals
are still possible and permissible in the XXth century.

Armed with an experience probably unique in the world, on
20 September 1952 M. Raoul Follereau addressed a petition
to the United Nations Organization asking that an international
statute should guarantee the rights of lepers and, if need be,
protect them against the many unjust strictures and cruel
superstitions to which they are subjected.

There followed long extracts from the petition quoted above.
Then the resolution went on:

> ... An appeal such as this cannot leave any man of goodwill
> unmoved, whatever his political or confessional allegiances
> may be. The humane and brotherly traditions of France place
> a duty on this country to defend those who remain "the saddest

of the world's oppressed minorities". Thus it is fitting that such a petition should be accepted and examined without delay and with all the attention it deserves.

These are the grounds on which we ask the Assembly to vote for the proposed resolution:

PROPOSED RESOLUTION

The National Assembly invites the Government to place before the United Nations Organization, in its own name, the petition recommended by M. Raoul Follereau on 20 September 1952 demanding the drawing-up of an international statute for lepers, and to give precise instructions to the French representatives in order that this petition may be placed on the agenda of the next session of the Assembly.

This vote and the dispositions that resulted from it have formed the basis of most of the laws, orders and regulations which have brought juridical liberation to "lepers" since that time.

THE ROME CONGRESS, ETC.

WHILE WELCOMING AND proclaiming the achievement of science which had made the "leper" an invalid like other invalids, I nevertheless added: But is curing him the same as saving him?

Let me explain. Since time began the man attacked by Hansen's bacillus has in fact had two illnesses:

he has leprosy

and he is a leper.

Leprosy? We know now that that affection is perfectly curable and contagious only to a small extent; we know it's an ordinary disease round which an idiotic and appalling publicity has been built. But what's the good of freeing a man from leprosy if he nevertheless remains a "leper"? If he goes on being ostracized? If he remains an outlaw and accursed?

We must therefore demand and insist that as soon as the doctors have declared the victim to be non-infectious, he must forthwith resume his position and work in society – without anyone wanting to punish him for ever for some inexpiable crime, in other words without his being condemned to be "a leper in perpetuity".

In order that the man stricken with leprosy will never again be a "leper" we must "cure the healthy" of the absurd, unreasonable and sometimes criminal fear that they feel for this disease and those infected by it.

To that end I planned to make an onslaught on public opinion by a demonstration on an international scale, a Congress "for the protection and social rehabilitation of lepers" which would bring together the most competent people in the field and have an impact capable of moving the world's conscience.

And I then thought of the Sovereign and Military Order of Malta whose charitable endeavour has persisted for a thousand years and done so much over the centuries for "our Lords the Poor".

I discussed my project with the Order's minister in Paris,

M. le Comte de Billy, and together we went to Rome. At a meeting on 7 July 1954 at the Knights' headquarters there, presided over by Count Angelo de Mojana who has since become Grand Master of the Order, I expounded the reasons in favour of such a Congress and suggested that the Knights should take the initiative. This proposal was adopted on the spot and the meeting asked me to draw up the agenda of the demonstration and decide on the main lines of the programme.

The Congress took place in Rome on the 16, 17 and 18 April 1956. Excellently organized, with care and generosity, it was a resounding success, and the Knights of Malta incurred claims on our gratitude that can never be discharged.[1] The Commission elected to produce a final resolution – it consisted of Dr Muir (Great Britain), Professor Gay-Prieto (Spain), Dr Doull (USA), Colonel Dr Aretas (France), Father Perlini (Italy) and Dr Rodriguez (Philippines) – asked me to draw up the text which was adopted unanimously and ran as follows:

The International Congress for the protection and social rehabilitation of lepers, meeting in Rome on the 16, 17 and 18 April 1956 under the sponsorship of the Sovereign and Military Order of Malta, and bringing together 250 delegates from 51 nations,

Considering that leprosy is recognized as being only a relatively contagious disease and capable of being effectively treated,

ISSUES THE RESOLUTION

—that the victims of this affection should be treated like the victims of any other affection (tuberculosis, for instance) without any discrimination;

—and that in consequence *all exceptional laws and regulations concerning lepers should be abolished;*

—that in countries where leprosy constitutes a social problem, a propaganda campaign should be launched to inform public opinion of its true nature and destroy the superstitions and prejudices attaching to this disease.

AT THE "INSTITUT DE FRANCE"

Not only the Legislative Assembly and important international bodies, but also the intellectual *élite* of France wanted to be

---

[1] The Knights of Malta have successfully continued their charitable enterprises on behalf of lepers, centred mainly round their International Committee at Geneva where our friends Robert Vernet and Dr Gilbert are guiding lights.

associated with our struggle and give public proof of sympathy and admiration.

In 1952 and then again in 1958 I had the honour of addressing the Academy of Moral and Political Sciences on the "Fight against Leprosy", and received valuable encouragement from MM. Boegner, Jacques Rueff, Gabriel Marcel, Léon Noel, René Cassin, Paul Bastid and many of their colleagues.

THE "ACADÉMIE FRANÇAISE" TO THE HELP OF LEPERS

The *Académie française* also brought flattering and resounding support to our brotherly "Fight", and announced that it would allocate a "Raoul Follereau Award" every two years to some outstanding figure in the campaign against leprosy.

Here is the announcement of the award as it appeared in the *Journal Officiel* of 6 April 1955:

By a decree dated 1 April 1955 the Minister for National Education authorizes the *Académie française* to allocate a prize to the value of A HUNDRED THOUSAND FRANCS every two years, to be called the Raoul Follereau Award, and to have as purpose "to reward a doctor or missionary, without distinction of sex, nationality or creed, who, by his work or example, has played an effective part in the Fight against Leprosy . . .

Recipients of the prize have been:

—in 1955, Dr Pierre Richet and M. Delord, director of the Valbonne sanatorium;
—in 1957, Sister Othilde, nurse at the Ducas sanatorium, New Caledonia;
—in 1959, Dr Montestruc, director of the Pasteur Institute, Fort-de-France; and Dr Féron, director of the Harar leper hospital, Ethiopia;
—in 1961, Father Goarnisson, doctor, founder and director of the *Ecole d'Infirmiers* in Upper Volta;
—in 1963, Father Clarisse, director of the Saints-Anges leper hospital at Ouidah (Dahomey);
—in 1965, the National Madagascan Association for Aid to Lepers and their Families (in homage to its president, Dr Raharijoana, who died on the eve of the allocation of the award);
—in 1967, Father Grémion, chaplain of the St Bernard leper hospital (Reunion Island).

"HAVE A GOOD TRIP, PRESIDENT!"

ALL THESE ACTIVITIES, and various others which were less showy but no less efficacious, held me in Europe only as long as was necessary.

I was more than ever convinced that I ought to go to the "lepers" myself to take them the good news: "You're going to get better: from now on, you're just medical cases like other medical cases, and tomorrow you'll be men like other men." And also so as to examine the needs of our poor friends on the spot and without intermediaries – the conditions of their life, the prejudices of ill-informed people of which they were the victim, and sometimes, alas, the violent or silent persecutions unleashed against them. And finally so as to mobilize, arouse and even shock public opinion with a view to "curing the healthy" of their fear and sometimes of their cowardice.

In the very year that the French Parliament voted for the resolution described above, the Emperor of Ethiopia, Hailé Selassie, had received me in Addis-Ababa and asked me to draw up a plan of campaign against leprosy in his country. "You must be frank, sincere and thorough," he had told me. I was not likely to be otherwise, as can be imagined.

Committees of help for lepers, created by these campaigns, sprang up more or less everywhere and prepared to take part in the struggle. Each wanted my advice – and a visit from me. And letters continued to pour in. "You've been twice to Martinique but never to us. Do you like their patients better than ours?" What could I do, except get into another plane? And continue my "trips round the world to the lepers"?

And how could I remember these journeys, sometimes epic tours, without mentioning – though I'd need a book to do so properly – the man who in Africa was my much-loved companion, who guided the "Fight" with such warm-hearted courage, and who is today a historic figure for all the lepers of that continent, and will soon be a legendary one: the supervising doctor, Pierre Richet? It was he who, among so many other things that can be said in his praise, had the idea of mass-treatment by the organization of circuits with cars or even bicycles to take medicines to people's homes. This is called Richet's Plan at the WHO.

I had known him at Hanoi where he directed the Health Service. Since then we've never left each other even when separated by thousands of kilometres. Every year we've toured Africa together, Africa which he knows better than anyone else in the world, and loves for all the good he's done it. In 1957 he, my wife and I covered 6,783 kilometres by car, along African tracks – in a single journey! So memories aren't lacking. . .

And then, when it fell to him to present me with the insignia of an officer of the Legion of Honour (this happened at Adzopé), he decorated me with his own cross, which had previously been worn by the great Muraz; and it wasn't protocol that threw us into each other's arms but the happy embrace of two comrades who had become two brothers in the service of the least happy.

*   *   *

However, the day came when my personal means and those put at my disposal by my family were no longer enough to meet the expenses of my travels, even though I was always given such generous hospitality on my way. On the other hand it was unthinkable that even a minimal part of the funds laboriously collected for help to the lepers should be allocated to my journeys – although on many occasions they would have been a positive investment. Our Administrative Council, which managed and was responsible for our treasury, agreed with me.

So there was only one solution: to make a special appeal to those of our friends who understood the need for these tours and their beneficial effects, while pointing out that their response to this appeal should in no way reduce the offering they were in the habit of sending me every year for the lepers.

To obviate any possible confusion, they were asked to put on the back of the cheque or money order destined for this special collection, "Bon voyage, Président!" ("Have a good trip, President!")

That year I was 500,000 francs down on my travel budget. They sent me 5 million. And with what enthusiasm and zeal!

These testimonies appeared in our bulletin for April 1952:

From a very sick man:
1,300 francs for the "new expedition of Love". I shall put something aside every month so as to help you, having been laid up myself for twenty years. Have a good trip, President!

From a working man:
Six hours of my work. Have a good trip, President! And thank you for allowing us to help you.

A small gold medal:
Having no ready money available, I'm sending you a small gold medal to help you continue with the magnificent work that you've had the courage to undertake.

Her hair . . .
My sister, who is a nun, has asked me to send you the small sum realized from the sale of her hair, so as to contribute to your work. Have a good trip, President!

I haven't much to live on . . .
I can only send you 20 francs because I'm ill and can't work. So I haven't much to live on, but still I'm sending you this sum with all my heart for your journey.

Taken from my food:
I'm sending you a few stamps. It's not much, but as it isn't taken from my "superfluity" but from my food, I hope you'll accept it, little as it is. And of course without sending a receipt for it isn't for you to thank us, but for us to thank you for your gift of yourself.

The end is near:
Please find enclosed two small notes for the "Fight against Leprosy".
It is a widow's mite.

I'm old (90) and ill. I can hardly see any more. The end is near; I was determined to send you this before it comes . . . May God bless your work, your effort and your courage.

*   *   *

Enclosed please find 400 francs to contribute towards the re-soling of the dear shoes that have paced the world so bravely and fearlessly. Good luck, dear President. I'd like to live a hundred years and double my offering every year.

1,000 francs. To strew happiness on your way. Have a good trip, President!

1,200 francs. So that you can put a little more in your luggage.

1,000 francs. I prefer going without clean sheets. Have a good trip, President!

300 francs. So that the President will have a good trip. From four little brothers and their grandmother.

1,500 francs. So that our President can take some goodies to the lepers. We thank him for being our dear ambassador. May the Angel of the Lord go with him.

1,200 francs. Thank you for the joy you give me by allowing me to help you.

600 francs. Have a good trip, President! Having unfortunately not been able to find a place at your lecture at the Opera House in Lyons, I'm happy to send my little contribution to your new "expedition of Love".

100 francs. I admire your mission. Herewith the mite of a former colonial, under-privileged and war-crippled.

800 francs. I'm 76, a textile worker and still at it. I ask only for your prayers that I may be able to continue working. Have a good trip, President!

* * *

In view of this success we decided to renew our appeal every year, not only so as to cover my travel expenses but so as to guarantee the publication of propaganda material (pamphlets, tracts, films) which was becoming daily more important; and also to cover the expense of the badges, records and posters which we distributed in six languages all over the world on the World Leprosy Days.

And our friends' generosity was such that every year I had enough left over to distribute individual help to the most urgent and tragic cases all along my route.

Thus – and it is my pride and honour – during those journeys which now total nearly two million kilometres I was the bearer of the inexhaustible and sometimes heroic charity of our friends.

So that I could then write that I carried a hundred thousand hearts in my heart.

60 YEARS: 60 CARS

ONE OF THE most touching proofs of my friends' attachment and generosity was given me on my sixtieth birthday. I spoke about this at the meeting held later at the Châtelet theatre in Paris to mark the event, and attended by all the ambassadors of French-speaking Africa and Madagascar, each of whom brought a message of goodwill from their Heads of State.

"So . . ." said I, "– as you all know it, there's no reason why I shouldn't admit it – I'm now sixty. As my birthday drew near I suggested to my friends (for as you all know, I've never been kept awake by timidity) that sixty candles on a birthday cake were all very well, but were really only good for being blown out. What I'd like was for the candles on my cake to be replaced by the sparking-plugs[1] of sixty cars which would allow of sixty new circuits of leprosy treatment to be opened in Africa and Asia.

"Sixty cars! It was a mad idea, I agree. And I'd hardly suggested it when I began to regret it. But my regret was short-lived. It was soon submerged by hope, then joy, then by a huge joy. Then came uneasiness. Why? You'll soon see. When my birthday was over and I totted up what I'd received, I realized that my friends in France, Belgium, Switzerland, Italy, Luxembourg and Canada had given me 104 cars.

"104 cars! Good Lord! Was I 104 years old?

"104 cars! Not even a millionaire has ever received as much on his birthday.

"And to cap all, I've never had a car of my own and don't even know how to drive!"

* * *

These are the people who won the "Fight against Leprosy". It's their love that makes my strength. It is because of them and in their name that I have set out so often, spoken in so many

[1] In French the word for candle and sparking-plug is the same: *bougie* (Tr.).

places. It is because of them and in their name that I shall set out again and speak again.

Two testimonies

From the Minister of Public Health, Mali:

My dear President,

In glancing through the review *Mission de la France* I discovered that on the 17th of this month our President, our dear "Vagabond", will be sixty years old, thirty of these years having been devoted to the cause of mankind, to bring about "true compassion". I couldn't let the occasion pass without joining the Council of the Order of Charity to celebrate the sixtieth birthday of the man who initiated and still wages the fight against leprosy.

Happy birthday, my dear Raoul; all the Mali lepers say to you: "Many happy returns and a long life, for you must bring your great fight to unconditional victory, the battle of mankind against leprosy."

Dr Sominé Dolo.

From a Vietnamese leprosy victim:

Father dear,

Happy birthday! My thoughts are with both of you in deep affection.

In fact I've been thinking about your birthday since the beginning of the year because I wanted to celebrate it in a special way. To this end I've prepared with the help of our friends a little booklet, and in spite of the delays and setbacks that happen in such cases I even hoped at one moment that it would be off the press by 17 August.

It's my birthday present, Father. Even without having read it yet, you must know that every word and every line is full of you.

And from the depths of my heart I share with you, Mother Madeleine, the joy you are feeling during these days of celebration. There will be many more, and on one of them a hundred of your children will come from a hundred different countries to wish you a happy feast-day. It'll be quite a Tower of Babel, but it will be the only valid United Nations because, gathered around you, we shall represent the Nations United in Love. And naturally your humble son shall be his country's representative.

VICTORY

THE FIRST VICTORY bulletin was published in the press in 1959. Here it is:

Geneva, 11 August. A Commission of experts of the World Health Organization has just recommended the suppression of leper-colonies.

According to the Commission's report, these are in fact a medieval survival in that they do not correspond with the demands of therapeutics.

Thanks to spectacular treatment by the sulphone compounds, leprosy can henceforth be viewed as one of the countless infectious diseases that can be treated at home.

The report points out that leprosy is only slightly contagious among populations whose general state is satisfactory.

One by one, timidly at first, as if they couldn't believe it, the former "lepers" came out of the places where they had endured such suffering.

And Society is gradually curing itself of its fear and cowardice.

The first repercussions are coming to us from all the corners of the world . . .

Dahomey

From the Saints-Anges leper hospital, Father Clarisse writes:

I've just baptized the son of one of my leper families. Luc is a fine baby. He's Ernest's and Cécile's fifth child.

After the baptism, I married Pierre and Catherine. Both are well on the way to being cured. Each of them has a wedding ring (the ones you gave me). And now the tom-toms are re-echoing, songs are ringing out and joy is bursting forth everywhere. Making them men like other men! Perhaps I'm happier than they are.

Mauritius

From Madame Nella Ythier, whose activity in the service of leprosy victims is so admirable, and whose friend I am so proud to be:

The leper-colony is slowly emptying. Three young men have found work outside as carpenters and have set up house in a village near Moulin-à-Poudre so as to go for treatment now and again. A young married couple has done likewise.

On a visit I made last Wednesday I saw the most moving thing in the world. A victim called Pâquerette, married a year ago to a boy from the colony, was sitting in a flower-filled room holding a new-born baby in her arms – a magnificent baby, rosy as an apple, and the pride of its parents.

We've bought a little chain which we took to her with the medal which you brought with the wedding-rings on your last visit. And that's not all. On 8 June we shall celebrate an important marriage: the daughter of a victim whom we brought from Rodrigues with her four other children and hospitalized in an orphanage. The two eldest are married already; the third, in her turn, will have her own family. The marriage will be celebrated in a church at Port-Louis, and the reception will be held in a well-known restaurant beside the sea. After that our admirable mother will go and look after her eldest daughter's children while she, the daughter, goes on a trip with her husband. She's asked us for a sewing-machine to do dressmaking so as not to be entirely dependent on her children. So now, yes really, there are no police at the leper-colony except to make music!

And all that thanks to you: thank you on behalf of our poor friends.

Martinique

In my book, *Des hommes comme les autres,* I had told this story:

1951. – That year it was the eminent Doctor Montestruc who at our request presided at the distribution of prizes. As this fine man of medicine is also an excellent speaker and rich in love, his success was deservedly great. In the tireless fulfilment of his role, he went on and on crowning the happy little girls.

But the endless procession suddenly halted. Two or three seconds, no more. The doctor had held a child's hand in his own longer than usual. He had caressed her face. But he'd said nothing. When the ceremony was over he spoke to the headmistress. This child had leprosy. It was only in its earliest stages and she wasn't infectious. But she must have treatment.

He took charge of this, and meanwhile she went on with her studies at home.

Two years went by. She was cured.

The headmistress then kept the promise she had made. The child – now almost a girl – was taken back into the school. She went into the fourth form. As if nothing had happened.

And nothing had in fact happened, except that a human being had been spared a most horrible fate. Because everyone had had the courage of their love.

1961. Ten years later I received this note:

Dear Monsieur Follereau,

You probably remember the little schoolgirl who was diagnosed as ill by Doctor Montestruc at the distribution of prizes in 1951.

It is I who am now writing to you. I have passed my baccalaureat and have been appointed a teacher.

I wanted to let you know the good news. . . .

Brazil

Doctor Martins de Barros wrote to me from São Paulo:

Do you remember the girl who gave you a bunch of carnations as you were leaving? She was a former victim of tubercular leprosy who had been put in hospital at the age of three. After which she received no more news of her family. She grew up alone and did her studies by correspondence; she learned shorthand and even started learning typing with the help of pencils as her hands are atrophied. Today she's nearly twenty-eight and never has positive tests. Having no family, she's obliged to live in the hospital.

On the day of your departure it was the first time she'd ever seen an airport, and it was also the first time that anyone had kissed her. The next day she told me she hadn't been able to sleep, so great was her emotion. "It was the first time in my life that I'd had a kiss from anyone. . . ."

I tell you this story because we're trying to rehabilitate this former victim within society. Thanks to you, she truly believes that she can leave the hospital and live like other people. I remember your words: it needs so little to make someone happy.

Peru

After visiting Lima, I received the following letter from Madame Lucila Flores de Tejada Sorzano, leading light of the Inter-Aid Association for the lepers of Peru:

> You will doubtless be happy to hear that Vicentia, to whom you gave a bracelet on your visit to the leper-colony at Guia, has now left.
>
> You will also be delighted to learn that forty-six cases have recently been freed at San Pablo. Several of them have found work locally; the others have returned without any difficulty to their families.

I could happily multiply these testimonies.

But the most touching proof that I received of this victory was probably the "public confession" of a victim who greeted me in a small Madagascan village with the following somewhat improvised words, spoken in the name of all his comrades:

> On your first visit here you said a lot of things about our forthcoming cure. You seemed like a prophet, telling us:
>
> ". . . You will all be cured; you will go back to your homes; you will see your families again; you will have healthy children, etc. . . ."
>
> We listened to you and we thanked you for your kindness, but, deep down, *we didn't believe you.*
>
> But now these things are happening. *We see that we were fools.* You told us the truth, and in fact you said only half of what is happening to us.
>
> We are cured, we are cared for, some of us have gone home. We have emerged from the darkness of misery and despair, and are returning into the midst of human society. You see in front of you a lot of little children who look hale and hearty. They are our children.
>
> All this, dear Benefactor, is a result of your efforts.

So I repeat for the hundredth if not the thousandth time: Why not elsewhere? Why not everywhere?

* * *

Coming home from one of my first tours of the world in the early days of the "Fight against Leprosy", I found a letter from a "leper" which said, "Here, everyone who despises us, everyone who ill-treats us, *is afraid of you*".

Though I had such anger in my heart I couldn't help feeling happy at this.

Some years later another "leper" (from Burma) wrote me this overwhelming phrase, "YOU ARE OUR FREEDOM". This lit up my path and determined the remainder of my life.

Even more than their benefactor, I have wanted to be their friend. The person who represents them, listens to them, defends them.

I have wanted the neglected, the abandoned, the doomed, in the world's filthiest leper-colony in the depths of the remotest bush, to know that I shall fight for them, right to the end of the battle and right to the end of my strength. Because they are men, and I am a man. And we love each other.

"WORLD LEPROSY DAY"

Among the enterprises that I've inaugurated in the context of the "Fight
against Leprosy", the most spectacular
and certainly the most efficacious has been
"World Leprosy Day".

THE IDEA CAME to me in the course of a conversation in 1953 in
an enchanting garden in Nîmes. I was talking to a young priest
who had just attended one of my lectures and was filled with
enthusiasm for the "Fight against Leprosy". Abbé Balez has
remained my faithful disciple and very dear friend ever since.

Abbé Balez was thinking along the lines of a day of prayer for
"lepers". This excellent suggestion gave me the idea of organizing
an annual demonstration on a world scale – a demonstration that
would constitute simultaneously a means of coming to the help
of leprosy victims, a sort of universal mobilization of hearts and
minds in favour of those whom I called the saddest of the world's
oppressed minorities, and a revolt against the cruel and often
tragic fate reserved for them.

Abbé Balez, who was in a way the spiritual father of the project,
was also the first to applaud it, and has never stopped contributing
to its success by means of articles and the spoken word. I
take this opportunity of acknowledging my gratitude, esteem and
affection.

* * *

I gave myself twelve years in which to attain my goal. Here is
the text of my appeal in which I announced the first World
Leprosy Day:

On 31 January 1954, 360,000 Catholic priests, together with
their millions of faithful, will read at Mass the Gospel for the
third Sunday after Epiphany.

"At that time," writes Saint Matthew, "after he had come
down from the mountain, large crowds followed Jesus. A leper
now came up and bowed low in front of him. 'Sir,' he said, 'if

114

you want to, you can cure me.' Jesus stretched out his hand, touched him and said, 'Of course I want to! Be cured!' And his leprosy was cured at once."

At their own good time, hundreds of thousands of Orthodox priests and Protestant pastors, together with their millions of faithful, will read and meditate on the same story which belongs to all Christendom.

When this page has been read, as it's read every year, will it be turned, as it's turned every year?

In the past we didn't know.

We knew there were lepers, but we didn't know there were *ten million lepers.*[1]

We believed it legitimate – cowardly, but legitimate – to flee from them and abandon them.

Leprosy was very infectious, we said.

We thought it was incurable.

. . . But today?

Today when we have an effective cure, the sure means of making a leper into a man, of not only curing him but bringing him back to life.

Shall we leave millions of human beings to rot and die when we can, truly, treat them, and probably cure them?

This 31 January shall be their day.

One day in a whole year!

Who can refuse to give it, and thus be forgiven so much selfishness, so much cowardice?

It's not our intention to set up solemn, imposing yet power-less committees, nor to dictate orders outside which everything would be vain.

All we hope is that on that day Christians, all Christians, and, following their example, all men of goodwill, shall say to themselves:

There are millions of lepers in the world.

Why them and not me?

Fed, clothed, housed, protected, what have I done for them?

Each will give what lies in his power. Priests, their Mass; religious communities and the faithful, their prayers; every-one, a thought, a tenacious, obsessed thought, a thought that will reach anguish before the most grievous and unjust misery in the world.

Each will do what his heart dictates.

In towns or villages near a leper-colony (as I have already

[1] 15 million, as we now know (1966).

proposed in the course of my travels) children will prepare songs for "Leper Day", and dances and short plays. Mothers will make cakes and goodies. And they will go together and make a visit of friendship to those who have been banished for too long.

On that day the leprosy victim will feel himself, by Christ's miracle, truly reunited to all Christendom worthy of the name.

On that day the leprosy victim, even if he is tortured by his leprosy, will no longer be a "leper".

Elsewhere people will organize meetings – if they can – at which the ignorant and unthinking will be told of the distress of those whom our selfish terror condemns to a double death. And they will make a collection, the proceeds of which will go preferably to a missionary or a doctor of the region whose dedicated work in foreign lands is the pride of all. They will thus associate themselves with the "Fight against Leprosy" at one point or another of its huge battlefield, and bring valuable help to one or other of the sublime Armies of charity.

But above all, the concern to muster material means should not allow the essential element of this day to be overlooked, which should be, first and foremost, a lucid and sorrowful awareness of the appalling condition in which millions of outcasts, our brothers, struggle for life, and, secondly, an immense prayer to Him who, two thousand years ago, healed our poor friends with a simple smile.

Every year I renewed this appeal, clarifying and enlarging on our directives.[1] On the Second Day, I said:

We ask you to examine what you can do without delay. For everyone can do something.

Last year's success, which was so happy and beneficial, must be developed and multiplied this year. "Leper Day", already celebrated in all the continents, will be truly *universal* this year, because each of you shall have willed it.

*   *   *

On the Third Day I asked not only for individual visits but mass demonstrations. And a commitment:

---

[1] No one should be surprised by the repetitions that occur in these texts. Just as "it is not only one day in the year that we must love", so it is not only on one day that we must say the truths that upset our habits, disturb our prejudices and shake up our little daily egoisms.

Festivities will be organized in treatment centres (which must never again be thought of as "leper-colonies") and to these you will flock in your hundreds.

... And you will also go to the remote, isolated, squalid hut where the leprosy victim – made a "leper" by our selfishness – still lies in hiding because *he is afraid.*

You will go and set him free by your love.

In various parts of the world, the "Fight against Leprosy" is now nearly won; such as the Black African country where 2,200 patients were being treated in 1951, whereas today nearly 100,000 come to receive the liberating injection.

Why those and not the others? All the others?

By means of the MASS DEMONSTRATION which is World Leprosy Day, the nations will put this question before the world's conscience.

But what purpose would be served if a victim were rescued from leprosy but still remained a "leper"? If through our base egoism and imbecile fears we refused him – though not or no longer infectious – the place that is his right, the respect and friendship that are his *right?*

29 January will be a day of commitment.

Personal, collective and national commitment so to act that *the victims of leprosy may never again be lepers.*

* * *

My appeal on the Fourth Day shed further light on this commitment and outlined its future development:

Let there be no mistake about it! The freeing of the leper, with the triumph over two thousand years of terror that it involves, will go down in human history as a victory comparable with that of freeing the slave. Then this century, branded as it is as "the century of the atom bomb", can rehabilitate itself by becoming the century of the conquest over leprosy.

And this Day, outstripping the goals that it proposed for itself, will be a first step in the great mobilization of men of goodwill to alleviate man's suffering.

... By participating in the Fourth World Day for the protection and social rehabilitation of lepers, and by demanding that they may become "men like other men", we shall wage and win a huge battle against the universal want that corrupts and dishonours this century – want that lies at the root of all hate and all war.

On the Fifth Day, I recalled the immediate aims of our great demonstration of brotherhood:

If someone said to you, "This man, this innocent man, is condemned to death; but one word from you could save him," you'd shout "Reprieve him" with all your strength.

That's what I'm asking you to do today.

But it's not a matter of a single man, but of several million men whose fate largely depends on each of us; of several million men condemned to exile, outlawry and death without having committed any crime except that of being ill.

I mean the lepers.

To *ensure* that leprosy victims shall be tended as other sick people are tended, with respect for their dignity and their freedom as men, and *to cure the healthy* of the absurd and often criminal terror that they have for this disease and for those stricken with it – this is the twofold aim of Leprosy Day now celebrated all over the world, and taking place for the fifth time on Sunday, 26 January 1958.

Every year its message goes further, to reach those who have never known hope in the depths of forest and bush. Every year its call arouses a greater number of consciences and moves more hearts. Millions of forgotten and abandoned lepers, formerly the world's outcasts, today see themselves *adopted* by a more enlightened public opinion whose voice daily grows louder and more urgent in demanding that they should be cared for, respected and loved.

It is in this sense that their reprieve and salvation lie in our hands.

. . . If we all thought about these wretched people, about the pointless cruelty of their lot, and about the means of helping them, then those responsible would have to take it into their heads to do something in their turn.

Between their bombs and their rockets, may those who lead the world take time off to save these twelve or fifteen million men for whom public opinion today demands a reprieve. That is *our hope* and *our aim*.

* * *

But there were other battles to be waged in the world. We gave a preview of them in our appeal on the Sixth Day.

WHY THEM, AND NOT YOU?

This terrible and salutary thought should impose itself on

your consciences not only on 25 January. It's not only on behalf of lepers that it should obsess you.

For there are other forms of "leprosy" besides leprosy.

Forms that are much more contagious and much more deadly.

Two-thirds of mankind haven't got enough to eat.

WHY THEM, AND NOT YOU?

There are 700 million people in the world who have never seen a doctor.

There are over a milliard human beings who can't read.

WHY THEM, AND NOT YOU?

600 million children go to bed hungry.

WHY THOSE CHILDREN, AND NOT YOURS?

On Sunday, 25 January 1959, the Sixth World Leprosy Day, we shall think of all these immense miseries that science could overcome if love demanded it.

For it is by loving the world that we shall save it.

* * *

The appeal of the Seventh Day was still more direct, in the hope of striking at everyone's heart:

Stop fiddling with the knobs of your radio, Sir.

And Madam, leave off your housework.

Come and sit down beside each other.

And listen to me.

Do you want to save 15 million men?

Do you want 15 million men to have the right to live and be happy like you?

It's in your power.

I'm referring to the most wretched, saddest and most abandoned of all mankind: the lepers.

In 1959, in the twentieth century of Christianity, I have seen them in prison, in lunatic asylums, shut up in disused cemeteries or else dumped in the desert, surrounded by barbed wire, with observation-posts and machine-guns. Lepers? I've seen them naked, starving, screaming, desperate. I've seen their wounds swarming with flies, their filthy hovels, the pharmacies empty, the guards with their guns. I've seen an unimaginable world of horror, distress and despair.

Is it going to go on? Are we going to let 15 million men rot and die when we now know that they can be treated, cured and saved?

That is my question.

I

The "Fight against Leprosy" should be waged every day, because every day the number of its victims increases (Eighth Day).

Let the celebrations this year be better than ever. Let there be more of you and may you be more determined than ever. But on condition that you don't rest on your laurels; that you don't say when you get home, "I've done my duty; that's it for this year". While, when the musicians have gone and the lights have been put out, the sick find themselves alone and abandoned again: lepers.

It's not only one day in the year that you must love them.

It's not a matter of a yearly examination of conscience: that's too easy.

It's a matter of daily commitment.

And you, the minority too unaware of your happiness, who eat three times a day; you for whom leprosy is no more than the recurring subject of baleful novels, don't say as an escape and a let-out, "I don't know any lepers, there aren't any lepers here so there's nothing I can do".

You can do a lot. All of you.

You can think about them. Talk about them, talk for them. You can refuse to be happy alone, while 15 million beings who are our brothers reel beneath the yoke of the most pointless and odious of segregations.

If we all set to, then they must hear us! The top people – the giants who have stopped being men – must stop playing with the moon for a moment or making weapons for our suicide, so as to bend over the 15 million lepers who have every right to become men.

Civilization means to love each other.

*   *   *

On the Ninth Day a crucial statement was recorded, and with what joy!

50 million? 60 million? More? How many of you were listening to your radio on the day when the marvellous, un-believable news was broadcast to thirty countries?

When from Radio-Lausanne the Doctor-in-chief of the Leper Service of the World Health Organization said, "I affirm that of the two-and-a-half million lepers currently being treated, over half are already *cured*".

. . . So fear and despair and execration are now over. But not the fight. That isn't over, alas!

Two-and-a-half million victims under treatment, the WHO tells us.

But there are 15 million lepers in the world! How about the others?

No one's found time to deal with the others, to study the question, work out plans, release credit, or whatever; even give up two bombers (as I've been demanding for seven years) whose cost would be enough to treat all the lepers in the world. . . .

Seven years! Oh, people who eat three times a day aren't in a hurry. . . .

15 million lepers in the world. From two to three million treated. The others – 12 million! – are waiting. They're waiting to be remembered so as to be cured.

The trouble is that leprosy doesn't wait. Every day hands are mutilated for ever, feet putrefy, eyes close.

Does that stop anyone from sleeping?

And here are the directives for that Ninth Day:

Those who can will swell the joyful crowds going to deliver the sick by their love. While prevailing on those who guide or inspire our destiny to fill their posts properly, to give an example and open the way!

The others will proclaim the good news far and wide: one-and-a-half million lepers are cured. And they will denounce the inadmissible scandal that twelve million others remain without care, without help and without love.

So that this mobilization of consciences, this rebellion of our hearts, may compel those who lead the world to think a little more of the men who suffer even if this means thinking a little less about the moon.

Because we think that it's more important – and more worthy of men – to tend 15 million of their kind than to play bowls in the stratosphere.

* * *

January 1963: Tenth World Leprosy Day. The thirtieth anniversary of my first appeal on behalf of "the saddest of the world's oppressed minorities". Hence the more personal tone of this message:

30 years. A whole life that has passed like a day. And here I am almost an old man now, but prodigiously enriched by serving the Poor. I shall bequeath my treasure to you. It is contained in one word: love.

To love. Not for a day, fleetingly. Not such-and-such a person who already loves you. But to love every day and all the earth, to love everything in the whole world, to love the fellow being in some remote land, to love the foreigner just near you.

In freeing "lepers" from their disease and the appalling curse that follows them, we shall also be freeing ourselves from another and infinitely viler and more catching "leprosy": fear, selfishness, cowardice.

*   *   *

The appeal for the Eleventh Day had a ring of victory.

What have I seen during my travels this past year?

Certainly – and still in too great numbers – wretched, doomed, abandoned lepers. But also – the dawn at last! – lepers working and singing, lepers building, carpentering, shoe-making, painting, weaving. Lepers who are "lepers" no longer even if not yet freed from their leprosy. Because they have become men like other men.

Their life belongs to them: they earn their living. They are responsible and respected. They work. They're men. So they sing.

They drive lorries on the roads of Senegal; they're carpenters or masons at Adzopé or Choquan; fishermen at M'Balling; farmers in Dahomey. In Mauritius they make furniture for the townsfolk.

Similarly I have seen them in India working the power knitting-looms of Seplenatam, making toys at Vellore, table-fittings and even elastic at Karigari. Elsewhere they are nurses, office boys, night watchmen, newspaper sellers. I even found one of my first "children", now completely cured, who had become headmaster of a school in a capital city of Africa!

And all these miracles accomplished with nothing more than a little courage and a lot of love.

Thanks to a few men who have had the courage of their charity, I've seen victims of leprosy – having been taken away from their leper-colony prisons where they were buried alive – installed where they rightly belong: in hospitals, even in special wings at the heart of urban hospital units. Just like any other invalid.

And I didn't hear tell of any resultant catastrophe.

I've seen this here and there . . . but not everywhere.

Why not everywhere?

At Clarac hospital in Fort-de-France, on World Leprosy Day, I saw a crowd of visitors thronging round the stalls and buying up the things that had been made by the sick during the previous year. And no one, as far as I know, was contaminated. So?

So let people stop – at last! – thinking of leprosy as an exceptional disease, and of the person affected by it as a creature apart.

Leprosy is sometimes contagious. It is natural and necessary that steps should be taken to check the contagion. As it is for all other contagious diseases. No more, no less.

The "leper" is curable. He must get himself treated: it's not only a duty but an obligation. But he demands to be recognized as what he is: a man. Armed with the same rights, protected by the same laws, subject to the same civic and social disciplines. He asks for no favour. He refuses all exceptional treatment which, however generous, would constitute a form of segregation.

He doesn't need pity, but justice and love. He rejects the state of individual or collective beggary to which our hypocritical virtues have too often reduced him. He wants to be a man, nothing more. A man who works and sings.

In defending him against a Society that has despised him for too long, against those who shamefully take advantage of his misery and his misfortune, or who use him (with disarming candour) to forge some shoddy heroism for themselves, we are serving man, hence all men.

*   *   *

1965: my twelfth appeal. There is already a note of conclusion.

. . . Having seen with my own eyes the immense suffering and distress of the lepers of the world, I protested some time ago: "Shall we leave 15 million human beings who are our brothers to rot and die when they can be treated, cured and saved?"

From all over the world you answered me. Organizations sprang up everywhere to prevail on society to tend leprosy victims and treat them as what they are: men. To insist that leprosy victims should never again be "lepers".

127 countries now celebrate the Day that is dedicated to them. Setting the example as they should, kings and heads of State go yearly to shake hands with those whom their people had formerly execrated.

Is the work finished? Certainly not. The fight will go on for as long as a single person needs our help and our love.

But the movement that has been created is irreversible. We have opened eyes and hearts that can never now forget. Henceforth the problem of leprosy will weigh on the world's conscience. And the world will be freed of it only by freeing the men whose sole crime is to be ill, the men whom our ignorance or cowardice has too often condemned to "leprosy in perpetuity".

To say that there are 15 million lepers in the world is too easy. 15 million times over there is a human being attacked by a disease that is often benignant and perfectly curable. The tragedy is that this disease is called leprosy, and that sensational drama and cheap novels have made it an instrument of terror and doom.

To be able to tend this victim, cure him, and put him in the way of becoming a man like other men, the "healthy" must simultaneously be "cured" of the often criminal panic that they have for this disease and the man stricken with it.

When the healthy are cured, then the former "lepers" become men, men who work and sing. Some whom I had previously seen in prison, in lunatic asylums, shut up in cemeteries, surrounded by barbed wire, with observation-posts and machine-guns, I have found again as workmen, employees, peasants, working and earning their living. And earning at the same time the pride of being men.

So let's say it again – and we shall say it as often as is necessary – WHY NOT EVERYWHERE?

The "Fight against Leprosy" doesn't only consist in controlling the bacillus, in detecting a victim, in waging war on the former leper-colonies. It is also fought within the heart of each of us. It's the struggle between the age-old terror that we've inherited and the courage of our finally enlightened charity.

It is for this final test of brotherhood that I've alerted you and gathered you together every year for the past twelve years.

We must press on with our Fight – our battle so different from others. When I began it, almost alone, "informed" people (informed in what respect, O Lord?) turned away and said: "It's been like this since the beginning of the world. He won't be able to change anything. It's impossible."

Impossible? Only one thing is impossible, and that is that we, the terribly happy people, should be able to go on eating, sleeping and laughing while the world around us weeps, bleeds and despairs.

And this is why our Fight should henceforth reach out to all the leprosies.

To those a hundredfold more deadly leprosies such as hunger, poverty, slums.

To those thousandfold more infectious leprosies such as cataleptic apathy, blind egotism, and cowardice that seeks a funk-hole so as the better to run away. . . . And distrust which defaces mankind. And hate which dishonours it.

Against all leprosies and for all men.

With one weapon only: Love.

Dictatorial techniques, sterile exploits, vainglorious records – that's what we have if the heart does not play a part.

A civilization without love is an antheap.

So, my dear friends, my dear marching companions, let's press on with our brotherly Fight, and let's extend it to the scale of the world and its woes.

As for myself, I'll stay before you or beside you till my strength gives out.

As long as there's one man to be cured, one wretch to be consoled, one "leper" to be freed, as long as there's one famine that could be avoided or one prison where injustice reigns, neither you nor I have the right to sit back or be silent.

RESULTS

EVERY YEAR, as we shall see, World Leprosy Day was to extend its scope and its benefits. Every year it was to win over new countries and fresh hearts.

Here follows a quick survey of its amazing ascent as shown by a few figures and testimonies.

1954

For the first time a unique and wonderful sight was to be seen on the Day: processions forming in towns or villages near leper-colonies. Children, their arms full of flowers and cakes (cakes made by their mothers), going to the "lepers", opening their doors (doors that would never again be shut), entering without fear, giving the sick – overcome by joy – their little presents. And then dancing for them, singing for them, telling them stories. . . . And smiling, smiling at those people who had never been smiled at before.

1955

In nearly 60 countries, 150 radio or television stations announced the Second World Leprosy Day.

MADAGASCAR

Les Nouvelles Malgaches of 31 January informed us that a special train was needed on the Day to transport the 2,000 people who went from Tananarive to Mangarano so as to visit lepers. *The High Commissioner suspended by special order all the exceptional laws still imposed on lepers.*

1956

72 countries. 400 radio or television announcements.

In Rome Cardinal Tisserant, Dean of the Sacred College, said his Mass for the lepers. He was henceforth to do this every year.

With him, and in union with the Pope's prayers, thousands of Masses were celebrated all over the world.

Many ceremonies also took place in Reformed churches and mosques . . . and even in Buddhist temples.

INDONESIA

The French Ambassador informed us: "Your record was broadcast over the Indonesian radio and followed by translations in English and Indonesian. *The Minister for Public Health organized visits of school-children to leper-colonies.*"

NEW CALEDONIA

The Minister for Public Health wrote to me: "In a common gesture of solidarity, the Government, the General Council and the people took part in the Third World Leprosy Day. The High Commissioner and the president of the General Council, surrounded by all the dignitaries of the island, attended a festival that took place at the Ducos sanatorium on that day.[1] With a view to associating itself as completely as possible with your campaign, *the General Council unanimously voted a sum of two million francs for improving the sanatorium's equipment.*

"Thus not only is the moral climate of the victims of Hansen's disease developing daily more favourably under your inspiration, but also the community is allocating considerable sums to them and granting them more material well-being."

1957

80 countries celebrated the Day. Every year a small inroad was made into selfishness and fear.

MARTINIQUE

Doctor Montestruc, to whom lepers – and not only those of the West Indies – owe so much, wrote:

"It was a wonderful day at the Hansen sanatorium of Fort-de-France. After Mass, the crowd of visitors rushed to the stalls covered with handwork done by the patients. Embroidery, toys, beautifully decorated pottery, books bound with great craftsmanship, everything went in a moment. It is now certain that –

[1] Which the government of New Caledonia has recently renamed "the Raoul Follereau Centre".

except for absurd exceptions – the ridiculous fear of objects made by the sick is disappearing."

A victim wrote me:

"It was an absolute triumph. Do you know that after the concert, at 8.30, there was a dance. And we all danced for the best part of the night. It was wonderful. Our dear doctor couldn't restrain his tears. . . ."

1958

83 countries. Success was getting organized.

BRAZIL

From the well-known Brazilian leprologist, Dr Ernani Agricola:

"The programme broadcast every Tuesday by the National Service for Leprosy was almost entirely devoted to the Fifth World Leprosy Day. We sent out your message. On 26 January your communication was broadcast again on the Brazilian wavelength and published in its Portuguese translation in the papers. I'm sure that this Day will have had a huge success all over the world as it is directed by the 'Vagabond of Charity' whom I myself prefer to call the 'lepers' Mahatma', that is to say their great soul."

EGYPT

The foundation of the "Assistance Society for the professional and social rehabilitation of lepers".

From Dr Youssef Georgi Gabrail, Cairo:

"Here we celebrated the Fifth World Day by the creation of a lasting good work, the 'Assistance Society for the professional and social rehabilitation of lepers'. After the showing of a film on leprosy, we listened to your stirring appeal, and your voice, so full of love, immediately won us a large number of members: official personalities, doctors, religious, and people from all classes of society. Thanks to World Leprosy Day the work is launched and will soon bear fruit. If by some lucky chance you can come and visit us, we and our lepers will give you a heart-felt and enthusiastic welcome."

NEW ZEALAND

From the French Ambassador:

"I had your appeal broadcast at the University on the day. In the course of the coming weeks it will be heard in other universities, schools and colleges."

1959

The demonstrations were so brilliant and so persuasive that the public Powers were drawn into the "Fight against Leprosy" in their turn.

UNITED NATIONS ORGANIZATION

UNICEF sent out through the world press agencies a communication that said:

"Sunday 25 January will be the Sixth World Leprosy Day. The United Nations Children's Fund states that 12 million men are affected by leprosy; Africa alone has 3 million lepers, that is to say three Africans out of every hundred are lepers."

On this occasion UNICEF announced that it anticipated opening a credit of *one milliard, 250 million francs for the fight against Leprosy in Africa.*

FRANCE

M. Jean Berthoin, Minister for National Education, addressed a circular signed by his own hand to all teaching personnel to "associate the youth of France with the crusade".

UNITED STATES

The largest United States organization in the fight against leprosy, the Leonard Wood Memorial (American Leprosy Foundation) sent us the following telegram:

"On occasion Sixth World Lepers Day wish to extend congratulations on your accomplishments in campaign against fear and prejudice. Doull and medical staff Leonard Wood Memorial join me in best wishes future success. Crowther."

THAILAND

From Dr Ramon Miquel, WHO's representative in Khon-Kaen:

"Radio-Bangkok broadcast your record to the whole of Thailand. Two of the main papers published your appeal, *The Bangkok Post* and *The Bangkok Tribune*. Their Majesties the King and Queen of Thailand listened to the appeal and read the message. Your way of speaking to men's hearts moved everyone even to tears."

ETHIOPIA

From M. Gingold-Duprey, director of the paper *L'Ethiopie d'aujourd'hui*:

"On 25 January Addis-Ababa radio broadcast your words which were also transmitted in Amharic and were warmly received in Ethiopia. I am told that local festivities took place almost everywhere this time, principally in the leper centres of Harar, Chachamaneh and elsewhere. At the Zenebe Worq hospital near the capital, a 'clinic' for lepers has just been inaugurated, the existing premises having been developed and enlarged. I personally have your magnificent efforts very much at heart, and the Ethiopian press often refers to your exploits which give hope to the unfortunate and strengthen our hope in a better world."

INDONESIA

From Dr Blanc, an expert of the World Health Organization:
"At Djakarta we had a very good Leprosy Day, with an official meeting presided over by the Minister of Health in person. More than *a thousand people* assembled at the hospital of Tangerang. There were ten speeches, of which one was by the Minister, one by the director of the Leprosy Institute and one by your humble servant. All had as aim to show those present that leprosy is now a curable disease. Between whiles a group of lepers gave us mimes, songs, music and dances. *A communal meal* was eaten on the premises to close a moving day, in the course of which many presents were given to the lepers."

1960

148 reports reached us from 88 countries.

CAMEROON

Cameroon made World Leprosy Day a National Festival.
Statement by the President of the Republic:

The Seventh World Leprosy Day will be celebrated throughout the whole of Cameroon. Its founder, M. Raoul Follereau, will come from France for the occasion and will attend, at Yaoundé, the official opening of a pavilion wing for leprosy-surgery built thanks to a gift from the Order of Charity of which he is president. Throughout the whole country the healthy must show brotherly feelings towards the sick on that day. The doctors responsible have already received all the necessary instructions from the Ministry of Public Health, and in particular from the head doctor of the S.H.M.P. But the success of Leprosy Day cannot be complete without the participation of the public powers.

That is the reason for this letter.

I ask the prefects, under-prefects and mayors to mark the day by taking their friends on a brotherly visit to the leper-colony nearest their homes, but I also ask them to start immediately helping the doctors responsible for the fight against leprosy to overhaul the infirmaries and huts of the leper villages, and also their approaches. Our solicitude on behalf of the most disinherited of men will have the value of a symbol in the eyes of the world. A. AHIDJO.

This appeal elicited a magnificent response, and 7,000 parcels were distributed in 50 centres of treatment.

CANADA

Throughout the whole of Canada, French-speaking and English-speaking alike, the Seventh World Leprosy Day enjoyed a greater success than the year before.

Fifty radio stations broadcast the message – in Raoul Follereau's voice in the French-speaking provinces, and in Sir Laurence Olivier's in the English-speaking ones.

GUADELOUPE

From M. Ernest Bonnet, president of the Committee for Aid to Lepers, whose dedication is so admirable:

"On 30 January Raoul Follereau gave a talk in the huge Place de la Victoire at Pointe-à-Pitre. *More than six thousand people* were there, among them the under-prefect of Pointe-à-Pitre, the president of the General Council, etc. It was the mayor, M. Dessout, who introduced the 'Vagabond of Charity'. After the talk he conferred the accolade on him, saying, 'You have cured Guadeloupe of fear of lepers.'

"The next day a crowd estimated at 2,000 went to the Hansen sanatorium at Pointe-Noir to wish the lepers a happy day – *these lepers are those who were formerly confined to Desirée Island.*"

JAPAN

From Father Anouilh:

"I know of no greater peaceful revolution than yours. A whole world has changed, or is on the point of doing so. You haven't been the hammer that drives the idea in, but the stylet that lances the abscess. *Fortior gladio calamus.*

"As I wrote you, I got your talk at the *Maison internationale* of Tokyo published in *Le Journal catholique* in an excellent translation by M. Matsumoto, director of the *Athénée Français.* I'm enclosing the two articles with this letter. I added that visits, letters or other demonstrations of sympathy towards our sick were altogether to be desired on Leprosy Day organized by you throughout the whole world.

"Result: Joy on the part of the lepers for the splendid text, countless letters, specially from children and youth groups."

1961

116 countries. VICTORY.

The Indian Union fixed the World Leprosy Day as 30 January, the anniversary of Gandhi's death, and declared it a National Festival.

*   *   *

Reports of the Eighth World Leprosy Day gave rise to various observations.

For the first time there was the active collaboration of many sovereigns and Heads of State who went in person to visit the lepers.

In Bangkok the King and Queen of Thailand themselves presided at the celebrations at the leper colony, and they were accompanied by their guests, King Leopold and Princess Liliane of Belgium.

In Senegal, the president of the Republic, M. Léopold Sédar Senghor; in Mali, the president of the Republic, M. Modibo Keita; in Madagascar, the president of the Republic, M. Tsiranana; at Chad, the president of the Republic, M. Tombalbaye – all went personally to visit the lepers.

The celebration in Cameroon started with an appeal broadcast by the president of the Republic, M. Ahidjo; in the Indian Union by a message from the president of the Republic, His

Excellency Rajendra Prasad; in Greece by an audience accorded to myself by the King and Queen.

The presidents of the Republics of Upper Volta, Niger and Dahomey interrupted the sitting of their joint Council so as to visit the sick of Ouagadougou together and take them their good wishes.

* * *

For the first time several countries of eastern Europe took part in our manifestation of human solidarity, thus giving it its universal character.

Reports reached us from Albania, Poland, Czechoslovakia and Yugoslavia, as well as cuttings from articles appearing in the press of these countries and texts of broadcasts.

Furthermore in the course of many demonstrations, notably in Africa, the Diplomatic Corps made a point of going to visit the lepers, thus showing with everyone else their compassion and friendship towards the saddest of the world's oppressed minorities.

* * *

Finally this universal Day was a huge act of prayer. An act of prayer which went beyond confessional and racial frontiers and united all believers in a single cry of love towards Him from whom all love comes.

While, as every year, His Eminence Cardinal Tisserant, Dean of the Sacred College, was saying his Mass for lepers, I was receiving a moving message from the Very Venerable Lama Che-Wou-Ming, director of the Chinese Buddhist Association and president of the Ling-Yuen temple (Formosa).

While Vatican radio was broadcasting our appeal, the pastor in charge of religious instruction for Lausanne radio was devoting his broadcast, relayed by the English network, to World Leprosy Day.

Already translated into eighteen languages, the "Prayer for all the poor of the world" was published in Arabic and thus was uttered simultaneously by Christians, Jews, Moslems and Buddhists.

All the religious communities of the Lebanon made a collection that realized two million francs, while at Westminster a meeting was held jointly by qualified representatives of the

Christian hierarchies: Anglican, Catholic, Lutheran, Presbyterian, etc.

*   *   *

But the most original and symbolic and certainly the most touching of these demonstrations took place in the Santa-Barbara (Greece) centre for treatment[1]. An eye-witness described them as follows in *Mission de la France:*

> ... The programme included ... a communal lunch with the sick. It was ... let's say, a bold idea. In the same room – that's one thing. But at the same table, using the same utensils, drinking from the same glasses, breaking the same bread. Who would dare to come?
>
> Who? Oh, if only we had had enough room! We had hoped for fifty guests in addition to the sick. But when a hundred and fifty had arrived, we had to turn the others away. Then try to find seats for the ones we'd let in. . . .
>
> We had to eat in relays. And many people ate standing up. Raoul Follereau went from table to table, clinking glasses with all the sick, holding arms, in the Greek manner.
>
> Then suddenly – who started it? – the merry winding steps of a farandole took possession of the room. And the sick, with their poor mutilated feet, were dancing. . . . And the hands of their friends from Athens clasped and upheld their own poor stumps. . . . It was a sublime moment during which no one thought of his suffering, his miseries or himself. Charity had swept away, renewed, recreated, conquered everything.
>
> And to me this farandole seemed like the chain of love which will one day unite the whole world in its gentle hold.
>
> Blessed be our poor friends whose afflictions will have forged its first links.

*   *   *

Sporting events took place between sick teams and those of the neighbouring towns.

Matches took place at La Valbonne (France), Adzopé (Ivory Coast), Toussiana (Upper Volta), Bamako (Mali), Agoudou Manga (Central African Republic). And even between two sick teams: the leper-colony of N'Den against the one of Sangbélima (Cameroon).

Cinema shows took place by the hundred, not only for the

---

[1] The celebrations were put forward a week so that Raoul Follereau could attend them, before setting off for Ouagadougou.

P.-A. Pittet

1. RAOUL FOLLEREAU.

2. Père Peyriguère, the great missionary, a friend of th author.

3. The author with Professor Mitsuda, the great leprologist, at the Lepros Congress of Tokyo.

"I'm hungry."

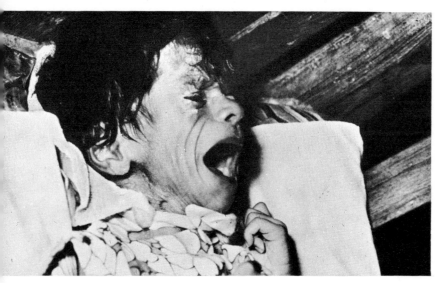

A little old man of . . . two.

P.-A. Pittet

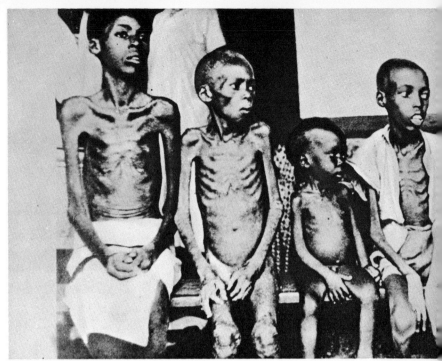

6. When love deserts the world . . .

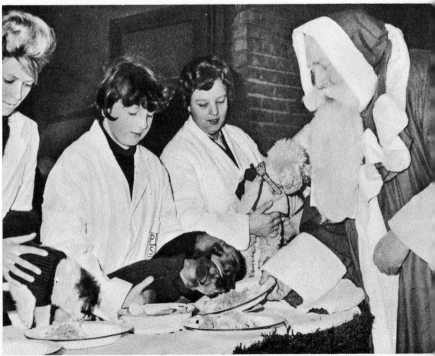

(7) . . . Christmas is for the dogs.

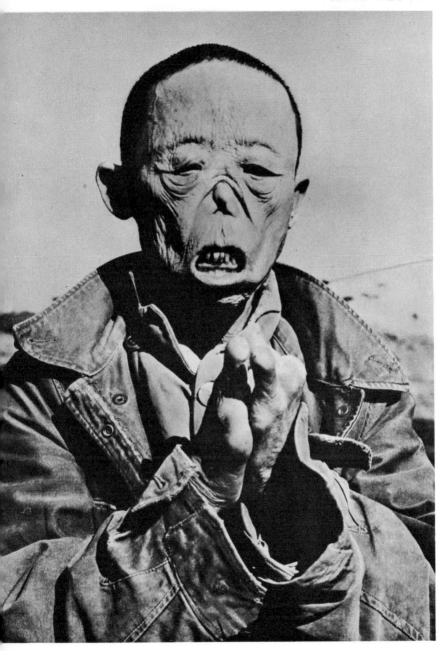

) . . . on the leper, . .

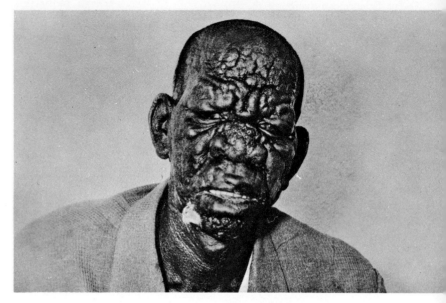

(9) . . . the outcast, accursed, . . .   P.-A. Pi

(10) . . . and sometimes treated like the worst of criminals.

Today, Science can overcome the disease—

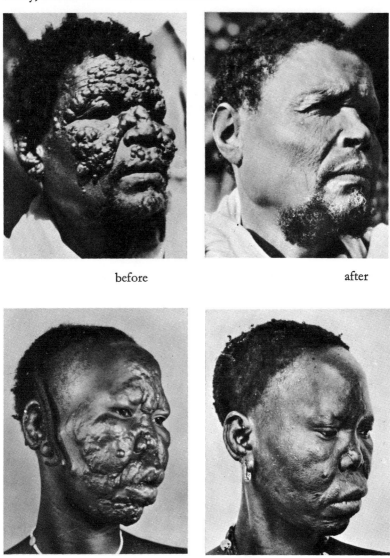

before   after

before   after

11. Treatment of leprosy with sulphone drugs.

—We have to overcome society's curse

12. In Africa

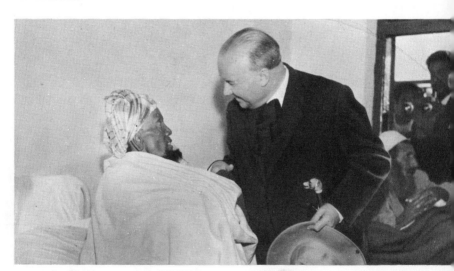

13. In Asia.

(14) a street, . . .   *Ivory Coast Information*

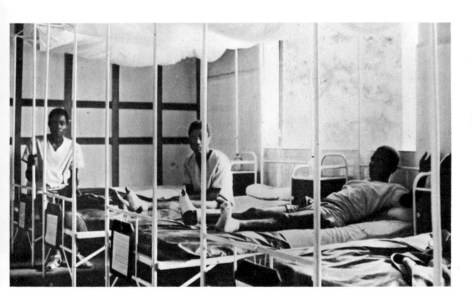

(15) . . . and the hospital . . .

Where leprosy is no longer a curse.

16. With Dr Claire Vellut, at a mobile treatment centre formed simply by pulling the vans up at the edge of the road

17. With the late Mgr Mathias, Archbishop of Madras, and Sri T. N. Jagadisan, a former leper and now General Secretary of the Indian Association for the Relief of Lepers.

18. Dr Schweitzer, a few months before his death, with the author's wife, who for more than thirty years has accompanied her husband on his visits to all the leper colonies of the world.

AND EVERYWHERE . . .

19. The liberating medicines are brought to the most remote villages.

(20) The author has spoken . . .

(21) . . . in theatres . . .

(22) . . . and even cathedrals.

For his sixtieth birthday his friends gave him

(23) . . . a hundred and four cars.

24. Youthful enthusiasm. The campaign has so far produced over 1,500,000 signatures, . . .

(25) . . . an audience with Pope Paul VI - 4 July 1964 - and . . .

(26) . . . a conference at the Press Office of Vatican Council II. Mgr Vallainc, General Secretary of the Vatican Press Services, is shown introducing the author, who spoke of his thirty-year-old campaign "against all the leprosies of the world".

27. At Father Damien's tomb on the Island of Molokai.

28. A welcome back to the Congo, and (29) to Tahiti

REMEMBER . . .

The price of an aircraft-carrier . . .

(30) would feed 400,000 men for a year—

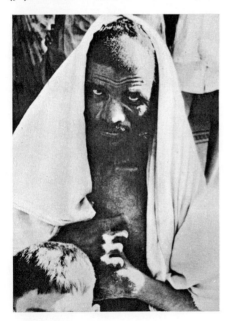

(31) including . . .

(32) us?

lepers, which is good, but in leper-colonies (which is better) to
which healthy guests were invited (Charlot Festival at Ouagadougou, Upper Volta), and even *in the public cinemas of the town* to
which the lepers were invited (which is perfect). The sick often
went "to town" to give a show to their healthy friends. For
instance the tom-tom organized on the main square of Ouidah
(Dahomey) by the sick of Saints-Anges and attended by several
thousand people. And the theatricals given before packed houses
at Kumbakonam (Indian Union), Fort-de-France (Martinique),
etc.

*   *   *

Here are a few other reports – among so many:

From Acarouany (French Guiana):
A dance closed the festivities "which went on very far into
the night".

From Mauritius:
"A lot of people. There was such a warm, cordial atmosphere
that no one thought of leaving. The night took us by surprise
while the festivities were in full swing."
The report received from Bertoua (Cameroon) states that "the
dance was opened by the important people present" but soon
"everyone was dancing".

From Tahiti:
". . . Cars were parked over more than 500 metres outside
the village. All the religious orders and important people were
there. Not only the presents, but the sympathy shown them, and
the songs sung for them, made of this 29 January a real festival
for the sick of Orofara. And it was with all their hearts that they
danced and sang for their visitors in their turn."

From Malaysia:
"Thousands of little coloured calendars were distributed with
the slogan: 'Leprosy is curable', as well as clear and precise
information about the disease and the ways in which everyone
can help in the care and social rehabilitation of the lepers.
"Collections were made for the sick of Malaysia throughout the
country. Everywhere public opinion was mobilized and turned

K

upside down, following the wish of the founder of the Day to whom all the press paid homage."

Some consequences

The president of the Republic of Senegal wrote to me:

". . . I am not unaware of the relentless fight that you've been engaged in for thirty years for the suppression of leprosy in the world.

"In Senegal we are in such deep sympathy with the purpose and value of your crusade that we are working out a ten-year plan whose object is to eradicate leprosy in this country.

"I made a point of presiding personally at Leprosy Day.— LÉOPOLD SÉDAR SENGHOR."

Dr E. Khoury, Lebanese Minister for Public Health, announced in a broadcast talk that "the Government will allocate a sum of 500,000 Lebanese pounds for the fight against leprosy".

The Minister for Public Health of the Ivory Coast announced that a sum equivalent to 5 million new francs will be devoted to converting Adzopé into a real Leprosy Institute comprising an important service for social rehabilitation.

*   *   *

Glancing through the enormous number of reports that have reached us, we pick out:

From the head doctor of Medical Assistance in Dire (Mali):

". . . I'm sure that the Day has had a salutary effect on minds, because a few days after it *many lepers came to be treated.*"

From the director of the Pasteur Institute, French Guiana:

". . . But the most important aspect in my view is that, as a result of their yearly repetition, these demonstrations have now had an influence over their habits. They are playing a large part in modifying the attitudes and behaviour of the public with regard to lepers."

From the treasurer of the Committee for Help to Lepers in Managua (Nicaragua):

". . . But the thing that touched us most of all – which might seem strange to anyone but you – was seeing the people who went into their rooms, who talked to them, who smiled at them, coming away happy, without disgust, surprised at seeing these men and women living like human beings, for everyone thought that going to visit them was an act of heroism. During the eight years that we've been concerned with them, we've received plenty of gifts, *but our sick had never been visited.* So we can say that the Day was a success."

From the director of the National Service for war against leprosy in Vietnam:
"I notice that the mentality of our lepers has completely changed. They have become more disciplined and more aware of themselves. Did you know that on the day of the festival they composed a song in your honour? Truly your efforts have not been in vain and I'm sure that every Vietnamese leper carried the name 'Follereau' in his heart."

* * *

Realizing the immense success of the Day, I wrote in our Bulletin:

Our civilization, martyrized by progress, nevertheless retains in its labyrinthine depths one road that opens on to the sun! What is needed in order to solve so many insoluble problems is a common denominator. And here in the midst of the clamour of fanaticism and the howls of demagogy a voice can still make itself heard, a voice so sweet yet so strong that the motorized hatreds hold their breath. Love chasing out fear, love coming first, love stronger than discord and suspicion and hate and death. That is the marvellous lesson of the marvellous Day.

But the Fight against Leprosy is only a chapter, the first chapter in this great battle that *everyone*, whoever we are, wherever we live, must wage against the *real leprosies* – much more infecting, alas, than leprosy – which are poverty, hunger, selfishness, fanaticism, cowardice. We have learnt how to attack these leprosies in the service of lepers – how to fight them and conquer them.

If we've been able to contribute to the deliverance of so many hopeless, doomed and outcast men, why should we not inspire other fights, fights on the scale of world suffering? The Fight against Leprosy can serve as an example and open up other paths. . . . What we have done and what we do every day for lepers can surely be achieved *against all leprosies.*

We believe this with our whole heart and our whole faith.

For too long men have lived *side by side.*

Today they must *live all together.*
We must teach them to live *for each other* tomorrow.
The only truth is to love each other.

1962

MESSAGE FROM JOHN F. KENNEDY

President of the United States of America

In proportion as our knowledge advances and our understanding grows, hopes of a final victory over leprosy become ever more bright.

On the occasion of the Ninth World Leprosy Day it is my pleasure to salute the people and organizations which throughout the world have devoted their efforts to this struggle and brought help and hope to the victims of this ancient enemy of man.

To all those who are united in this world-wide campaign to alleviate the sufferings of these victims, I wish the greatest success in the years to come.

JOHN F. KENNEDY

ALLOCUTION

broadcast over Teheran radio by

H.M. FARA DIBA PAHLAVI

Empress of Iran

Dear Countrymen,

One of the scourges that has afflicted mankind for centuries is leprosy which affects the whole world not excluding our own dear country. Not long ago its victims were banished, chased from their native towns and imprisoned in some place far away from their homes and families. Happily today, thanks to new discoveries, we know that if leprosy treatment takes place at an early stage, not only is the danger of infection eliminated but also the sick can pursue their normal life, like everyone else.

In addition to the obligations incumbent on the Minister of Health and the sanitary departments in all that concerns these victims, and in accordance with orders issued by His Imperial Majesty the Chahanchah, an Association, under Our patronage, was recently founded in Teheran.

The purpose of this Association is to help lepers by putting them under observation instead of shutting them up. Villages will be built where they can devote themselves to agriculture, so that they can again be reintegrated into human society.

The 8 Bahman, 28 January 1962, has been recognized as World Leprosy Day throughout the whole world, and is also recognized by Us as Leprosy Day in Iran. So I hope that you, my brothers and sisters, will hold out your generous hands to these unfortunates who are deprived of everything, for they need your help and assistance.

To you, lepers of Iran and the world, I am happy to tell you that the Association for aid to Lepers will stop at no sacrifice on the sacred road of your happiness.

LETTER

FROM THE VENERABLE LAMA CHE-WOU-MING

spiritual leader of the Buddhists of China

. . . I acknowledge you as the apostle of leprosy victims, and pay homage to your great efforts on their behalf.

I shall not fail to give your message on the Ninth World Leprosy Day the greatest possible publicity among my compatriots in the Chinese Republic; I shall stress that opinion must understand that the ill against which we are fighting is a disease like other diseases and no complex of any kind should be attached to it. I am constantly in touch with official broadcasting services, and also I shall write an article in the next number of the review Bouddhisme chinois. *You can rest assured that the Ninth Leprosy Day will be celebrated among us.*

In answer to your good wishes, I sincerely hope that the fine work that you have undertaken will prosper; I have in my heart an enduring memory of your visit of three years ago and beg you to believe in my devotion.

1963

CAMBODIA. Creation of a National Committee to combat Leprosy. Its president, Ung-Hong-Sath, former Minister of Public Health, wrote to us:

I have the honour and the pleasure of bringing to your notice the birth of the National Committee to combat leprosy in Cambodia – of which I am president.

The founding of this National Committee is undoubtedly a direct result of your last year's message addressed to His Royal Highness the Prince Norodom-Sihanouk, our national leader who, concerned as are you with the plight of all who suffer, has in his turn launched an appeal so that the fight against this terrible scourge may be intensified in Cambodia.

Our National Committee has as its aim to unite men of good

will, to gather in gifts of every kind, to help the public powers in the line of action they have always followed, with a view to alleviating the condition of leprosy victims.

It is thus that on the occasion of the Tenth World Leprosy Day the Committee was able to hand over to the leper-colony crèche blankets, kitchen equipment, food and anti-leprosy medicaments to the value of forty-six thousand riels (about 460,000 old francs).

So you see, President and Founder of the Order of Charity, what has just been done in Cambodia to alleviate, as far as this is possible, the lot of our leper brothers, to whom you have dedicated yourself for the past thirty years.

We have not done much and we want to do more and better. And for this reason we would be most grateful if you would give us the benefit of your long experience.

We shall always be deeply grateful for an indication, any suggestion that you would like to make with a view to helping us to make our compassion more effective – the compassion that, following Buddha our Master, we feel towards all beings and particularly towards those of our brothers who are plunged in the ocean of suffering.

1964

The King and Queen of Belgium visited the lepers

Polambakkam

A hundred kilometres south of Madras, lost among huge bougainvillaeas always in bloom, hidden by syringa bushes as tall as trees, there are houses that play hide-and-seek with the sun. Is it a dreamed-up landscape or a fairy-story?

It's better. For lepers, it's a paradise.

This centre was created in 1955 by Dr Hemerijckx, sent out specially by the Belgian Foundation to combat leprosy. In 1960 it was handed over to the Indian Government which is currently in charge of it but asked the team then working there to continue with its management.

A girl who smiles

When Dr Hemerijckx, the well-known leprologist whose goodness and learning are both legendary, had to give up Polambakkam so as to take on heavier burdens, which he accepted because they enabled him to do still more good, he handed the settlement over to his assistant. His assistant was a young woman, Claire Vellut, sent out by the International Women Auxiliaries. At that time she was hardly more than thirty. She was, and is, both smart and pretty. Of course she has the certificates necessary to assert her authority: doctor in medicine at Louvain University, pupil of Professor Maisin. Those are her qualifications. But it's her smile that wins the day.

23,000 treated: 16,000 cured

The Polambakkam Centre pursues its war on leprosy over an area of 3,000 square kilometres. This includes 884 villages totalling a population of 550,000 inhabitants of whom about 4% are affected with leprosy. Five doctors are engaged in the campaign, with about fifty helpers, nurses, laboratory assistants, physiotherapists, social workers and so on, under the direction of Dr Claire Vellut, and they are ceaselessly on the go throughout the region. Fifty-two mobile units, set up for the most part on the side of roads, bring treatment and the necessary medicaments to the sick where they live. Each unit is visited at least once a month by a doctor and his assistants.

At Polambakkam itself there exists – for serious cases requiring surgical intervention or more intensive supervision – a hospital ward of 45 beds, an operating room for reparatory surgery, two laboratories and a physiotherapy department.

Thus over the past ten years 23,000 victims have been treated with skill and love. It can be estimated that 16,000 of them are now cured.

It was for the purpose of honouring their countrymen, identifying themselves with the campaign and celebrating the victory, that the Belgian King and Queen came to spend the Eleventh World Leprosy Day at Polambakkam.

Over each victim the tireless sovereigns shed their youthful radiance. To each they said the right word, the word that leaves a great sweetness in the soul. No word of mine could possibly describe what those sad and suffering victims received that day in the way of light, hope and joy – given in one clasp of their outstretched hands, in one smile from the King and Queen who projected on to each face the wonderful light of their own happiness.

1965
A Message from President Lyndon Johnson

Following in the steps of President Kennedy, President Johnson of the United States addressed a very cordial message to all the American organizers of World Leprosy Day.

For the first time the four great American organizations for aid to lepers decided to unite their efforts so as to make of the Day a real national festival.

At Bamako, 100,000 people

A HUNDRED THOUSAND PEOPLE – that was the official estimate – went to the Marchoux Institute on the Day to wish the lepers a happy festival.

Together with Raoul Follereau himself, all the government of Mali and the whole of the Diplomatic Corps were present.

In his speech Dr Dolo Sominé, Minister of Public Health and president of the "National Raoul-Follereau Committee", said:

. . . When President Follereau became aware of the destitution and suffering of men, he thought up a dream (for great men are all visionaries): to bring things about so that love for each other should form a current of brotherhood and solidarity, and thus the most disinherited would be able to find loving concern from the more privileged.

. . . Repudiating ostentatious almsgiving, he made an appeal to men's consciences, to true charity, in order that each of us should clearly see that we haven't the right to be happy alone. He has fought tirelessly against the absurdity of our prejudices and our criminal selfishness by means of lectures and the press. He has travelled the world so as to create a little more love and concern among men. Committees have sprung up everywhere and he has founded World Leprosy Day, celebrated by more than 125 countries all over the world. The result of this remarkable crusade on behalf of lepers has been an awakening of the consciences of men of good will. All have answered his call, rich and poor (and often the poorest!). The leper's fate is improving with proper treatment, but it is improving still more with the new spirit that has been created among the healthy.

The material means at President Follereau's disposal have been entirely made over to the service of our sick: means of locomotion so as to treat them in rural areas, buildings to shelter them, medicaments, etc. So now is the moment for us assembled here to show him our gratitude officially.

In recalling the courageous and humanitarian activities of our friend, President Follereau, we cannot fail to mention his wife, who for more than thirty years has been at his side, helping him and supporting him in his work. So we hope that you, dear companion of the "Vagabond of Charity", will also accept our deep and respectful gratitude.

M. Alain Peyrefitte, French Minister of Information, presided over the Day in Reunion Island

Father Grémion, chaplain of the leper-colony, wrote:

Do you remember? On the first Day, twelve years ago, there were twenty-five of us and all we had as presents were three bottles of white wine and two packets of biscuits.

How many this year? Two thousand. Perhaps more. With, first and foremost, the Minister of Information surrounded by the mayor and all the authorities of the island.

There was a very poignant moment: when our dear Adrien, coming out of Mass, went up to the microphone and in a voice full of emotion warmly thanked the Minister for having come. It was all televised. Don't you find an immense victory there? And that the little flame lit by you ten years ago has become a huge fire?

Then the whole day became a huge fête for the people and there was always a dense crowd round the stalls where the Lions Club, the Legion of Mary, our Committee, the Youth Movements, and so many others were giving of their all.

This year a happy innovation was a great attraction: a temporary post-office installed in the leper-colony by the Philatelist Club of Saint-Denis. It was a great success, and I should say that at least 10,000 letters were stamped at the leper-colony on that Day.

It really was a triumph, and, from the financial point of view, altogether successful. I can't give you exact sums yet, but I should say that we've gone beyond a million C.F.A. (French W. African francs). So this year again we can help our dear sick families and do something to improve their lot.

Once again this little Reunion Island has given a perfect example of charity. And now we're already looking forward to the Thirteenth Day and your presence here which always means so much to us.

The Hansen Sanatorium of Martinique would henceforth be known by the names of "Follereau-Montestruc"

Uniting in one gesture of admiration and affection the "Vagabond of Charity" and the man who for the past thirty years has been not only the saviour of the lepers of Martinique but also their protector and father, the Administrative Commission of the Clarac Hospital of Fort-de-France decided that the adjoining Hansen sanatorium would henceforth be known as "Follereau-Montestruc". This was a just and well-deserved tribute paid to the great leprologist whose voice is listened to at every international congress, and to the good father who has been so beloved by the sick for over a quarter of a century.

DOCUMENTS

"You HAVE added a new chapter to leprology," declared Dr. Montestruc, director of the Pasteur Institute of Martinique.

In 1960, in introducing Raoul Follereau to the packed audience gathered in the club-house of Fort-de-France, Martinique, Dr Montestruc – the victor of the "Fight against Leprosy" in that country – recalled the "unforgettable moment" that had marked the end of the final session of the VIIth Leprosy Congress in Tokyo.

It was 19 November 1958 and it was 12 noon in Tokyo. In the great conference hall on the fifth floor of the Sankei building the work of the Congress was drawing to a close.

Dr Davey of Nigeria, the last speaker before the closing speech by the Secretary General, Dr Hamano, had the task of summarizing all the scientific novelties contained in the various communications presented in the course of the previous days. His intervention finished with an examination of the Technical Commission's report on the social aspects of leprosy. In the normal way leprologists, men of science by definition, are uninterested in the social aspect of a disease which they are nevertheless fighting with all their faith and tenacity. But on this occasion one felt that something had changed, and those of us who have an ear for what goes on behind the scenes had no doubt that the intervention made at the plenary session the day before by Raoul Follereau was not unconnected with the changed attitude. And when, in the course of his magnificent speech, Dr Davey cried out, "Everyone behind Raoul Follereau to win the Fight against Leprosy", a huge ovation filled the congress hall. So, as I have already said on the air from the French broadcasting station of Fort-de-France, whatever rewards are bestowed on you, even the great ones that lie in wait for you, none, my great and dear friend, will have the significance of that demonstration.

Of course it was flattering for our national *amour-propre*.

But there was more to it than that: the leprologists of the whole
world rose up in an access of enthusiasm to welcome you, who
are not a doctor, among them. For those leprologists had
suddenly realized that you had added a new chapter to leprology; the sociology of leprosy would henceforward have its
place, side by side with the chapters on its immunology, its
bacteriology, its epidemiology and its therapeutics.

... This little episode that I have just recounted is intended,
ladies and gentlemen, to bring home to you how decisive has
been Raoul Follereau's action in the social domain of leprosy.
... He has obliged everyone, including leprologists, to look the
truth in the face, that is to say to acknowledge that leprosy is
an infectious disease like other infectious diseases, and that a
leper is an invalid like other invalids, that is to say with a right
to the therapeutic care necessitated by the state of his illness,
and also and most of all to the sentiments of kindness and
charity accorded to other invalids. That is the big, the immense
achievement of Raoul Follereau, so you will understand why in
time to come millions and millions of victims will have their
minds and hearts turned towards him.

But Raoul Follereau's achievement doesn't end there. I
would like to remind you of the material help he has brought to
lepers in the form of money, medicaments, every kind of
vehicle from homely bicycles to the most up-to-date jeeps so as
to enable the sick in all areas to have medical attention, har-
moniums for hospital chapels, cinema apparatus and other
amusements for the entertainment of the sick. Nothing has
been forgotten. At the moment when all the top people are
talking about aid to the underdeveloped countries, they have
here a magnificent example before them.

But there's still something more. For this liberal action in the
social domain of leprosy appeared so revolutionary and even
dangerous to many people that leprologists were forced to
think before deciding where they stood, then to follow Raoul
Follereau in his beneficent action of which the applause of
19 November 1958 was the stirring proof.

One day in the perhaps not very distant future I shall open
a file in which facts of epidemiology and immunology have been
accumulated over nearly thirty years – showing, with something
of the rigour of an experiment, that, in the mechanism of
leprous infection, contact with the victim is only an epipheno-
menon, and that it is not by avoiding everything that may seem
to be a focus of infection that contamination will be avoided

(witness the woman who, believing her taxi-driver to be leprous, threw herself out of the taxi while it was going and fractured her leg). For inevitably one day or another, in a country where leprosy is endemic, one will come into contact with a source of massive contagion without even knowing it. And on that day a new organism, unused to resisting slight contaminations, will have nothing with which to face this massive infection. And that is how one becomes a victim of the severest forms of leprosy. At the risk of perhaps losing the respect that some people seem to have for me, I can assure you with the most complete conviction that, for my part, I have nothing to fear from these massive contaminations because my organism has set up a state of resistance, shown by a strongly positive lepromino-reaction and acquired as the result of years and years of contact with Hansen's bacillus.

All this is to assure you, ladies and gentlemen, that it is not only for reasons of sentiment or affection that leprologists have followed and backed up Raoul Follereau in the magnificent crusade of kindness and charity that he has undertaken, but because they have understood that in him they had the decisive element for winning the Fight against Leprosy.

SPEECH DELIVERED

BY M. CYRILLE ADOULA

president of the Council of
Ministers of the Republic of the Congo
on the occasion of the XIth World Leprosy Day, 1964

Ministers, Excellencies, dear sick brothers,
Today is leper day, leper festival day, your day.
Not only you, the sick, but everyone here will join with me in paying homage to the first man to break the barrier that separated lepers from the rest of mankind, to the man whose example has triumphed over all prejudice and all cowardice. The whole world is today united in the tribute that I'm paying in the name of the Congolese Government to Raoul Follereau.

. . . Just now, while we were distributing the parcels brought you by the Lions, my wife and I took it on ourselves to embrace some of you. This gesture shouldn't surprise you, but this gesture doesn't come from us. We were following the example of Raoul Follereau, for one day when he was given a garland of flowers by a girl in a leper-colony, he kissed her. The whole world should follow this example, for your disease should not outlaw you from society. You are men like other men. You must not lose heart, nor a taste for life. We are convinced that you are men capable of working, of earning your living, and we are here to help you.

I have come here today to tell you how concerned about your lot are the Head of State and our Government. We shall do everything we can to make your life happy, and to see that the healthy do not keep away from you.

In the olden days lepers were condemned to death, to solitude, to abandonment. I have heard this from Follereau himself. But he has thrown down these prejudices; he has been the first to break the barriers. At first he was alone, but now he is no longer alone. We are with him, and I hope that all the governments of the world are with him, bringing him every possible material aid, but also the humanitarian aid which you both need and deserve.

And that, my dear sick friends, is all that I have to say to you on this memorable day, this day that the whole world should celebrate with rejoicing, conviction and love.

SPEECH BY DR LAMBIN

Minister of Public Health in the
Republic of Volta, on the XIIth
World Leprosy Day, 1965

At a time when acts of violence are unhappily the order of the day, it is infinitely comforting to take part in a demonstration inspired by a spirit of love, charity and hope; I mean, the XIIth World Leprosy Day which we are celebrating today. For us here in Ouagadougou, the festival has a particular brilliance owing to the presence among us of the founder of this Day of human solidarity, President Raoul Follereau and his admirable wife. It is a great honour for our capital and our whole country to have been visited this year by the "Vagabond of Charity".

[After giving a brief picture of leprosy in Upper Volta, where more than 30,000 victims have already been declared cured, and where 13,000, no longer showing any sign of the disease, will be declared cured as soon as they have undergone adequate treatment (in one of the cantons the number of cures has reached the exceptional figure of 80.6%), the Minister paid tribute to all the national and international organizations that contribute to our brotherly fight, then went on:]

But the thing that is greater than all this is the hope that you, President of the Order of Charity, have managed to awaken in the hearts of "the saddest of the oppressed minorities"; it's the transfiguration of wretched people, treated in the past as noxious beasts, so that now they have access to all the benefits of mankind, now they are men, women and children like everyone else. And you have contrived to achieve this miracle in our selfish, cruel and cowardly world. You are an example and lesson to the whole world. You have taught us that all victories are possible once we can touch hearts. I would like to paraphrase Jean Nocher and say that you have managed to prove three truths that are to be venerated as modern sanctity:

One man alone really can awaken the universal conscience. He can do it because all victories are possible against any kind of indifference, defeatism and fatality. But on one condition: that courage is put at the service of love.

This threefold demonstration is of crucial importance to us.

May I remind you, my dear friend, of a striking remark made by a leper in the course of his speech:

"We were crucified. It's you who have torn out the nails."

Such a phrase must surely be the reward for your life.

TO THE SCALE OF THE WORLD

The world press released this information in October 1965:

The Fight against Leprosy launched throughout the world thirty years ago by Raoul Follereau and continued by him almost single-handed for so many years, was crowned and consecrated in the course of the first international colloquy held in Brussels on 2 October 1965, at the instigation of the "Friends of Father Damien", at which were assembled representatives of all the great organizations involved in the fight against leprosy from Germany, England, Belgium, France, Italy, Luxembourg, Switzerland, as well as from the Sovereign and Military Order of Malta. In asking the Vagabond of Charity to preside at the meeting, then in appointing him Honorary President for life of the European Committee of liaison with the Associations fighting against leprosy (ELEP) the delegates paid deserved tribute to Raoul Follereau.

This was confirmed at the meeting in Antwerp on 1 October 1967, when a delegate proclaimed: "We are all your sons or your god-sons."

And here is the testimony of "The Leprosy Mission":

The Council of the Leprosy Mission send sincere good wishes to Monsieur Follereau on the occasion of his retirement. During the many years of his compassionate service to the cause of lepers and sufferers throughout the world, M. Follereau has shown an enthusiasm and devotion which has stirred the hearts of many people. His life has been an example of what can be achieved when energy and vision are contained in a crusade on the behalf of the poor and neglected. It was M. Follereau's initiative which led to the founding of World Day for Leprosy Sufferers, which he celebrated in more countries each year, and thousands of leprosy patients owe him a great debt for his share in arousing world-wide concern for them.

The Leprosy Mission joins with other workers in the field of leprosy to congratulate M. Follereau on his achievements and wish him continuing happiness in the future.

THE TRUE VICTORS

AFTER THIRTY YEARS of fighting against leprosy, sometimes alone, but never disheartened, surely I have the right to say: the battle has been won.

Certainly there remain, and will doubtless remain for some time, pockets of resistance, ethnical or political communities who don't know or don't want to know, and scattered everywhere those dreadfully happy people who live enmeshed in their own squalid selfishness.

Certainly there remain, and will doubtless remain for some time, victims of leprosy. But henceforth there should never be "lepers". And who in the world today is ignorant, even if he pretends to be, of the two revolutionary truths (and oh, what a fine revolution it is!) that have enabled an age-long terror to be run to earth, subjugated, strangled: that leprosy is only a very slightly contagious disease, and that leprosy is a curable disease?

Lepers are invalids like other invalids, they are men like other men.

The fight against absurd fear, squalid cowardice and destructive selfishness is won.

The myth of the leper as doomed, desperate and accursed has gone for ever. The victim condemned to "leprosy in perpetuity", the outlaw, the social outcast, the "leper", will in future be nothing but a monstrous exception.

*   *   *

I must now pay tribute to those people whose ardent and often heroic love has been a source of strength and joy to me. . . .

Father Damien and the missionaries, by their courage and love, had trodden the first paths.

The doctors, by the discovery and perfecting of the sulphone drugs, had condemned the disease to death.

But there remained the man to be delivered. He had to be given confidence so that he could show himself, emerge from his hiding-place and his despair.

Once cured, he had to be saved by being made "a man like other men", a man who works, a man who feels responsible and respected.

It is for him that I've gone round the world thirty-one times in thirty years.

*   *   *

I've left Orly or Le Bourget fifty times with my bags full of medicaments, my heart full of hope and courage. And I've returned fifty times empty-handed, but with my heart overwhelmed yet full of joy. . . .

As my friends know, it's a long time now since I've leapt up the steps of the gangway two at a time. Sometimes during these last months I've had to be hoisted to my seat. Though sometimes unable to walk a kilometre on foot, I always chalk up my hundred thousand kilometres a year. . . .

But for how long?

For a long time I haven't dared slacken my pace and look backwards so as measure the path traversed, to take breath, to pick up strength. I was so frightened that age, fatigue, illness might catch up on me. Now it's happened.

But I have the right and the duty to say, because today everything proves it, that with you, thanks to you, we have won the greatest victory in the world, a victory that isn't measured by fifteen million living people left to die, but by fifteen million semi-dead people brought back to life.

As long as I have the strength, I shall go on.

I shall go on because those who were the first to understand me, help me, love me, are still there, silent, fervent, invincible.

For in this struggle, which was essentially a struggle and a victory of love, it is they who have won. I have merely been their spokesman, their messenger, their envoy.

Fifty times I've left Orly or Le Bourget with thousands and thousands of hearts within my breast. . . .

The hearts of the poor and the insignificant. Ambassador of the poor to the poor – that's what I've been.

And this evening, in the twilight gently invading both my

study and my life, it is to them that I dedicate my efforts and offer in homage all the joy which, through them, I've been able to give. . . .

*   *   *

Perhaps the greatest lesson of the Fight against Leprosy will be not so much the sick who have been cured, the lives that have been saved, the men who have been freed, as the truth that I've so often repeated: without love, nothing is possible; with love, nothing is impossible. . . .

And this testimony: if one man, even alone to start with, plies his pickaxe every day in the same direction, without turning round or getting distracted, if he goes on with this without missing a single day, his eyes fixed on the goal he's set himself, if he plies his pickaxe every day, whether the ground is rock or clay, he always ends up by hacking out a path. . . .

That's the memory I would like to leave with you. . . .

TESTIMONIES

IN RESPONSE to the wishes of the organizations sponsoring the publication of this work, we have added to the documents assembled by the founder of World Leprosy Day, and to his own written account, some of the testimonies from people of all kinds who have followed Raoul Follereau's career during the main developments of the Fight against Leprosy.

(Publisher's Note)

STATEMENTS BY

> DANIEL-ROPS of the *Académie française;*
> FATHER PIRE, O.P., Nobel Peace Prize Winner;
> JEAN ROSTAND of the *Académie française;*
> GENERAL WEYGAND of the *Académie française;*
> ROGER FERDINAND ⎫
> PIERRE LANGEVIN ⎬ reported by Jean Vernet.
> FRANÇOIS VEUILLOT ⎭

1951

The Vagabond of Charity[1]

Don't ask him about his health: he'll look at you with surprise, then dreamily, as if you'd asked him a very unexpected question, or the answer to some difficult problem. Then he'll talk about something else.

And don't ask him if he's had a good trip: he won't remember which one you're talking about.

He's everywhere. You'd think there were two, three, ten Follereaus in the world. Yet as soon as you're near him, you realize there couldn't be a copy.

The Indians of Bolivia saw him landing one day from an

---

[1] Quotation from *Raoul Follereau, le Vagabond de la Charité* (Raoul Follereau, Vagabond of Charity) by Jean Vernet (Vitte, 1951, out of print).

altitude of more than 4,000 metres; the Blacks, crossing their lagoons by canoe; the Bedouins, contemplating (from the back of a camel) the sun rising over Palmyra; and the Tuaregs, turning up one fine evening in the most remote oases of the Sahara.

Over the five continents he takes his ineradicable rheumatism with him – which he treats with the greatest contempt. (We'll see which will give in first. . . .)

Wherever he is, he's the same: rotund, jovial, with eyes that laugh without stopping noticing, and that black cravat, and that cane topped by an animal's head which could be a bear or a dog – both almost legendary throughout the world.

The Americans call him the "Vagabond of Charity"; the Blacks of Africa, the Apostle to the Lepers.

*　　*　　*

Ever since 1925 Raoul Follereau has been travelling all over the world as a messenger of Charity. He has given thousands of lectures in almost every country.

He has spoken in the most improbable places and sometimes in the most unexpected conditions. In front of nearly all the Kings or Heads of State governing the world; to the lepers in the heart of virgin forests, and even from the pulpit of Tours cathedral.

He was a guest of Gabriele d'Annunzio in his palace at Gardone; he was with Jean Mermoz on one of his first flights across the Cordilleras of the Andes; he was . . . Oh! if only he'd write his memoirs!

*　　*　　*

The striking thing about his life is its splendid unity, centred entirely round Charity.

As a young man he started out on a literary career that promised to be brilliant. When he was twenty-five he was billed at the Comédie-Française where the great tragic actress, Madeleine Roch, declaimed his work at a "Poetry Afternoon".

As a playwright he produced works some of which – for instance *Petites poupées* or *Les nouveaux chevaliers* (in which he tells of his first trip over the Andes) – reached a thousand performances.

But which of his poems had the honour of being read at the Comédie-Française? *Credo*, in which Raoul Follereau declares "I believe in the God of Love", and *Redemption*.

And *Petites Poupées* is nothing but an eloquent and moving plea on behalf of the poor, the unfortunate and the abandoned.

So the man had already revealed himself through the poet. And his exceptional destiny "along the highways of Charity" was there in embryo.

*   *   *

When he founded the "League for Latin Union" before the war, he defined its aim thus: "To defend Christian civilization against all paganisms and all barbarisms. . . ."

When a journalist asked him in Rio de Janeiro what he meant by Christian civilization, he replied, "Christianity is revolution through charity".

*   *   *

There followed the spiritual encounter with Père de Foucauld, the three trips to the Sahara, the hundreds of lectures given in France, Europe, South America, so as to build the church of El Golea near de Foucauld's tomb, and the chapels of Adrar and Timimoun.

But the field of his charitable activity was to grow ever greater.

And quite naturally he found himself concentrating on the men who are the most abandoned, the most forlorn, those who are ostracized and feared: lepers.

In the course of hundreds of talks delivered in France, Africa, Belgium, Switzerland, Canada and the United States, Raoul Follereau collected the millions of francs required for the building of Adzopé, the town "where leprosy no longer brings down a curse . . .".

A prizeman of the Academy of Moral and Political Sciences, Follereau received the *Prix Montyon* twice (in 1947 and 1950) from the French Academy (the *Académie française*).

*   *   *

He is certainly one of the best speakers of our time, one of the most passionate, one of those who possess to a supreme degree the capacity to evoke and persuade. After one of his talks a blind man made the astonishing remark: "For the first time, I SAW."

The great Catholic journalist, François Veuillot, described as follows a lecture given by Raoul Follereau in the *salle* Luxembourg of the Comédie-Française. It was on behalf of lepers.

From the groundlings to the gods, the house was packed. What extraordinary spectacle had they come to see? And who were those peculiar usherettes moving so swiftly and deftly between the rows? Yes, they were white-clad nuns. And who were those amazing figures in the dress-circle? None other than the Cardinal-Archbishop of Paris and the Papal Nuncio.

What play were they all waiting to see?

One minute more, and we would know. The curtain rose and there was the stage. But the décor was disconcertingly sober, not to say bare. A small table with a glass of water on it; and, not sitting behind it, but standing near it, a man.

This was the only character in the show that was about to take place before our eyes. And yet it was great drama, epic, stirring, marvellous, and it kept the audience with bated breath for over an hour and a half. The evocative phrase and tone of voice made the audience really see the landscape and action. Better still, they were brought to life.

. . . Raoul Follereau, the speaker, or rather the witness whom we acclaimed yesterday, is now going off – in the manner of ancient bards or medieval troubadours – across France and the world, singing.

*   *   *

Another journalist, Pierre Langevin, drew this amusing portrait of him in the *Courrier de l'Ouest*:

Shall I admit it? I've a weakness for this devil of a man. I like everything about him: his frank laughing eyes, his round pink cheeks, his old-fashioned cravat, his stomach that will soon protrude. I like most of all his extraordinary gift for taking an audience where he wants it, making it laugh or cry as he desires, or rather as the subject demands. For Raoul Follereau, who is an orator as they don't make them any more, who is a sort of force of nature, a perpetually bubbling spring, who could easily let himself be carried away by the richness of his temperament or be pushed by the enthusiasm of his audience, who is naturally fond of vivid phrases and strong emotions, Raoul Follereau is anything but a demagogue: he's a man of consistent good faith.

*   *   *

It is this sincerity and absolute disinterestedness that kindles his friends' enthusiasm and compels everyone's admiration.

It's because he's incontrovertible that his personality imposes itself and his example inspires so many young hearts in all parts of the world.

It is difficult to gauge today the extent of his influence; but it is certainly greater and above all deeper than one would think. . . .

In the course of one of those huge meetings to which Follereau's name draws such large numbers of people, Roger Ferdinand, the well-known author of *J3* and president of the Society of Playwrights, greeted him in these terms:

"You are, Monsieur, a lawyer. And the cause that you've been pleading for twenty years in all the courts of the world is the best cause of all. And that's why you always win your case. But what a very odd lawyer you are, in all truth, considering that you've never asked for a fee. . . ."

*   *   *

Such is Raoul Follereau, Vagabond of Charity, Apostle to the Lepers and Messenger of Brotherhood.

May the world, bowed down by every kind of selfishness and woe, listen to his ardent voice and rally to his motto which is his whole programme:

CHARITY WILL SAVE THE WORLD

Jean Vernet

1959

Father Pire, O.P., Nobel Peace Prize Winner:

I have spent some hours with Dr Schweitzer, doctor of the virgin forests, and with Raoul Follereau, Apostle to the Lepers.

Let us pay deep reverence to these saviours of humanity. They are saviours because they are first and foremost true men themselves, men of great stature. For them, yes means yes; for them, a suffering being is eminently to be respected; for them, Love should have first place in the world. How good it is to know such fine fellows! Yet what they teach is so simple; that each man should stay humbly in his place and plough his furrow where God has put him. Neither one nor the other wants to draw a throng of people to Lambaréné or the leper-colonies – generous people, no doubt, but romantic, confusing true Love that gives itself with the superficial impressions provided by brushing shoulders with suffering – though this brushing shoulders is soon

seen to provide nothing romantic whatsoever. So let everyone
stay in his place. Let the student study, the housewife cook, the
workman do his job, the apostle give himself. And let each think
about all beings. Each is responsible for everyone, each is
responsible for the whole world.

1960

M. Daniel-Rops, of the *"Académie française"*:

Will the Lepers' Apostle have the Nobel Peace Prize?

The news has not yet got around, and yet it would be very
desirable if it did get around. First in France, then among those
all over the world who are still friends of France, those who still
see in her a witness to a certain concept of man.

So: twenty-two Governments have taken the initiative of
proposing a Frenchman for the Nobel Peace Prize: Raoul
Follereau. These Governments were immediately followed by a
host of social and charitable organizations belonging to other
countries. All, both Governments and charitable organizations,
with two exceptions, belong to what is called the "Afro-Asian
group" from Cameroon to the Lebanon, from Thailand to Angola.
That is to say the proposal has come from the very places where
the work of Raoul Follereau, the Lepers' Apostle, is seen and
known.

No one will deny that this man, who has been travelling the
world for twenty-five years in the service of a cause, is somewhat
eccentric – with his large hat and floppy bow-tie and general air
of "Montparnasse 1925". But he almost alone has made this
cause urgent, immediate and present to us, and deserving of all
our sympathy: the cause of lepers. Leprosy, the appalling disease
that spread terror in the towns and villages of the Middle Ages,
has been so well tracked down and stamped out in the technically
advanced countries (there are only a few dozen cases a year in
France) that we forget that in other parts of the world it still
afflicts countless beings. For twenty-five years Raoul Follereau
has been reminding his contemporaries of the fact; for twenty-
five years the "vagabond of charity" has been travelling the world
to visit lepers.

"He is without doubt," says a letter addressed to Oslo by the
vice-president of the New Caledonian Council, "the man who has

held in his arms and kissed the greatest number of lepers. For it is in clasping their hands and kissing them that he has often given them back their dignity as men, and at the same time cured the healthy of the unjustified fear usually felt for this disease."

We have seen photographs of him leading a young woman to the altar in a wedding-procession in a leper-colony. We have seen him over and over again holding leper children in his arms. Innumerable audiences have heard him speak of his friends the lepers, and with a strength of conviction that transcends eloquence. He founded "World Leprosy Day" which is today celebrated throughout the world. He has written to all the leaders responsible for world politics to tell them that for the price of two atomic bombers all the lepers of the world could be cared for and treated and many, no doubt, cured. In over fifteen countries medico-social centres created to fight leprosy bear his name. At the recent Leprology Congress in Tokyo one of the speakers said, "Fifteen million human beings have staked their hopes on him".

Are not these singularly compelling qualifications for a candidature for the Nobel Peace Prize? How many among you can pride yourselves on having accomplished such difficult or disinterested work? Has Dr Schweitzer himself, or Father Pire, done more?

As we have said, this candidature has been put forward by the "Afro-Asian group" of countries. Would it not be desirable for this candidature to be put forward also by responsible representatives of the West? Could not the French Government be associated with it? And Nobel Prize winners whose "social sense" is well known – for instance the two whose names are mentioned above, and also François Mauriac, Hemingway and others? And even the *Academie française*, which has already, if I am not mistaken, honoured Raoul Follereau, would surely – why not? – add lustre to its name by taking up the initiative on his behalf.

So that at least here we may bear witness to this good man, this brave man, this man whose oft-repeated maxim is: the only truth is to love each other.

1962

General Weygand of the *Académie française*:

On 17 July 1956, in the course of a reception given in his honour at the Hôtel de Ville, Raoul Follereau received from the hands of M. Pierre Ruais, president of the Municipal Council, the medal of honour of the City of Paris. It was on the occasion of the twenty-fifth anniversary of his first journey along the highways of Charity.

Sur les Routes de la Charité is the title of one of Follereau's first books, for which it was my pleasure to write the preface twenty years ago. He conducted us across the African missions of the Sisters of Our Lady of the Apostles, for whom he was later to build Adzopé.

Raoul Follereau has been all his life on the highways of Charity. And on the earth. As a lover of statistics he has calculated that he's travelled nearly two million kilometres in the service of the Poor.

. . . Everyone knows what Raoul Follereau has done for those whom he calls "the saddest of the world's oppressed minorities". We know about his petition to UNO which was adopted unanimously by the French Parliament on 25 May 1954; about his open letters to "Our Lords of war and peace"; about his founding of World Leprosy Day which is now celebrated in all the countries of the world.

But statistics and documents cannot say everything. They cannot, for instance, describe the overpowering emotion felt by all those who have heard his voice throbbing in turn with holy anger and love. From the Châtelet theatre where thousands of Parisians flock every year to hear him, to the confines of the earth from Quebec to Tahiti, from Amsterdam to Mauritius, his brotherly but implacable voice has quickened consciences, stirred up courage, aroused hearts.

I've been told that during these last thirty years Raoul Follereau has distributed some two milliards of old francs to the poor. That's pretty good, but it isn't everything. It isn't even the most important thing. The thing about him that will endure is the example of a life totally devoted to the most wretched and abandoned of all men, of a man passionately dedicated to a great work of justice and love, of a campaigner who has won the "Fight against Leprosy" over our ignorance and selfishness, because he has commanded our attention not so much by skill as by courage and good faith.

1965

M. Jean Rostand of the *Académie française* :

A few days after the death of that most admirable of men, Dr Schweitzer, I wrote: "We have scientists and thinkers and first-rate writers; perhaps we've even got geniuses. But where are the apostles?"

Well, we've got one, just beside us, in the person of M. Raoul Follereau, whom I have the pleasure of welcoming today in this hall.[1]

We all know with what zeal, with what militant fervour, with what enthusiastic devotion, M. Follereau has for years put himself at the service of one of the most moving and pathetic causes that exist: lepers.

Appeals, articles, lectures, books – and above all journeys, to get to know these men so cruelly stricken in their flesh and their spirit, to make direct contact with them and bring them the moral comfort of his warm brotherliness. . . . Because of all this, Raoul Follereau merits the fine name of philanthropist, a friend of men. And by the persistence of his effort and the pertinacity of his concern he has also won the right to use the word "charity", that great word so difficult to say, because it has been devalued and compromised by too many Pharisees and thus easily seems suspect – unless the authority of exemplary activity and continuity is there to guarantee its genuine quality.

In 1954 Raoul Follereau addressed an eloquent appeal to the two "top men" of the time, that is to say to the two men who then disposed of the monstrous privilege of being able, with a single word, to unleash the apocalypse over the earth: "If you each give up one bomber, we shall be able to tend all the lepers of the world."

He made this overture again in 1955, then in 1959, and yet again in 1962. . . . The two masters of the planet had changed by then, but their successors continued not to reply, and to put the making of murderous aeroplanes before help to the lepers.

In order to fight the terrible disease efficiently, it sufficed – indeed it would still suffice – to donate to this "fight" a sufficiently large sum of money, because the required medicaments now exist, as everyone knows. There's no question here, as with cancer, of

---

[1] Speech delivered in the conference hall of UNESCO, 7 October 1965.

subsidizing research whose outcome is problematical, because discovery, at least in this domain, is beyond our control; the money employed in the treatment of lepers would be certainly active and operative; to refuse it is to permit them, to prefer them to go on suffering and dying.

Today Raoul Follereau has returned to the attack, with the fine frankness of an honest man. He's persisting and persevering, and he is enlarging his mission-field. He is begging now not only for his dear lepers but also for all the people, all over the world, who are suffering from hunger and poverty, and these form two-thirds of the world's population.

What does he want this time? Oh, it's quite simple.

He's expressing the hope that "every year, on the occasion of a World Peace Day, all the nations will agree to set aside from their respective budgets the price of one day's armaments production; this they will then pool to fight famine, slums and the great endemic diseases that decimate mankind".[1]

One day a year. One day for life, as against three hundred and sixty-four for death. It's a modest request.

But the new important fact in this crusade is that Raoul Follereau is no longer alone; he has with him, and behind him, a whole peaceful army whose effective force is growing every day. . . . An army of young people between 14 and 20 has signed his appeal. A million signatures have already arrived at UNO: a result of which Follereau has every right to be proud, for here we have a unique act in the history of modern youth that is so often accused of vacuity, but seldom called on to express idealistic enthusiasms. What a fine precedent! And the size of this success surely invites us to think that it is to the young that we must go if we want to check the escalation of war madness. Yes, surely we must put our trust in the young, given that the old have let us down so ignominiously. Is it not from the young – who are not yet contaminated with the virus of chauvinism, not yet perverted by the spirit of hatred and violence, nor by a stupid realism which has so often sent us to our doom – is it not from the young that we must learn the lesson of common-sense, wisdom and right reason? Is it not the young, who refuse to die as combat troops, who should undertake the task of reconciliation and world unification that seems more urgent every day if man is not to

[1] See below, Part 3.

succumb, stupidly and absurdly, to the effects of science and technics whose criminal use he was unable to control at the right moment? Is it not those who have a future before them who should see to it that there is a future?

Whatever, here and now, will be the results of his most recent overture, I'm sure that his enterprise is praise-worthy and that it will bear fruit in the long run, for it is always a good and healthy thing, and always salutary, to denounce in season and out of season the shameful disproportion that exists between the sums allocated to the preparation of armaments and the sums allocated to education, culture, hospitals, the protection of the old and infirm, medical and scientific research; between the munificence for what destroys and kills and the stinginess for what alleviates and saves.

I don't want to compromise M. Raoul Follereau in the very least in this brief speech, for his high idealism has always operated above the domain of political quarrels, yet I think I can say that he is one of those dangerous men, one of those subversive citizens, who prefers to see a hospital or a laboratory built to a factory for atomic bombers; I think I can say that he's one of those evil spirits for whom victories are not measured by corpses but by lives saved, someone who prefers to send sulphone drugs to lepers than missiles to I don't know whom. . . .

A philanthropist, I said, a friend of men; but one who doesn't see this friendship in vote-catching terms; who doesn't want to exploit it for personal or honorific ends; who is content – there's no danger in it! – to be president of the "Order of Charity"; who simply, naturally, carnally, biologically, feels for every man, whoever he may be and whatever may be his race, religion, philosophy or ideology, the sympathy and the compassion (it's the same word) that one owes to one's neighbour from the simple fact that he carries within him – as the great and irreplaceable Schweitzer said – that value and mystery which, as one respects it in oneself, one is bound to respect also in others.

Part Three

LOVE ONE ANOTHER OR PERISH

ATOM BOMB OR CHARITY?

IN 1948 I PUBLISHED the casualty figures for the last war which had just been established by official sources.

This was the list:

14,450,000 soldiers and officers killed;

29,650,000 soldiers and officers wounded or disabled;

2,800,000 civilians killed in the bombing;

21,245,000 displaced persons;

11,000,000 interned in concentration camps, where a great many of them had died;

3,500,000 gassed, burnt, murdered;

32,000,000 homes destroyed;

16,800,000 administrative buildings, offices or factories destroyed;

100,000 kilometres of railway-lines destroyed;

1,000,000 kilometres of roads destroyed;

10,000 bridges and viaducts destroyed.

To say nothing of churches, schools, hospitals, museums, theatres, and all those things which can never be repaired, compensated, or reconstructed. . . .

This is what hatred leads to.

And I added:

"And yet, if even the smallest part of the ingenuity and money that men have dissipated for the purposes of killing and destruction had been devoted to healing, the relief of poverty, and teaching, there would be such happiness in the world today.

"May this lesson of blood and terror finally awaken our consciences and our hearts.

"Charity alone can save the world."

* * *

This was the starting-point of a campaign that was to find its most powerful expression in the appeal I launched a year later – in 1949: Atom Bomb or Charity?

Although this appeal has been published already in several of my books, I must include it here, since it is from this manifesto that my campaign, "Love one another or perish," was born:

ATOM BOMB OR CHARITY?

. . . At least, now, it's simple. . . .

There is no place for equivocators, temporizers, those who make a base compromise with life.

Today we must choose, immediately, irrevocably. Men must learn to love one another, to understand one another; man must learn to live for man, or all men will be destroyed, all men, and all together.

True there has always been warfare and strife. It began with Cain and Abel. But Cain only killed Abel.

There has been progress since then, and progress has become an immense machine for murder. Tomorrow one man, one alone, one man's madness could annihilate humanity itself.

For who can guarantee that a thousand, two thousand, ten thousand atom bombs dropped on the world won't mean the end of the world?[1]

*   *   *

But all this was inherent in the Creation, in the earthly Paradise. God willed it, with all else.

God allowed man to discover how to split the atom, and left him free to use his knowledge as he would.

If man so wishes, he has at his disposal an inexhaustible supply of energy and warmth.

No one would be cold.

Soon no one would be hungry.

But if man wishes otherwise, it's the destruction of the world, the disappearance of mankind.

Which fruit will man pick from the Tree of Knowledge of good and evil?

*   *   *

Whatever happens, the atomic age is the end of the world; the sort of world where each could live for himself, think only of himself, and make his own respectable, hypocritical little kingdom.

It's the end of that sort of world, or just of the world.

[1] Alas, in 1966 it would need far fewer. Such is progress. . . .

Man must learn to live for man, or all men will be destroyed, all men, and all together.

CHARITY! CHARITY!

Charity opposing the atom bomb: that is the war that is beginning.

It is a momentous struggle.

Only charity can wipe out the atom bomb from men's hearts.

Because the atom bomb is like charity.

Its terrible strength is that nothing along the road to death can make it pause.

One atom destroys another, and the next and the next.

It's a chain of destruction, unlimited, and perhaps limitless.

The man who drops the bomb knows nothing of the number of corpses sprawled across the earth.

Therefore, have charity.

One good act, one true gesture of friendship creates a feeling of joy.

From one feeling of joy another one springs.

A chain of happiness, unlimited, and perhaps limitless.

The man who does something good never knows how much good he has done.

Atom bomb or charity?

Chain of death or chain of love?

We must choose, immediately, irrevocably.

*   *   *

Two thousand years ago, he told us. But men crucified him for saying it.

And because his disciples spread the word, men killed his disciples.

But they could not silence the gentle, holy voice that, for two thousand years, has ceaselessly repeated:

Love one another!

CHRISTIANITY IS A REVOLUTION
BROUGHT ABOUT BY CHARITY!

A crusade, then? Why not?

Do you think to save the world with politicians' speeches or round a conference table?

For our aim is to save the world, from itself, and its atom bomb.

A world that no longer dares to believe, because it has been taught to deny; that no longer expects, because of all it had been promised.

To save the world.

To teach it a new approach to life, an alert and joyful friendship.

To tell it that the only happiness is that which one gives to others, that the wicked are the truly wretched, that only the selfish are alone.

Charity, light of our lives.

Charity.
Not alms-giving.
Money corrupts all things, even the true meaning of charity.
Charity has nothing to do with money.
It's an act of love, the gift of oneself that ennobles and repays the effort and renunciation with joyfulness.

Charity, source of all joy.

Charity, that knows neither class, nor caste, nor race.
Charity, that breaks down frontiers;
Charity, that rejects all warfare;
Charity, stronger than death.
Charity, God's law, and reflection of his eternity.

* * *

I once dreamed. . . .
A man came to the Seat of Judgment.
"Look, God," he said, "I have kept your Law, done nothing dishonourable, wicked or impious. Lord, my hands are clean."
"Doubtless, doubtless," replied God, "but they are also empty."

Atom bomb or charity?
We must choose.

* * *

.... And first we must learn to live for others.

If we could only think of something other than ourselves, realize that at every moment in our life, while we are eating and sleeping, and wasting our time, or even worse, there are people, millions of human beings, our brothers in Christ, dying of hunger, dying of cold; if we could only think of others we could not go on eating like pigs, sleeping like logs, in mindless contentment.

If we could only imagine the misery of others we would become like men.

*   *   *

We shan't solve everything, of course.

We can't revive the earth, and we haven't the power to restore life.

The poor, cold dead will not reopen fearful eyes to laugh tomorrow in the daylight of the world.

Thousands of simple lives have ended in mass graves.

But there are still the living, still people to protect, and a world to rebuild.

We shan't finish everything but we can accomplish something.

If all of us, all together, now, do what we can, more than we can, I mean, then some will be saved.

Then, inspired by our example, others will copy us, do better than us, I mean, and they will be followed by others again. And others will copy them, I mean, do better than them.

A great chain of love will encircle the world.

Chain of love or chain of death, we must choose, immediately, irrevocably.

*   *   *

A crusade?

Yes.

As long as there is a helpless creature starving on earth, cold, persecuted; as long as there is famine on earth that could have been avoided, imprisonment without cause, Christ's message of love will not be fulfilled, Christianity cannot relax its struggle, neither you, nor I, will have the right to keep silent, or to rest.

Atom bomb or Charity?

The supreme struggle has begun. But victory is sure:

Charity will save the world!

This appeal was translated into fifteen languages and hundreds of thousands of copies were distributed. It was not without effect.

In 1957, Queen Elizabeth said, in her message to the Commonwealth: "There will never be peace on earth until we have goodwill among men. Scientists talk to us of chain reactions. We must apply this principle to the greatest force of all: love for our fellow creatures."

In 1958, Nehru reiterated: "*The world must choose between Buddha and the H bomb.*"

"Amritsar (India), 9 February. – Before an audience composed of militants of the Indian Congress Party, Mr Nehru said today that the world would have to choose between the message of Buddha and the hydrogen bomb. There was no other choice."

. . . But nations continued with undiminished enthusiasm to make and stockpile even greater numbers of increasingly horrible weapons of death.

And to dissipate in this shameful and senseless way the wealth of the Poor.

160,000 deaths a minute

Nearly twenty years ago I wrote: "Who can guarantee that a thousand, two thousand, ten thousand atom bombs dropped on the world won't mean the end of the world?", and I was afraid of being thought a "defeatist", as we said in those days.

I laugh at my naïveté now.

At this moment in time it is estimated that a single little 50-megaton H bomb – the small version, as it were, death's poor relation – would annihilate everything within an 80-kilometre radius of the point where it fell.

Now, it is thought that the U.S.A. and the U.S.S.R. already possess reserves of weapons whose power is equivalent to billions of tons of TNT. In order to make sense of this macabre jargon, remember that in 1943 the city of Hamburg was devastated by . . . 230 tons of TNT. And 600 bombers were needed for this great achievement.

Here is another measure of "greatness" – shall we say? If the equivalent of the total number of explosives used in the Second World War were exploded *every day*, it would take over a hundred years to exhaust these existing reserves.[1]

[1] Taken from *Face au Péril*, by Louis Lippens.

You must admit that our "civilization" has something to boast about.

Mr Khrushchev had no illusions when he said, "In the sixty hours immediately following a declaration of war, there would be anything from 500 to 700 million victims." 160,000 deaths a minute! You can't deny that it's a neat bit of work!

President Johnson confirmed these figures when he stated in Congress that the atomic explosion in Hiroshima twenty years ago would seem no more than a "pale spark" beside that of a modern nuclear device. He also pointed out that one bomber nowadays carries weapons whose force is greater than that of all the bombs that were dropped during the Second World War put together.

The admirable and courageous John Kennedy said a few days before he was assassinated that man must put an end to war, or war would put an end to man.

Love one another or perish: there is no other choice.

Mass-butchery

Of course it all costs a lot of money: we have some idea of how much already. Some idea . . . that's all.

Here are a few of the costs in detail, as given by the most competent suppliers: that is to say the War Ministry.

Tax-payers in France and other countries should know that in 1962 the death catalogue offered the following selection at "prices defying all competition" (there's no mistake about that):

An armoured tank medium size	180 million F.[1]	
A Frelon helicopter	500	,, ,,
A Mirage III aeroplane	700	,, ,,
A Mirage IV (bomber)	$2\frac{1}{2}$ milliard ,,	
An anti-submarine fighter plane	2	,, ,,
A squadron escort plane (Galissonnière type)	9	,, ,,
A battery of Pershing guns	30	,, ,,
An aircraft carrier (without aircraft)	40	,, ,,

Even though they don't emphasize that there are models to suit all pockets, it must be admitted that the choice is large and – to connoisseurs – tempting.

[1] I have given the prices in Old Francs because we all used to put away our hard-earned savings in this currency.

But what use is a solitary tank, or an aeroplane by itself, let alone an aircraft carrier "without aircraft"? We can't be bothered with detail in this game. But, to be serious and to look at things in a more reasonable light: the equipment for an armoured division in fact costs 200 milliard francs. An aircraft carrier – this time complete with its machines and escort ships – can be obtained for a more modest 100 milliard francs.

But now let's consider the star-turns!

A Polaris-type missile comes at 550 million francs.

An atomic-powered submarine costs about 40 milliards.

But wait a minute! That's without weapons or nuclear warheads.

It's like buying an Easter egg in a sweet-shop. You must ask if its filled or empty. In the above-mentioned case it's empty.

How about the "filling"? This will give you some idea:

A factory for the separation of isotopes comes at 350 milliard francs (these are still the War Ministry's figures).

*   *   *

Yes indeed, it is a lot of money.

An American senator calculated after the last war that each of his sons killed had cost the United States 50,000 dollars. I commented that that was enough to make a corpse blush with shame.

But not at all. That was death on the cheap. "Mass grave" status. If there is ever another "last war" you'll see. Granted that you're given the time. . . .

You can easily understand that in the circumstances, and in view of such huge outgoings, the armaments people haven't time to spare for the poverty of others. The poor should realize that, they should pull their weight, be patient. . . .

What do you expect? You can't prepare for the end of the world and at the same time give the means of life to those who may survive.

And this is why, even after the war is over and peace has been re-established, unnecessary death persists – more hideous, more scandalous, more intolerable than ever.

Each year hunger accounts for more victims than that last holocaust killed in five years.

On this planet there are 800 million human beings who have less money to live on in one year than a French labourer has in one month. Cardinal Suenens wrote recently: "For seven mothers in every ten, their child will not live to see his fifteenth birthday." He will die. Of hunger.

Do we need other figures? There is no lack of statistics. Nor of statisticians.

Of every thousand children born in Sweden, twenty will die before they are one year old.

Of every thousand children born in India, a hundred and twenty-five will die before they are one year old. They will die. And these ones will die of hunger.

But how can they be fed? A labourer in Asia has to work ten times as long as his European or American counterpart in order to buy a litre of milk.

As for those who survive, the average expectation of life in India is thirty, while in Europe it is between sixty and seventy. Why? Because an Englishman spends 7,500 O.F. a year on his health, while an Indonesian spends 150. And even if an Indonesian wanted to call in a doctor more often, where would he find one? There is a doctor for every 1,000 people in Europe, and one for every 20,000 in Asia.

Once in Pakistan a leper came to us in a state of indescribable exhaustion and misery. But it wasn't leprosy that had eaten away his torn and blood-stained feet. No, it was walking. This man came from a small remote village in the Himalayas, and in order to reach us he had walked 1,200 kilometres. Yes, on foot. 1,200 kilometres he had walked before he found a doctor to help him. How had he survived such an appalling journey? One dares not think of it.

An American investigator wrote: "If you tried to feed a rat on what a Bengal peasant eats, the rat would die." The man, of course, dies too, but as he's used to suffering he lasts longer.

But meanwhile what are the lucky people doing? – those who live in the rich, powerful, sparsely-populated countries?

Empty stomachs and bursting stomachs

The lucky people, the frightfully lucky people are doing nothing. They don't want to know. They take care not to upset their stomachs.

And they read their newspapers without turning a hair, without a pang, even those "news items" that careless or cynical editors have placed side by side. Such as:

"There are 38 million refugees in the world", and "Parrot inherits 20,000 dollars."

Such as: "There are 15 million disabled people in the world," and "American leaves 3 million dollars for the upkeep of his racehorse's grave."

While 400 million children are starving, starlets use 250 litres of milk for their daily baths.

While millions of men die of cold, they are making heated kennels for lap-dogs.

And these very lucky people, in their comfortable slippers, look at a photograph of the actress climbing out of her milk bath, or at "Momma's little doggy-woggy" in an astrakhan or mink coat lifting its leg outside its centrally-heated hotel.

The eternally narrow-minded

But what about the Christians? What have they to say about all this? They do exist. They are legion. Statistics – ubiquitous things – show that there are more than a thousand million of them. That's quite something. . . .

Yes, but too often what Christians!

They are also called "right-thinking".[1] Doubtless they think of themselves all right, and not often about anyone else. They are quite certain – and with a disarming sincerity – that as long as they observe the forms, say the right things, go through the motions, *their* salvation is assured.

And that with this assurance of *their* salvation their duty ends.

Whether God will be satisfied with that? This is a question they never ask themselves. Truth to tell, it would be the crowning offence. After all, they've always received the right sacraments at the right times, and for baptism and marriage there were flowers and the organ! They eat fish on Fridays, go to Mass on Sundays. Even High Mass on special occasions. They pay their contributions regularly, subscribe to the parish magazine. And on leaving church they give a little something to *their* poor man (because of course the poor man, too, is theirs, like their seat in church), and murmur, if time permits, those few vague words of hope that the lucky ones so revel in.

[1] *"Bien-pensant"* in the French which also, of course, means a faintly pejorative "pious". (Tr.)

They do what they've been told to do, and they don't do what they've been told not to do. So it's obvious that God owes them a place in Paradise. Furthermore, this place is reserved; they've paid for it in advance. Nevertheless, if they meet an exhausted nursing-nun coming out of hospital, or a missionary just returned from his lepers, you may be well sure that they'll say devoutly, "Pray for me". After all, it's always a good idea to refresh the Lord's memory. What can you lose?

For them religion is an insurance policy against the fires of hell.

* * *

Yes, of course, other people are in want. . . . They've heard about it from the pulpit, and their edifying books have been tiresomely full of it, particularly of late.

They'd like to have the courage to make Chancellor Séguier's words their own – who is reputed to have apostrophized St Vincent with: "The poor were with us before you, Monsieur, but they didn't stop respectable people from sleeping. Now they're all over the place. Upon my word, one would almost think that you invented them!"

And when they go to sleep, these eternally narrow-minded people ("the *petits-bourgeois* of eternity"), they recall the comfortable maxim of their childhood: "Each for himself, and God for all."

* * *

"He who robs a man of his clothes shall be called a thief; and he who neglects to clothe a naked man when he could well do so, is he worthy of a different name?

"To him who is hungry belongs the bread you are storing; to him who is naked, the coat you have put aside in a cupboard; to him who is without shoes, the shoes mouldering in your room; to the poor, the money you are hoarding.

"Thus you commit as many injustices as there are people to whom you could give."

Thus spoke St Basil, over sixteen hundred years ago.

And St Augustine added: "The superfluity of the rich belongs to the poor."

But the eternally narrow-minded think deep-down that these men were over-enthusiastic; in today's parlance, trouble-makers.

That their words might "disturb the peace" and should be read only in Latin.

For they're law-abiding folk and they don't want any trouble. They're for the established order and the golden mean.

It remains for these good Christians to be Christianized.

That is to say, they must be taught to love.

Love is not giving but sharing

St Augustine – we always come back to him – said:

"You give your bread to whoever is hungry. But it would be better if no one was hungry."

Charity is not the same as pitying people. Pity is a sickly form of love in which we piously revel; it's the pretext for giving oneself a certificate of "kind-heartedness".

"How I pity him!" So saying, the terribly lucky people feel that a large part of their duty has been done. For the rest they rely on charitable organizations and even National Assistance (we live in an age of progress, after all).

This is not good enough! The poor, the sick and the unhappy need more than sugared words and crocodile tears. And they despise and reject the travestied charity of officials who hand them forms to fill in from the security of their pay-desks.

It's not a matter of giving them a little from our excess, but of making room for them in our lives.

*   *   *

We must have the courage to recognize that we can't solve social problems with Christmas trees or hunger with collections.

The poor, the sick and the downtrodden feel a need, however dimly, to find themselves; to know that they are men like other men, that they have a right to live and a duty to hope. We must procure for them the means of providing for themselves and their families by their own efforts, not give them the small change from our purses; we must share their suffering, their anger, their hopes and their joys and let them share ours: for this is to love them.

Are we sharing our prosperity?

Have individuals and countries even reached that elementary stage of sharing out wealth?

These figures will speak for themselves:

Each American citizen spends 1,450 francs per year on defence and gives 77 francs to the underdeveloped countries.

Each Soviet citizen spends 732 francs per year on defence and gives 43 francs to the underdeveloped countries.

Each French citizen spends 475 francs per year on defence and gives 84 francs to the underdeveloped countries.

And yet . . .

For the price of a torpedo we could give the slum children 16,000 days of holiday.

One tank costs as much as 84 agricultural tractors.

With the money that is spent on a really up-to-date bomber you could build thirty schools with twenty classrooms each.

For the price of an aircraft carrier you could feed 400,000 men for a year. . . .

If the balance is not righted quickly, very quickly, it will be a catastrophe.

Starvation will hasten the end of the world.

The instruments of death must be transformed into tools for rebuilding life.

To this end I made the petitions which follow. I reproduce them here without comment.

To this end I called for "a day of war for peace", entrusting to the youth of the world this last effort of a man of goodwill who, after fighting for so long, still believes in the power of love.

PETITIONS TO STATESMEN

1944

THE WAR. I wrote to President Roosevelt from the village where I had taken refuge:

> One day this war will be over. It will end, like all other wars, where it should have begun – in Peace.
>
> On that day I would suggest to all of you, today's and yesterday's allies, today's and tomorrow's enemies, that you prolong the fighting for a day. On paper, that is to say.
>
> The money that has let you go on killing for so many years could easily be made to last for one more day, couldn't it?
>
> The war budgets would not be closed until twenty-four hours after hostilities had ended. The war would go on costing money for a day and a night but would do no damage.
>
> The hundreds of millions saved at death's expense could be put into a common fund and all could co-operate in the reconstruction of some of the things that are the property, safeguard and honour of humanity and that war has destroyed by the way, as it were, without even noticing or intending.
>
> That would give the opportunity of a first peaceful contact between nations who, since they have not managed to wipe one another out, will tomorrow find themselves obliged to get along with one another.
>
> And for your own people, after so many years of hopelessness, bloodshed and despair, it will be a first sign of hope.

But my request went unheard in the chaos of war.

1954

First Letter

To General Eisenhower, President of the USA, and to M. Malenkov, Chairman of the Council of the USSR.

Presidents,
Gentlemen in Power,

Will you read this letter? If it ever reaches you, I think you will.

Even if you do not answer it to me, you will have to answer it in the depths of your own hearts.

For you both have a heart, hidden though it may be beneath a soldier's or a proletarian's uniform.

But definitely beating.

Do you ever take time off to listen to it? If you do, I pray that it will remind you of the hundreds of millions of other hearts all over the world that often beat more quickly because of you . . . for, because of you, they may stop beating altogether.

I am a man of goodwill. Like you. But I have explored other domains of suffering. I still believe in goodwill. And that is why I am writing to you.

You, Gentlemen, are the two most powerful men in the world. I know that that does not mean much; the powerful are rarely free to do anything but harm.

But what I am going to ask you to do is very little. . . . Almost nothing. . . .

Give me one aeroplane, each of you, one aeroplane, one of your bombers.

Because I have heard that each of these war-machines costs about five milliard francs. . . .

Now, I have estimated that with the price of two of these death-dealing machines *all the lepers in the world* could be treated.

One plane less on either side would not change the balance of power. . . .

You could both go on sleeping peacefully.

I would sleep considerably better.

And millions of poor people would sleep for the first time. . . .

You are the demi-gods of our century.

In former times demi-gods were feared and worshipped from afar. I do not remember whether people loved them; they were too remote. . . .

It is the same with you. You are so remote that you may never read this letter.

And yet I am sure that you are good, and that you do really want peace and happiness for everyone. . . . But you are too remote. And too remote from each other.

Do you not think that this would be a good opportunity to "do something"?

Ten million people do not represent the sum total of those in need, but they represent quite a considerable amount of need.

Two bombers! And we would have all the medicaments necessary to treat them. Two aeroplanes – when all you want is that they should rust in their hangars and never be brought out again.

They won't altogether solve the problem? I know. But just give me those two planes, and we'll be on the way to solving it.

And what hope will be born in the hearts of millions of needy people, not only the lepers. . . .

At the moment, however, I alone am hoping.

But I'm hoping so hard that you will hear me, that finally you will hear me. . . .

if it is pleasing to God,

to the God in whom only one of you believes, but who loves you both.

1955

Second Letter

To our Lords of war and peace

Gentlemen in Power,

This time I address my letter to you all. To you, the Lords of war and peace.

I feel great confidence in writing to you. The world has seen you on its screens, and it has seen you smiling: so it is beginning to hope.

We are sure that each of you – taken separately – is a man of goodwill. But when you were all together in the past you immediately looked less reassuring. . . .

But, thanks be to God! you are all now agreed on the necessity of reaching an agreement: that in itself is enough nowadays to make millions rejoice.

So it seemed to me that this was an opportune moment to ask a favour of you, a great amnesty:

A favour on behalf of millions of innocent people condemned to suffering and death.

I mean, the lepers.

Afflicted with disease much less contagious than tuberculosis, they are, for the most part, victims of a type of social excommunication that causes them as much, and sometimes even greater, suffering than the actual illness.

They can now be effectively treated and often cured, and yet too many of them are condemned to "leprosy in perpetuity".

On 20 September 1952, I sent a request to the United Nations Organization. I asked for the closing down of "leper-prisons, leper-cemeteries and mass leper-graves for the living". I also asked that a Lepers' Charter should be drawn up which would make it obligatory for civilized countries to treat their sick, and to guarantee them a return to life and liberty as soon as they were found to be non-contagious.

I have never received a reply. I wrote again. A waste of time.

The French parliament voted unanimously for a motion approving this request and asked that it be entered on the agenda for the next meeting. Nothing was done.

You, gentlemen, who have the power, to whom should I turn now?

Presidents, secretaries, commissars, counsellors, delegates, attachés, I don't know which official to try next. Can you find out, you who are so powerful? . . .

For three years lepers have been dying in their thousands when they could have been treated and perhaps saved. . . .

Doesn't that thought prevent someone in the UNO from sleeping at night?

I have been told that "the matter is doubtless under consideration. . . ."

What sort of consideration? And who is considering it?

In the meantime, death is not "considering". It threatens millions of people who, with a little less "consideration" and a bit more courage and charity, can still be rescued from misery and despair.

*   *   *

I wrote a letter to the President of the USA and to the Chairman of the Council of Ministers of the Soviet Union.

It was exactly a year ago.

The letter was respectful and polite. Some must have thought: naïve as well.

I received no reply. Neither from one nor the other.

. . . I think it must have been the only time when they both thought alike.

And yet, I was not very demanding. I said to my two illustrious correspondents:

N

"Give me a plane, each of you, one of your bombers. The latest model, of course.

"I want them because I have been told that each costs five milliard francs.

"Now, I have estimated that with the price of two of these death-dealing machines all the lepers in the world could be treated."

I understand now from their silence how clumsy my request must have seemed. Two bombers, indeed! You can't play games with things like that! Their entourage of generals must have shrugged their shoulders. . . .

I am not offended.

But I will not give up.

And now, since the world is in the mood for loving its neighbour, I have returned, incorrigibly, "to the charge".

This time, my idea is simpler . . . and it is so very simple . . . .

Gentlemen, you who have the power; statisticians – a pitiless race – have told us that the budget for armaments in the three great countries of the world (United States, Russia, Great Britain) had reached the sum of 750 milliard dollars in the year 1954.

For those of us who buy our bread with francs that makes TWO HUNDRED AND SIXTY-TWO THOUSAND MILLIARD. . . . Not a sou less.

It is an impressive figure, you know.

And then I began to reflect.

Experts say that there are now two and a half milliard people on the earth. That must be less than a milliard families. With the money that is spent on guns, planes and bombs, one could have given each of them an income of 262,000 francs last year.

262,000 francs income! Nobody would have felt the poorer for it.

But there would be no more poverty today.

And then if there was not so much misery, the chances of war would be reduced, you know. . . .

My suggestion is absurd? I could admit it cheerfully.

But you must prove it to me first.

Gentlemen, you who have the power, lords of war and peace, will you never agree to set aside the thousandth part of what you have squandered over the years for death, hatred and destruction to heal the poor and feed and educate them?

It is man who asks this question, every man of every race. Whether you remain silent or not, he will either rejoice over your action, or note your indifference: there is no way of escaping his judgment.

But I am sure that you will answer. I can tell it from the way you smile in your photographs.

And you will unanimously come to the aid of the lonely, of those without hands to applaud and without voices to shout. . . .

Bossuet said: "Cursed be any knowledge that does not lead to love."

If it were to win the "Fight against Leprosy", this century, tainted as it is by your atom bombs, could be rehabilitated.

Then history would consider you with its Great Men. . . .

1959

Third Letter

To General Eisenhower, President of the United States and to Mr Khrushchev, Chairman of the Council of Ministers of the USSR.

Presidents,

At last you have met each other. The masters of the world are finally going to talk in person. People everywhere are at once hopeful and fearful. We know that there is almost nothing you cannot do for human happiness, but – inevitably– we think first and foremost of the disaster that could result from a disagreement.

But we know also that your hearts work like our own, and only really want to work for the peace of the world.

It is because I am convinced of your good intentions that I am writing to you.

I am an ordinary man, such as you might find in your own countries. A man who would like to be able to go to sleep at nights knowing that everyone else is content.

That is what gives me strength and faith.

And authorizes me to write to you.

Gentlemen, you who represent the two great powers, are you willing to save 15 million men? The most abandoned and pitiful of all, who are so wretched and so alone that they have no idea to which political party they belong.

Fifteen million innocent people infected with an illness that the World Health Organization has just declared to be only slightly contagious and perfectly curable, and who are yet only too often condemned to a most horrible death: the lepers.

Would you, *together*, sign a reprieve for 15 million men?

Would you be willing that your *first* point of agreement should be to deliver 15 million men imprisoned by ignorance, selfishness and cowardice, those three leprosies more catching than leprosy and more difficult to cure?

You can do it. With one word. By giving up, each of you, one of those machines of which you have so many that no one would even notice if one were to disappear from your vast hangars.

Each of you could give us one plane, a bomber.

One of those machines that is both a technical masterpiece and the terror of your civilians.

For the price of these instruments of death, we could buy enough medicine to treat and often to cure all the lepers in the world.

What does it matter to you if there is one less plane in the USSR and one less in the USA! The balance would not be disturbed. . . .

But if the report of your meeting announced that: "The two great powers have allied themselves in order to win the 'Fight against Leprosy' ", believe me, the 15 million lepers would not be the only ones who would rejoice. And it would cost you each no more than a bomber. To win such a great victory!

. . . Don't you feel like thanking me?

It is death to go on with the arms race. And we shall all die with you. For nothing. Because of you. And neither of you wants to go on killing. You just haven't found any other way of behaving.

It would only be a tiny step towards disarmament if you were each to give up a bomber.

But that could be just the start. . . .

And you might feel so happy about it that you would be inspired to continue. . . . Until the last bomb and the last leper. . . .

That is all I have to say. And if I have had the audacity to say it, it is because I am sure that there are millions, here and everywhere, among your people and ours, who will be glad that I have done so.

And now, act in accordance with your consciences and hearts
I shall go on hoping.

1962

A Message to Heads of State throughout the World

I am confident that this letter will reach you all.

Even if you do not reply to me, you will have to reply to it in
your hearts.

It is to your hearts that I am writing.

I am a man of goodwill and for thirty years I have fought a
difficult battle and experienced both cruelty and fraternal love
in it.

Now I am almost an old man, but one who still believes in
goodness.

This is why I am writing to you. To you and all the other
Heads of State, to ask a favour, a great amnesty: a favour for 15
million innocent men who have been condemned to the worst
possible death: the lepers. I have a right to speak for them: I have
spent all my life caring for them.

They are infected with an illness that was once accursed and
hopeless, today they can be cured. Two million of them have already been cured and delivered from the wretchedness that
oppressed them: that is the proof that it can be done.

Millions more, however, remain without treatment, help or
love: the "Fight against Leprosy" is not over.

Then, stupefied and horrified, as all men worthy of the name
must be, by the fabulous sums spent on armaments, I made a
calculation. If all the powers, large and small, had in 1962 given
100 francs to the treatment of leprosy for every million they
squandered on preparations for war, all the lepers in the world
could have been treated.

A million for killing: a hundred francs for curing. It is so simple
and seems such a negligible proportion that one cannot imagine
any country refusing.

Will you set an example, and give some, perhaps, a lesson?

The gesture that I have proposed, whatever the material
results, has supreme symbolic value. It would pave the way for
that transformation of instruments of death into tools for rebuilding life on which depends the very salvation of humanity.

While certain people defy each other or play bowls in the

stratosphere, the world rushes with the speed of an avalanche towards the greatest disaster of history.

The undernourished in 1938 made up 35% of the world's population. They account for two-thirds of the population today. In ten years they will represent three-quarters of it.

If our human conscience is not stirred by a great wave of love at some time during this century, man's starvation will hasten the end of the world.

ONE MILLION for killing: ONE HUNDRED francs for curing. Will you listen to my appeal?

A country does not become great by being powerful or rich, but when it is capable of extending love.

If you will undertake, on an equal footing with the greatest world powers, this gesture of human solidarity – or show them what their duty is by undertaking it – you will be proclaiming that no one on this earth – individuals, nations or countries – has the right to be happy alone.

History will judge then which were the great countries.

The "Follereau precedent"

In his authoritative book, *Malthus et les deux Marx,* M. Alfred Sauvy, professor at the Collège de France, mentions under the above heading my first letter to the two Power Men: "If each of you were to give up one bomber we could treat all the lepers in the world."

"Of course," he goes on to say, "the Power Men did not reply that time, but the idea had been planted and it will be taken up. It is such a promising line of argument that one keeps on coming back to it."

M. Alfred Sauvy is himself an example of this, since my initiative provides him with his concluding argument.

If a spokesman could get up and speak very loudly for that million, in the words of Raoul Follereau, making them even more telling, he would address all the advanced countries in the following terms without separating Marx from Malthus:

"You rich peoples, you have three-quarters of the world's wealth and you are committing the crime of squandering it. However important they seem, your internal disputes look very petty when compared to the lives of millions of people. A generation ago butter and guns were weighed against one

another. The latter won. And now today the choice is between
your guns and our butter, or to be exact, between your missiles
and our bread. For it is our bread that you squander, and what
is worse, our chance of bread tomorrow. If a disaster does
happen one of these days to our planet, and if there is a his-
torian left to describe it, you will be accused of having committed the most terrible crime in human history. The crimes
of a Caligula, an Attila, a Hitler, will pale in comparison with
what you are planning: to use for killing some people what
could give life to others."

Millions of men, even when without arms or money, can
make themselves heard. The more tense and close to violence
the attitude becomes, the happier the two prisoners will be,
in their heart of hearts, to be released.

And in a generation or two, perhaps men will say: "When
humanity emerged from its subservience to nature, it wavered
for a time, drunk with its own power. No one could have fore-
told that it would come down on the side of right. It was
perhaps just a matter of luck that the right men were there at
the time. That's not important, the fact is there. Humanity has
entered upon the great period of construction."

After all the world only needs to become conscious of its
own existence and to channel fear into the right paths. A
moment's enlightenment would be enough.

TWO MESSAGES TO
THE YOUTH OF THE WORLD

1961

Don't say "I'm hungry"

WHEN YOU feel like eating, don't say: "I'm hungry!" But think of the 400 million young men and women who won't eat at all today. For half the youth of the world is starving.

If you have a cold, don't say: "My God, I'm ill!" But think of all those who are suffering, of the 800 million people who have never seen a doctor. And especially of the 15 million lepers whom the world has cursed, when 12 million of them are still without treatment, help or love.

What was their crime? To be ill.

To be affected by an illness which we now know is not very contagious and can be cured. But this illness is called "leprosy". It causes shame and fear.

And fear – a real leprosy if ever there was one – continues its termite-like work. . . .

In order to find, treat and save the twelve million sick who are still prisoners of our stupid fear, and to "cure the healthy" of their senseless and sometimes criminal terror, in 1954 I instituted World Leprosy Day.

Will you help me?

One day, when I was in Asia, I was called to the side of a girl with leprosy who was about to die.

She was young – twenty-two – and of above average height. I watched helplessly as she shook herself free of her hideous existence in a series of little jerks. When she was dead, I was overwhelmed by the desire to weigh her. I lifted the still-warm little heap of bones and carried it over to the scales. That twenty-two-year-old leper weighed twenty kilos. . . . Now you know what she died of. . . .

Because it horrified and sickened me, I was told "That's the way it's been since the beginning of the world. You'll never change anything, it's hopeless!"

Impossible? The only impossibility is that you and I should go on eating, sleeping and laughing when we know that there are women of twenty-two who die because they weigh only twenty kilos. . . .

Will this state of affairs continue? Shall we let millions of human beings die and rot when we could care for them, save them and cure them?

That is the question.

That is the question that you must answer, you – no one else; you – no one else, by bringing to this world-wide reunion of human solidarity your support and your love.

And, of course, without thinking that you've done your bit at the end of the day.

Well, that's that for a year!

No, you can't love on one day only.

* * *

And so, your love is brave and pure, and would like to extend beyond our poor friends and combat distress, outrage and suffering on other fronts. . . .

When you feel like eating, don't say: "I'm hungry."

* * *

. . . It starts with a fainting feeling. . . . A mysterious sort of numbness rising up slowly and relentlessly from the legs to the stomach. Sometimes it's a monstrous sort of dropsy, and the skin stretches to bursting point, and sometimes does burst . . . sometimes it's the opposite, the body dries up. The muscles waste as if some invisible and insatiable animal were devouring you. . . .

And then, slowly and amidst terrible anguish, death.

But what is this horrible illness?

Beri-beri, the result of starvation.

You have never seen it?

I have seen it for you.

And having seen it, it was a long time before I could sleep again.

And now you understand what I am trying to say.

It's not a question of letting fall a half-hearted tear: that's easy.

You must realize, and not accept any more.

Don't let *self* be the centre of your universe – or the members of *self's* family – while waiting for *self's* little place in Paradise.

Refuse to take a self-righteous little rest while others are crying out in despair all around you.

Don't accept the kind of existence that always dismisses the rest of mankind.

Don't accept that negative Christianity that the narrow-minded have stifled in a labyrinth of formulas and taboos.

Refuse to be happy alone.

Never give up when confronted with poverty, injustice or cowardice. Don't compromise, or draw back. Strive, fight.

Take the offensive!

Stop those responsible from sleeping!

You belong to tomorrow, demand happiness for others.

Build happiness for them.

The world is hungry for corn and love.

Let's get to work.

1962
It's up to you to Fight

I'm calling on you, the young of all nations. Because you have the greatest power in the world: the future.

I was about your age when I embarked on the "Fight against Leprosy". The people who had, so to speak, "arrived" – arrived where, for heaven's sake? – looked at me with suspicious curiosity. There always had been lepers, and so there always would be: it was simple and final.

For thirty years I tried to stop those responsible from sleeping. Today two million lepers have been cured: that's an achievement. But there are still millions without treatment, help or love: the "Fight against Leprosy" isn't over.

Thirty years ago I was like you. But now I'm almost an old man, and yet I think I'm still like you. My strength is failing, but my heart is still as young as yours; setbacks haven't weakened it.

I repeat: will you help me? Will you become the relief force, take over from me, carry on the fight, make the last assault, win through? And over and above our immediate aim, will you win that great battle – the only one that matters – against ignorance, selfishness and cowardice?

A few years ago I wrote this to the two Power Men – the giants who have ceased to be human; "It is death to go on with the arms race. And we shall all die with you. Without knowing why. Whether you wish it or not. Because you just haven't learnt any other way of behaving."

My words were not heard. Because they were those of a single person, speaking in the name of those poor people who have no hands to clap with and no voices to shout with.

Today I am calling on all the Heads of State in the world.

I am asking of them something that is immense, and yet very small, within the means of the less rich and less powerful.

Listen to what I have to say to them:

Stupefied and horrified, as all men worthy of the name must be, by the fabulous sums spent on armaments, I made a calculation. If all the powers, large and small, had in 1962, given 100 francs to the treatment of leprosy for every million they squandered on preparations for war, all the lepers in the world could have been treated.

A million for killing: a hundred francs for curing: could any country refuse?

While the Power Men are defying one another or playing bowls in the stratosphere, the world rushes with the speed of an avalanche towards the greatest disaster of history.

The undernourished in 1938 made up 35% of the world's population. They account for two-thirds of the population today. In ten years they will represent three-quarters of it.

If our human conscience is not stirred by a great wave of love at some time during this century, man's starvation will hasten the end of the world.

One million for killing: one hundred francs for curing. Will you listen to my appeal?"

That is what I wrote to those who have the power and the duty to reply.

And now, youth of the world, it's your turn to fight! If you make this cause your own, you will have the means of making yourselves heard.

Men have only this choice now: Love one another or perish.
We must choose. Immediately. Irrevocably.

You are the ones who must choose.

If you can achieve the symbolic conversion of the instruments
of death into tools to rebuild life, you will not only win the
"Fight against Leprosy", you will say "no" to fear and hatred
and fatalism.

In order to do that, there is only one necessity.

Be intransigent about the duty to love. Don't yield or compromise or draw back. Laugh in the face of those who advise
caution and waiting for the right moment, "maintaining an even
keel", those wretched champions of the "golden mean".

And then, above all, believe in the goodness of the world.
In every man's heart there are great reserves of love: you must
make him draw on them.

The worst thing that can happen to you is to be of no use to
anyone, for your life to be purposeless.

Be proud and exacting. Knowing that it is your duty to try
to secure happiness for all mankind, your brothers, you will not
let yourselves be bogged down in the shifting sands of procrasti-
nators and impotents. Look them straight in the face. Denounce
at the top of your voice. Don't let people trick you. Be yourselves
and you will win.

Perhaps my final duty will have been to indicate yours to you.
If I am speaking to you like sons, I think of you as brothers.

I was before you.
I am waiting for you.

A DAY OF WAR FOR PEACE

Letter to U Thant

Secretary General of United Nations Organization

Paris, September 1964

Dear Secretary General,

In 1944 – twenty years ago – I wrote to President Roosevelt from a small village in France where I had had to take refuge: one day this war will be over. It will end, like all other wars, where it should have begun – in peace. On that day I would suggest to you, to your allies and your enemies to prolong, in theory, hostilities for another twenty-four hours. I mean that for twenty-four hours the war should go on costing money, but do no damage. You could have found enough money out of all that capital that has let you go on killing for five years to carry on just for one more day, couldn't you? Then you could put those milliards into a common fund and we could all co-operate in the reconstruction of some of the things that are the property, safeguard and honour of humanity and that war has destroyed by the way, as it were, without even noticing or intending. After so many years of hopeless bloodshed it will be the first sign of hope for your people.

There was no reply.

In 1954 – ten years ago – I wrote to the two World Leaders: "Give up, each of you, one bomber plane and we shall be able to treat all the lepers in the world." There was no reply to this either. I tried the same tactic again in 1955. In vain. Then on 15 September 1959 – five years ago. This fourth letter was no better received than the others. At last, in 1962 I sent a message to all the Heads of State. . . .

Well, you may think, what incredible obstinacy. But there's no reason to keep quiet just because people don't hear men, is there? Or am I to think that these words: hunger, poverty, frater-

nity don't exist in any of the languages used at international
conferences?

And now I am making another attempt – no doubt the last
– to appeal to the conscience of the great powers and to the hearts
of all nations.

My confidence has been strengthened by your presence. You
belong to a country and a continent where there is no need to
learn about hunger and misery in school: too many, alas, know
all about it from birth. . . .

This is my request and it is exactly the same as the one I expressed twenty years ago:

Let all the members of UNO agree that every year, on the
occasion of a World Peace Day, they will set aside what they have
spent *in one day on armaments* to go to a common fund for the
relief of famine, slums and endemic diseases which are decimating
mankind.

One day of war for Peace. . . . Perhaps you will think that I
don't ask enough.

But this first transformation of the instruments of death into
tools for rebuilding life would be a glorious gesture, and could
assure the salvation of a humanity that stands by, its hands tied
and its mouth stopped, helplessly watching its own suicide.

In 1959 I wrote to Mr Khrushchev and General Eisenhower:
"It is death to go on with the arms race. And we shall all die
with you. For nothing. Because of you. Not because either of you
wanted to kill. But because you had never found another way
of behaving."

This would be a method. A modest one, to be sure. But it would
open a little door for hope.

Disarm in order to love.

That's what I should like to hear you say in the UN for me.
Because I am sure that millions of people who belong to the
member-nations would be glad to know that it had been said.

Let every country decide according to the promptings of its
conscience.

Whether they respond or whether they remain indifferent to
this last appeal, it will be remembered in the future. And no one
will escape judgment.

For my part, I shall go on hoping.

An Appeal to the Young

On the same day I wrote a message to the youth of the world, telling them about my letter to UNO and adding:

But my appeal risks being vain once more. Wandering from storey to storey, getting lost, being read in office after office, only to finish up like all the others in some oubliette in that Tower of Babel which has been the grave of so many hopes. . . .

But if thousands of other voices respond to mine; young, ardent, intransigent voices who will not put up with being silenced, and will rebel against silence as if it were an insult, then the wilfully deaf, the deliberately dumb, instead of thinking: "Oh, him again!" will say: "Them, already!" Them: those who have come to leap to the attack, to prevent the guilty from sleeping . . . while waiting to bring them to account.

Then people will have to hear you and listen to you.

Because, tomorrow, it is you who will be the great ones.

* * *

Therefore, write to New York. Immediately. Sign the forms proclaiming your determination in groups of ten.

If those who have the power and the duty to reply receive thousands of copies daily of the declaration of the wishes of the young, people will eventually have to take notice at all levels of the UN.

Which do you prefer, Young People of the World?

The most recent prototype bomber with all its equipment
> or 75 hospitals with 1,000 beds each?
>> In some poor countries medical facilities are only a *fiftieth part* of what is available in advanced countries.

The most recent prototype bomber with all its equipment
> or 30 colleges each accommodating a thousand students?
> or 250,000 teachers in that third of the world where *one in every two children under fifteen* can neither read nor write?

The most recent prototype bomber with all its equipment
> or 50,000 tractors
> or 15,000 harvesters?

These figures were taken from the UNESCO Newsletter (Nov. 1964).

Which do you prefer, young people of the world?

The most impressive Support ...

4 December 1964

His Holiness Pope Paul VI said in Bombay:

"Let all nations stop the armaments race and instead devote their energies and resources to giving brotherly aid to those countries that are in the process of developing. Let every nation that entertains 'thoughts of peace, not of affliction' and war, divert even a part of its military expenditure into a world fund for the relief of the many problems that beset so great a number of the disinherited (food, clothing, housing, medical treatment)."

Some Repercussions

From the Governor General of Canada

Dear Sir,

I have received and read with interest your letter of 8 July, in which you tell me about the wonderful campaign that you have undertaken on behalf of the lepers: "A day of war for Peace."

The aim you are pursuing should be supported by all men of goodwill. I beg you most earnestly to continue your efforts to secure for mankind, particularly for the youth, a future filled with peace and happiness. "Disarm in order to love" is a noble ideal.

I have had a copy of your letter sent to my government and they are actively working, have no doubt of that, towards a solution to the problem of disarmament and the maintenance of peace.

My wife would like to join with me in expressing sincere and friendly greetings to you.

GENERAL VANIER

From the President of the Republic of Lebanon:

Your appeal to all the nations of the world to devote the amount of money they would spend on armaments in one day out of their annual budget, towards financing tools for rebuilding life cannot fail to be imprinted on the heart of any Lebanese.

Lebanon, which is, within its own frontiers, a peaceful and friendly country and presents itself to the world as such, knows that peace can only come from justice and charity. We are happy to take part in this general mobilization against hunger, misery and disease (particularly leprosy, as you have devoted so much effort for so long to curing it).

In doing this, my country accepts its duty and its mission. We are determined to take part, whatever the obstacles and reversals, in the progress of humanity towards salvation.

In conclusion, Mr President, I should like to express my very high regard for you.

CHARLES HÉLOU

From the President of the Republic of Cameroon:

I am pleased to have received your letter of last July and to be able to tell you of my own personal interest in your generous proposal to transform the instruments of death into tools for re-building life, in the hope of making a better future for humanity.

Your campaign for "a day of war for peace" could only be well received by myself and by my government.

Allow me to express warm words of encouragement to you, and hope for favourable developments from your action.

I can also assure you that the Cameroonian delegation will be given appropriate instructions to give your campaign all necessary support at the next General Assembly of the United Nations, if the question comes up for debate.

May I wish you every success and at the same time express my deep regard and friendship.

A. AHIDJO

From the President of the Republic of Senegal:

On my return from America I found your letter of 20 September 1964.

I applaud your initiative "with ten hands", as we say in Senegal. It is initiatives such as yours that awaken public opinion and work on the consciences of Heads of State.

As far as the young people are concerned, the form you have sent me will be sent back to the UN with ten signatures. Others will follow.

May I express my sincere regard for you.

LÉOPOLD SÉDAR SENGHOR

From His Highness the Prince Norodom Sihanouk, Head of State in Cambodia:

It is with all my heart that I offer you my own support and that of Cambodia in your noble campaign "A day of war for

o

peace". As Buddhists we think of compassion as one of the highest human virtues and acknowledge your action as one which has a place in all that is great in the Western tradition.

I share your indignation at the scandal of riches and energy being used for war. My indignation is the greater because in Indochina alone hundreds of millions of dollars are being used to kill and destroy. Fortunately, Cambodia has been able to preserve peace and to work with success for the stamping out of the great endemic diseases of the past. But on our very doorstep in South Vietnam where the most modern weapons decimate the population, we can also watch the medieval scourges of leprosy, plague and cholera becoming more prevalent every year. . . .

Permit me to assure you of the support of my people and especially of our youth who will respond to your appeal in the manner you have outlined.

May I close by assuring you of my highest regard.

NORODOM SIHANOUK

From the President of the Republic of Gaboon:

In answer to your letter I have the honour to tell you that I was very moved by the terms of your appeal and that I have decided straightaway that the Youth of Gaboon will give you the maximum support in your campaign.

Like you, I am convinced that only weight of numbers can make any impression on the indifference with which your suggestions have until now been greeted by the powerful of this earth. I think that a small country like Gaboon can help by being consumed with enthusiasm for your cause, and that this could set in motion, at first in our own immediate neighbourhood, and then across Africa, an irresistible force that would make UNO give some thought to your problems and institute the "World Peace Day" for which you, first, gave the idea.

To this end I have asked the ministers of Work and Social Affairs, National Education and Public Health to meet here on 31 October 1964 to decide the details for the campaign for signatures that you have just launched in order to submerge the UN offices with the indictments of the youth of all countries.

. . . Wishing also to do more for your appeal, I shall not fail to associate my government with it by instructing our representative at UNO to draw the General Assembly's attention to your idea of instituting a "World Peace Day" and to support it in discussion.

In this way Gaboon, which is treating 6,000 lepers, will give full recognition to your unsparing efforts over the last thirty years to improve the lot of the hungry and the sick, by approving your gesture.

LÉON M'BA

From the President of the Republic of Dahomey:
I was extremely moved by your letter of 20 September and fully approve the ideals which inspire this new campaign. It is an action as elevated as all those you have previously undertaken.

I have handed your letter to our Minister of Youth and Sport.

I am sure that he will do his utmost to encourage the young people of Dahomey to give enthusiastic and unanimous support to your project.

May I offer you my sincere regards and my hopes for the success of your work.

S. M. APITHY

From the President of the Islamic Republic of Mauretania:
. . . I take great pleasure in writing to tell you that the government and people of Mauretania will give you their full support over your campaign for "a day of war for peace" and we shall do everything possible to encourage the young to take part.

We shall be very glad to accept your offer to send us all the necessary promotional material for the campaign, and we should also like to have two thousand petition forms.

MOKTAR OULD DADDAH

From the President of the Republic of Rwanda:
I have just received your letter of 18 May 1965.

The feelings you express there and which represent the most intimate aspirations of your life have made a deep impression on me.

I fully support your campaign for Peace, as it is my dearest wish to see the beginning of an era of peace among men. I feel that we should all hope for and work towards the time when all men without exception will only have one enemy to pursue: hunger, sickness and ignorance, and when all our money and efforts will be directed towards the improvement of man's condition.

You may rely absolutely on the support of our representatives to the various international organizations when the time comes.

May I wish you every success and reiterate my conviction that you will gradually overcome the lack of understanding and that your appeal will be heard by those who control human destiny.

Gr. KAYIBANDA

From the Minister of National Education of the Republic of Chad:

Further to your letter of 21 December 1964, I am pleased to be able to tell you that we shall be organizing a large-scale petition during the third term of the present scholastic year in response to your splendid campaign: "a day of war for peace".

The campaign will be under the patronage of our President, and he will thus lend his distinguished support to your efforts.

We intend to publicize this day widely among the young people, and we should therefore be very grateful if you could send us as soon as possible:

35,000 forms and 100 records.

I should like to express my thanks to you and assure you of my very high regard and admiration for you.

From the Minister of Public Health in Upper Volta:

Once again I must admire the initiative you have taken. I believe that it is only through such perseverance that the world conscience will be made to take positive thought about all the wretchedness that surrounds us.

First Victories

The Shah of Iran devotes a day's armament budget to the struggle against poverty.

On 3 May 1966, His Majesty the Shah of Iran announced that he had decided to offer "the equivalent of a complete day's military budget", that is 700,000 dollars (350 million Old Francs), in order, as he says in his message, "to give to the two-fifths of mankind who are stagnating in ignorance the hope of economic and social improvement".

At a meeting of the General Assembly of the World Health Organization, Doctor Dolo Somine, Minister of Public Health in Mali, demands a day of war for peace.

Here are the concluding words of the very fine and moving speech made in the General Assembly of the World Health Organization by Doctor Dolo Somine, Minister of Public Health in Mali.

Fellow delegates, it is because of the high aims of our Organization that I have thought it permissible to present for your consideration this manifesto addressed to the youth of the world by that great humanist, Raoul Follereau: "A day of war for peace". It has been signed by over a million young people of all nationalities and sent to the Secretary General of the UN in the hope of awakening the consciences of men and governments and making us realize that it is for all of us that the "bell tolls". In this way perhaps a little more love and brotherhood will operate in the world and so put us in a better position to overcome disease, ignorance and poverty.

One million, five hundred thousand Young People answered me

Here is what they said. . . .

A young student:

I just want to tell you how very much I admire you and to thank you for initiating "a day of war for Peace".

Although it is almost impossible to ignore the problems of peace and hunger in this day and age, you are the first to offer young people a useful plan of action. We have all heard enough talks and discussions on the subject of peace and hunger. . . . There are even films about it. Up to now, however, no one has ever shown us what we could do about it. All they wanted, after having played on our emotions, was a donation. Young people never feel that that is sufficient.

But you have given us real hope. There is something we can do, even though we are young and have no money.

I look after a girls' club, and I must tell you what a "tonic" your life and work have been for my girls. They can at last believe in Love as a force, the only one that can save the world.

I am absolutely certain that many of my girls have only discovered that life has a meaning because of you and your books.

. . . I do hope that we shall be successful, but even if your campaign is not a resounding success with the UN, I know that a lot of young people will find there is a new dimension to their lives and they will perhaps be able to accomplish something.

I know that many people will be saved, thanks to you. For myself, I have every confidence in you and am grateful to you for this hope in life.

A college chaplain:

I am writing to thank you because to us, and particularly to the young, you are a symbol of hope. We are proud to be able to say that you are a Christian.

I can promise you all my assistance and, as a priest, my prayers for your work, which is in the great tradition of John XXIII, Paul VI and the Council.

A Protestant clergyman:

Would you be kind enough to send me fifty forms to be signed in support of your appeal to the UN? The young people in my parish to whom I spoke about it have taken the whole thing very seriously and had soon used up the first batch that you sent me.

What I find most interesting about this is not only that the the young are collecting signatures, but that the campaign has given them and others a chance of looking at the problem of Christian commitment to the ideal of peace among men in a new and unusual light. They tell me that they have many discussions and talks about it among themselves.

One other thing I should like to mention is that I spoke about your appeal from the pulpit in Saint-Eloi church on Sunday 15 November. It was an "official" service, with all the civil and military authorities present, also representatives of all the old soldiers' associations. I thought it would be appropriate this year to use your appeal to illustrate the point I was trying to make in my sermon – how Christian virtues could cope with the tremendous problems of our era.

A youth-group leader:

I should like to tell you how important it is that you should carry on with your work for the poor. You could become the mouthpiece for millions of people who are no longer willing to accept a society that does not recognize human dignity.

I think that Christians today have to give this testimony, as it is set out in Schema XIII of the Council: the relationship of the Church to the modern world (especially to its poorest inhabitants).

Your struggle is a proof that Christians are awake and that it is time for action.

Please believe that you are not alone in your work. Thousands of people think as you do – in terms of unselfish love – but they are still afraid to say so. Your having taken the initiative will give them courage, do not doubt it.

At a J.E.C.[1] reunion where I was present, we talked to the young about it. I assure you that they listened and understood. I hope that this thought will give you courage to go on with your splendid work.

A girl of eighteen:
Everyone talks about disarmament and hunger in the world. Everyone talks and no one does anything. And now an adult, you, as it happens, has decided to act. First of all I am grateful to you and admire you for that. I am only eighteen and I was afraid that no adult would ever show us the right way to go about doing something. I believe in peace, real peace that comes from fighting against selfishness, not the sort that springs from indifference. I believe in love, and I think that peace and love are stronger than hatred, and have already conquered it. And everyone who signed the three forms which I shall be sending back to you shortly has the same faith and ideals as I have. I distributed the forms among the country people where I live, among members of the J.E.C. in Le Mans, and finally among my school friends. With the exception of one person, who approved in principle but thought it would not succeed, everyone was enthusiastically in favour.

I wanted to tell you about this heartening support because you have given us a hope that strengthens us. Thank you.

Other Repercussions

Thank you for trusting the young
Thank you for having thought about the young and for giving them the chance to devote themselves to a task in which they are not usually allowed to help.

Thank you for trusting the young.

We shall try to prove that we are worthy of it all our lives.

[1] *Jeunesse étudiante chrétienne* (Young Christian Students).

From a college in Toulouse

I have not stopped thinking about you and praying for you since you went to Caousou. I don't know how to thank you; your arguments have changed my life.

May God bless and keep you.

You have chosen to believe and hope

It is a curious coincidence. . . . I had been thinking about your untiring efforts for the "abandoned" during these past few days, when I received your latest appeal to the UN. Of course I shall support you with enthusiasm.

You have chosen to believe and hope when so many others are losing heart and denying that there is any goodness and brotherhood among men. Despite everyone and everything, do carry on with your mission: I am sure that there are millions of people who are with you in spirit, countless young people with a desperate conviction that love will eventually overcome hatred.

Young people are capable of great things

. . . I am overcome with amazement and admiration for the enthusiasm of the young. We found willing helpers among the Guides, the members of the J.E.C., the students . . . as soon as we began to talk about these petitions for Peace. Already all those that you sent to Miss B. (federal secretary of the J.E.C.) have been eagerly taken away. Older guides have been going round the children's homes with them. In the Faculty of Medicine students have been keen to take over the microphone after lectures to tell others about it. Yesterday, at a federal J.E.C.F. week-end, the militants unanimously decided to take the petitions round their school friends. . . . I could go on citing examples for ever. The best "scheme" came from a group of guides and students who wanted to hire a bus during the summer holidays and go from town to town holding evening discussions on the important problems that confront us. I hope that they can manage it and I shall do my best to help them.

I have been college chaplain for seven years and I also visit the secondary school, the local J.E.C. and the guides. I have drawn on this experience to learn some lessons from the campaign for peace.

1. The young are capable of great things . . . all they need is something to hang on to.

2. They see in you an adult who believes . . . who gives . . . who does not make do with words, but who can talk if need be.

3. Your book, *Une bataille pas comme les autres* (*A Fight that is Different*) – and the other books as well, of course – really is the answer to all their personal problems. I give it them to read and they're cured. We must distribute it widely.

4. Even if they don't get signatures for the petitions, they do communicate with other young people and have to explain and argue. Even this is a little victory for peace, is it not?

A breath of fresh air has come into our lives – thanks to you. Yesterday I met another chaplain who has come over to your side.

Thank you, Monsieur Follereau, for having enabled us to give something. Thank you on behalf of the young and for ourselves. What a struggle you must have! That is why I wanted to write this evening and say that you are not completely alone. I shall pray for you.

We needed your confidence

There were about twenty of us, divided in groups of six or eight, and we were reading your message.

I wish you could have been here! You would have seen that your confidence was justified.

We had often thought about the problem of poverty, but we are very weak, we needed your confidence, and the evidence of our faith!

We don't amount to much, but all together our voices cannot go totally unanswered.

Those who are all-powerful here on earth cannot go on playing deaf!

The youth of the world stands beside you

We were overjoyed to find that, in a world that is moving towards disaster, towards destruction through its hatreds and rivalries, there were still men whose ideal is love.

The youth of the world stands beside you, Monsieur Follereau; we want to love, as you do. Do not be afraid to speak, for millions of little voices are here to support you.—*Some Canadian students.*

Young people say: "Things must change"

Our teacher told us about your appeal on behalf of the unfortunate, and, as we understand it, you want the young to take part. My school friends all hope that this time the world's leaders will listen to your appeal for "a day of war for peace".

Don't give up hope, Monsieur Follereau, young people all over the world say: "Things must change."

We want to thank you, like all the unfortunate people whom you have helped.

From a Belgian educationalist:

The young want to have confidence in the future, but they can see that most of their elders don't care; as a result I noticed some who were beginning to have doubts about what to do. By your action you have given them confidence again, and for this I give you heartfelt thanks in their name.

Even if your campaign does not succeed in its main object (we all hope that it will go well, but we have no illusions), it will certainly give encouragement to all the young who hear of it and think about their future responsibility and the good they could do. This leads me to a formal conclusion: the world of love is taking shape.

On a petition from Nigeria:

Our petition carries the signatures of ten young people who are starving.

Young Men and Women of 105 Countries

One million, five hundred thousand of you replied to my appeal. I have dedicated these memoirs, testimonies and instructions to you

It is for you to say "No" to mankind's suicide.

In this world which totters from insolent squandering to desperate famine, from empty stomachs to ones that are bursting, you must demand that today's leaders take seriously their responsibility to you, the men and women of tomorrow.

With me, you asked for "a day of war for Peace".

From now on – and throughout your lives – you must demand peace every day.

Say "No" every day to war, to hunger and to death.

Accept this inheritance as a duty. It will enrich you more surely than any worldly treasure.

*   *   *

Three forces today command respect and attention in the world: numbers, might and money.

To set the weight of numbers, not at the helm of blind force or corrupt wealth, but at the service of a radiant love, that is your human task. The only truth is to love each other.

You won't obtain it by sitting on the fence, putting up with things, profiting out of them. You must build, defend, enlighten, teach. Nobody has the right to be happy alone.

If you can do this, you won't just have lived, you will have been worthy to live. . . .

I have spent the best years of my life fighting for your safety against the horrible absurdity of our weapons, against stupidity and distrust and virulent anger.

Now you must defend yourselves.

EPILOGUE

Lord, in the twilight of my life,
I am bringing you what I have done.

Your lepers,
their faces once defiled
now illuminated by hope
and awakened to dignity.

Divested of all hatred,
the pure joy of the wretched.

This evening, Lord, I offer you
the faith I had when I was young,
when I strove obstinately,
pursued great aims;
my fierce, ardent battles
which came out well
all my long life. . . .

But I offer you also, Lord,
my cares, my worries,
the dreary hours full
of fear and doubt;
my hopes betrayed,
all my dreams abandoned
and my illusions dead. . . .

Before your infinite love accords
to this vagabond who has lingered too long
in insubstantial solitude
and deceptive certainties
the supreme grace of arriving
at the Islands of Mercy,

I bring you, Lord, my exultations,
my hasty and imperfect efforts,
the great joys that were given me,
and all my little griefs.

My day draws to its close,
the obstinate struggles are over,
my work finished and my heart at rest.

The prize I would ask, if it is not sterile and unworthy,
the prize I would ask from the Master of the Vineyard:
Lord, do not stop loving us.

SELECTED EXTRACTS

It SEEMED desirable to the organizations sponsoring the publication of this work that, in addition to the author's own story and selected testimonies, there should be a brief anthology of his most characteristic writings over the past forty years.

Some of them are unpublished. But the majority are taken from works now out of print, though one or two appear in more recent books.

It was felt that they form part of a whole that should remain intact, and bear witness to the amazing unity of Raoul Follereau's life and work.

Extracts from: *Les Iles de Miséricorde* (The Islands of Mercy), 1933 (out of print).

HYMN

Azure waves, emerald waves,
and aquamarine waves,
angry waves, giant waves,
living waves,
waves that throb,
waves that sing and scold,
dark hearts
that beat with a whole world,
throbbing waves, living waves, free waves,
waves that leap to the light
like a second sky. . . .

Blue castles, dishevelled waves,
waves that coil and uncoil
their fairy hair,
green monsters, waves thirsty
for cruel pain,
livid-green waves that dispense
the poison of slow death,
black tombs that suck in and cradle
panting hearts,
waves of dream and horror,
young, dying, buoyant, cast down,
according to the ephemeral whim
of the eternal order,
beneath the sun which cures and kills
like an inflaming criminal,

I salute you . . .

*   *   *

I look at you and pray to you,
O waves, warm
and caressing,
aquamarine
or emerald,
waves that sing. . . .

213

I'm not afraid of you, shan't run away from you,
scolding as you are,
monsters frothing with foam and wrath,
wicked waves. . . .

I love you and love as well
the death you offer between the swell
of two billows, like a hidden shark;
death, the supreme reason-to-be,
you who have marked out for me
perhaps a mysterious rock
where one is drowned. . . .

For I know that, near or far,
one morning, one morning clear,
a morning drunk with joy and glory,
or else a poor sick morning, opal-coloured,
when the two lights
harmonize so purely
that one seems to be floating on the sky
in the manner of angels,
on such a morning,
on one such strange morning,
my waves, you will unloose your triumphal
     clasp. . . .
Beneath the sublime sun,
a peak
will appear.

It is the promised land
of all dead dreams;
no hand has marked it in
on sailors' maps;
mysterious trade-winds
have brought me its white scent;
and I shall be its godfather,
as I have already baptized it.

There I shall find images
and mirages
that give life . . . ;
Faith that mingles with Mystery,

and purity that sets free . . .
I shall tear away the rope
that binds me, and the shroud
that made my brow pale. . . .

And then for me, for me alone,
in the exaltation that lays low
the grey ratiocination of men on earth,
there will emerge,
at the tired prow of my little boat,

the Islands of Mercy . . .

PRAYER

O my destiny,
you who watch over the dreams
that await me,
I have bent my knees
to speak to you . . .

* * *

We:
the night, the sea
and me.
Which of us three gives the world its rhythm?
The movement of the stars,
the whim of the waves
or my emotion?

Who inspires you,
waves wicked
or caressing,
and who makes you,
my heart,
cry or sing in my breast,
for better or for worse?

What divine routes
do you tread, pale stars,
in the black sky?
Which of us three gives the world its rhythm?

The night, the sea,
and me.
What do I care, after all, for things that claim
to be understood?
Dreams, sweet dreams that await me,
I'm going to meet you . . .

*   *   *

Through what too tempting hope,
or too facile, or too bitter,
did I bend my two knees before the night?

And I pray:

O Night,
O gentle night, so wide, so pure,
so high,
night that cradles, night that murmurs, night
   that sings,
brilliant night
tender night,
welcome night,
beloved night,
warm with unexpressed sweetness,
containing so much goodness
that you throb
to my happiness;
O dearest night
in which the Three Maries
smile like three sisters . . .
receive me.

May the earth,
the earth deaf
to so many desperate cries,
may the earth,
the earth weighed down
with so many broken hopes,
disappearing like a fateful shadow
hand me over to the living abode of your
   blueness;

to the sacred baptism of the virginal waves,
that my eyes may become pure again . . .

*   *   *

And now, get up.
Wait . . .
The stars conspire together
to fix your destiny in an unknown sky.

*   *   *

Glide . . .
The wave is gentle and the night vigilant . . .

Glide as one breathes,
glide as one goes to sleep,
with a dream, with life
and passionless desires . . .
The breeze,
your accomplice,
blows like a hope in your fragile sails,
like the purest wings;

glide
towards I know not what
absolution.

Extracts from *Si le Christ, demain* . . . (If
Christ, tomorrow . . .), 1954.

IF CHRIST WERE TO KNOCK
ON YOUR DOOR TOMORROW . . .

If Christ were to knock on your door tomorrow,
would you recognize him?
He would be, as in the past, a poor man,
and certainly a solitary one.

He would probably be a workman,
perhaps unemployed,
or, if the strike is just, a striker.

Or else he'd be selling insurance policies
or vacuum-cleaners. . . .
He'd climb up endless stairs,

stop on endless landings,
with a marvellous smile
on his sad face. . . .

But your doorway is so dark. . . .
And then one doesn't see the smile of people
one wants to turn away.
"I'm not interested," you'll say,
before listening to him.
Or else the maid will repeat her lesson:
"Madame already has her poor,"
and she'll bang the door
in the face of the Poor Man
who is the Saviour.

*   *   *

He'd be perhaps a refugee,
one of the fifteen million
with UNO passports;
one of those whom no one wants to know
and who wander,
wander over the desert that the world has become;
one of those who really ought to die
"because after all one doesn't know where that
sort of person comes from. . . ."

Or else, in America,
he'd be a Black,
a Negro, as they say,
tired of begging a bed in the New York hotels,
like Our Lady, the Virgin,
long ago, in Bethlehem. . . .

If Christ were to knock at your door tomorrow,
would you recognize him?

*   *   *

He'd look tired,
exhausted,
bowed down as he is
because he has to carry
all the pain of the earth. . . .

Look here! We can't take on such a tired-
   looking man. . . .

And then if he was questioned,
"What can you do?"
he couldn't very well say: everything.

"Where do you come from?"
he couldn't very well say: everywhere.
"What are you expecting to get?"
he couldn't very well say: you.

So he would go away,
more tired, more bowed down,

with Peace in his bare hands. . . .

LORD, HERE ARE YOUR LEPERS

Lord, here are your lepers,
their hands absent, their faces tumefied,
the repulsive, the repulsed, the unclean,
who bear like your Cross
all the misery of the world.

Lord, here are your lepers,
their hands absent, their faces tumefied.

Lord, here are the real lepers,
the selfish, the impious,
those who live in foul waters,
the comfortable, the frightened,
those who have done nothing with their life.

Lord, here are the real lepers:
those who crucified you.

THIS MORNING . . .

This morning I ate.
Of course, nothing could be more normal,
more natural.
At lunch-time I shall eat, and again this evening,
like everyone else.

What do you say? Do you say
that everyone in the world doesn't eat?

Yes, so it seems; someone told me.
How very sad that is.
We're certainly not in heaven yet!

But people must know how to accept their lot:
after all, there's nothing anyone can do about it,
    is there? . . .
This morning,
I ate.

*   *   *

Certainly, yes, they didn't eat,
but what can I do about it?
Whatever I do
I can hardly, with my effort,
my poor effort, feed the world,
feed all those who are hungry in the world.
(One is always being put upon
as if
one hadn't worries enough!)
And then
I'm too taken up with my own affairs.

And they're all foreigners anyway . . .

As for myself,
I ate
this morning.

SHE'S A SPLENDID WOMAN

She's a splendid woman,
church-going,
edifying,
respectable, very respectable.

There's nothing to say against her;
she's an example, a model. . . .

She has her prie-dieu
in the front row in church,

it's covered with red velvet,
like that she can follow "her" Mass better
(because Mass is hers, too).

*   *   *

It's cold.
She's well muffled up,
so is her child;
she advances, looking ahead
in the direction of the church,
peaceful and without emotion.

She is going, as they say, to "make her devotions".

It's cold.
And even with her fur gloves
she can feel the cold.
So she hurries to get to the porch
without noticing the Poor Man waiting . . .

She says: I'm going to the Lord,
I'm going to pray to Christ
who loved us to the point of dying for us.
. . . And she passes by him without recognizing
   him.

She says to her child:
"Come and see little Jesus."
And the child – it's so cold! –
pushes aside the other Child there waiting,
poor and thinly-clad,
so as to get in quickly.

*   *   *

But yes, she's a splendid woman . . .
she's so sure of herself,
sure that she does good,
and that she does it well.

*   *   *

Whether God is pleased with her?
It's a question which, to tell the truth,
she's never put to herself.
She was baptized,

made her first communion,
was confirmed,
married,
all in church.
. . . And what flowers there were,
and lights, and the organ!

And then she prays,
goes to Mass on Sundays,
eats fish on Fridays.
She does everything she's told to do,
everything she has to do
so as not to go to hell;
in short, she does everything
that's done.

      *   *   *

Of course God is pleased with her!
Between ourselves, let me tell you,
he would be a bit hard
– and, in face of so many merits, very ungrateful –
if he didn't order the fatted calf to be killed
on her entry into Paradise. . . .
She has done everything commanded of her!
So . . .
– So what?
   – Nothing.

      *   *   *

By the door, in the cold, in the night,
God and his Son are waiting . . .

MY MONEY

My money, your money, our property:
Mine, yours, mine, yours. . . .
My capital, your goods, our possessions:
Mine, yours, mine, yours. . . .

One single world,
cushy, mean, enclosed,
in which we barricade ourselves.

No time to love.
Hundreds of millions of Poor, without bread,
  shelter, or support.

My money, your money,
My capital, your goods:
Mine, yours,
Mine, yours.
  It has been the Christian era for two thousand
    years. . . .

But when are we going to begin to be Christians?

SO MANY KNEES . . .
So many knees, so many knees
that have polished so many stones;
so much prayer, so much prayer
that has risen from everywhere. . . .

So many a steeple, many a steeple
storming up to heaven;
so many, so many hopes at rest
beneath their stone crosses,
so many dreams, so many prayers,
so much desire in poor breasts. . . .

So many, so many lives consumed,
so many great and valiant people,
Rudel and his loved one,
Damien and his lepers. . . .

So much enthusiasm afire
with truths past understanding. . . .
The Poverello in his joy,
St Vincent in his loving. . . .

And so many more, and others again,
all the artists,
all the apostles,
whose triumphant pain
cannot be born of chance:
Pascal, Dante,
Michelangelo, Mozart. . . .

And this little word: adieu,
the word that to death says 'no'. . . .
So much love and so much regret,
so much hope and so much prayer,
so many knees on so many stones,
all sing that he is there:

God.

MADAME

Madame, Madame,
you who walk in this garden,
lightly,
holding your child by the hand,
have you ever thought?

*   *   *

This evening,
this evening and indeed nightly,
after you have dined,
you'll go softly to the little room
where, in white sheets,
sleeps,
the living face,
your life's joy.
Gently, gently,
like an angel's caress,
you will touch with your fingertips,
then with your lips,
the little forehead buried in the soft pillow,
very lightly,
so as not to wake up
the happy little boy.

*   *   *

This evening, Madame, this very evening,
and henceforward nightly,
while kissing your little one,
your love, your own,
you will think
that there is on earth

another
child
as fair
as yours,
as innocent
as yours,
but who isn't asleep.

Who isn't asleep
because he's hungry.
And who weeps
because he's hungry.

And he'll be hungry
tomorrow,
next week,
and all days,
always.

He'll be hungry with 400 million others
who are hungry.

Why not yours?

Why is yours
fed,
sheltered,
protected?

Why yours, and not the others?

Madame, have you ever reflected?

LORD, WHAT HAVE WE MADE OF YOU?

Lord, what have we made of you?
An accountant, a cashier,
who pays out the change for good actions sold.

A magician,
who seeks vengeance and calls down curses.

A grocer,
who hands out little slices of Paradise
to hypocrites.

You whose power bursts forth in its totality
in the most humble impulse of love.

NO ROOM FOR THEM

He earned his living all right,
Only he didn't like being alive.
Ever since he was small, ever since he could remember,
life had been a terrible burden to him.
He was afraid to go out, afraid of others, of the way they
looked at him. . . .
Oh no, they didn't do him any harm. . . . But they
looked. . . .
And they laughed.
It was this laugh that made him suffer.
He was a hunchback.

* * *

Every day it was like this:
"Oh look, darling," a mother would say to her child, "look at
that little hunchback: isn't he funny!"
"Hunchback, hunchback," a man would cry, he wasn't bad,
but just cruel, and he wanted to impress his mates, "Hunchback,
come here so that I can touch your hump and have some good
luck!"
And the little hunchback bent his head and ran away.
It was like that every day.
It had been like that every day for years. . . .
Yet he felt no hate in his heart. He just realized that, in order
to live with others, you had to "be like everyone else".
He was a hunchback: no room for him.
Hunchback, hunchback, that's all he heard in his silence, in
his sleepless nights.
So he wanted to sleep. To sleep without hearing, to sleep and
to forget. . . .
Hunchback . . . hunchback.

* * *

He poisoned himself.

Of course it was only a "news item".
And of course there was only one corpse.
. . . But how many murderers?

*   *   *

In our absurd and cruel century, no room for the disabled!
No room for the lepers who number 15 million and who rot
alive! . . .
No room for those who are defeated in advance by sickness
or poverty. . . .
No room for old people, those "unproductive beings", those
useless mouths!
There are, in Europe alone, 12 million children either "dis-
placed" or in "compulsory exile".
They belong to no one, and no one wants to have to do with
them.
Before their sad innocence, before their weak little arms, doors
close; barricades are placed at frontiers.
No room for them! No room for them!
Such is the world.
So the world has been since the first day.
So it would have remained until the last day, if . . .

*   *   *

"And she wrapped him in swaddling clothes, and laid him
in a manger, because there was no room for them at the inn"
(Luke 2. 7–14).

*   *   *

Then, everything changed.
Because since that day we've known that everything will
change, that everything is on the way to change.
That a day will come when there'll be room for everybody.

*   *   *

And our hearts have sung, "Noel! Noel!"

*   *   *

And that's why the story of the little hunchback didn't end
with his miserable death.
Because before dying, he gave his eyes. . . .

Killed by human stupidity, he wanted his misfortune not to
be vain. When, at the end of his strength, he hurled himself
into darkness, he gave light to a blind man.

. . . So that there would be "room for him".

From his despair was born a hope.

*   *   *

Noel!

On that Night, in a manger, was born the child of Poverty
whose love was to shake the world . . .

Noel!

Ever since that night, no one has the right to be happy
alone.

THOUGHTS

Man is free in his life like the fish in the river: between the
source and the sea.

We must choose between knowing how to die and not living.

Those who fear death are those who have never lived.

The wise man knows how to make up his mind, free of prejudice.[1]

The sublime superiority of the heart! On earth we cannot
know God, but we can love him.

Holiness is the grace of doing the humblest things under the
sign of eternity.

I like the saints who are not angels.

Happy is he who lives in God;
Blessed is he who dies seeking him.

I don't know God, but I'm known by him: and that is what
Hope is.

How can we despair? We have so much sky above us.

Hope is the ship that leads to the discovery of the new world:
faith. But only charity can cast off the mooring rope.

---

[1] The point of this in the French is the word play: "*Le sage est celui qui sait prendre
parti, sans parti pris.*" (Tr.)

Charity is the most effective of prayers; because it's the most disinterested.

If charity only demanded that we should be charitable, where would be the merit and the joy?

Giving without loving is an offence.

A heart that is not aroused by poverty is very poor.

How can he possibly be happy? He only loves himself.

A person must have done a lot to realize that he hasn't done enough.

If one could go down into the depths of one's heart, how one would pity oneself. . . .

A civilization without love is an ant-heap.

Happiness is the only thing that one is sure of possessing when one has given it.

The reward is to have someone waiting for you.

Win heaven? Let's start by deserving it!

Extracts from *Tour du Monde chez les lépreux* (World Trip to the Lepers), 1953 (out of print).

FRIENDSHIP ISLAND

OUR LITTLE charter plane took off towards the Pacific and quickly gained height. It was a brilliant morning. Below us the green, purple and blue waves were casting recurrent silvery fringes along the beaches of Honolulu. But we hardly noticed that. We were looking for another piece of land, one that was tragic and mysterious.

The natives call it Friendship Island. But Friendship Island was for long a place of horror. It was Molokai.

There were over a thousand lepers there when Father Damen landed. They'd been taken from their homes, forcibly embarked, dumped on the island, abandoned. And Friendship Island re-echoed with their cries of hatred and despair.

Then Charity came. One man, one poor man, alone, whose goodness and heroism lifted hearts and shamed the selfish and cowardly. Father Damien lived with the lepers, caught leprosy from them, and died in their arms, so today Friendship Island has become a land of hope.

There were more than a thousand of them when Father Damien disembarked at Molokai, and he had nothing to give them except his love. But that was what they needed most, and first.

*   *   *

In every room at the hospital Father Patrick introduced me with the words, "He's a friend of Father Pierre."

You should have seen all the faces as they turned towards me, beaming with delight.

"Father Pierre, oh, how is he? When's he coming back? Oh Monsieur," said an old woman, "if only you knew how he loves us!"

Pierre d'Orgeval, a missionary of the Sacred Hearts of Picpus, spent the best years of his life among them, living their life, every moment of their life, tucking them up at night, playing the piano to them to soothe their sufferings and help them to sleep, then going to the chapel to pray to him who cured lepers.

By singing, he taught them to sing,
By loving, he taught them to live.

A few years ago he returned to France, his homeland, where the old missionary was given a triumphal welcome in his native village. But at Kalaupapa in Molokai the lepers still watch the horizon in the hope of seeing the "bird" that will bring him back.

Love, always love. It's only love that does everything.

*   *   *

The car rolled gently through the dream-like landscape, putting to flight now the mina-birds absurdly strutting about, now the enchanting Japanese turtle-doves with their unending cooing. We arrived. And there in the valley stood the first church built by Father Damien beside the first Protestant temple. Two apostles lived there who were also two friends. What a lesson and what an example!

Then we saw his tomb. Very simple, black with a tall cross and this inscription in silver letters:

SACRED TO THE MEMORY
OF THE REV FATHER
DAMIEN DEVEUSTER
DIED A MARTYR TO THE LOVE
FOR THE AFFLICTED
15 APRIL 1889.

The body is no longer there. The poor leper was taken from the land of his suffering and joy and forced to accept glory. The body was received in triumph by the Belgians, including the king. Meanwhile at Kalawao in Molokai the lepers continue to put flowers on his tomb. As with Charles de Foucauld in the desert, Father Damien's soul, with his love, remains on Molokai.

*   *   *

Back at the hospital.

He was sitting on his bed, blind, but smiling at I know not what. . . . Beside him was a guitar.

"Will you play us something?" asked Father Patrick. Then, to me, "He's a composer."

Play something? In spite of myself, I jumped. For this man had no fingers. At least he had fingers to just half-an-inch above the knuckles.

The leper hesitated. He said something aside to the missionary who burst out laughing. "He's got stage-fright."

Stage-fright! If he could have seen me at that moment, he'd have known which of us was frightened.

And then the thing happened.

With his fingerless hands, the leper played. Under his vanished fingers a tune was born, tender, sad and sweet. So sweet and sad that you could have wept (and it would have been such a relief to do so, if only the sick gathered around us were not watching us so intently. . . .).

A ballad, a gentle love-song, a song of peace and love. It swelled, faded away, came to life again, like suffering and hope.

A deep silence descended on Friendship Island. And the poor monstrous heads swung up and down in time with the tune. Now one could only see souls. And hideous death, death lurking in the shadows, dared not mock. For a moment something from heaven seemed to touch us. Father Damien had come back.

Q

THE ISLAND OF THE DAMNED

No, it's not some ghoulish fairy-story.
No, it didn't happen in the Middle Ages.

* * *

Taenga. One of the eighty-four Tuamotu Islands, coral atolls lost in the Pacific.

When the doctor passed on his yearly visit he examined a young woman. There were suspicious marks. "It could be leprosy," he said aside to someone. "I'll have to see her again."

Unfortunately he had said it too loud. No sooner had he sailed off than the village chief had the "suspect" woman seized. She was torn from her husband and five children, dragged to a canoe, and abandoned on one of the Tuamotus eight kilometres away. And her dog went with her.

Neither her own tears and cries nor the terrified dog's howls were heard. Fear of leprosy excused everything. Even crime.

This woman was twenty-five years old.

Six years passed.

For six years she was alone, alone with her dog. Trained to fish, the dog provided her with her miserable rations. Meanwhile every week a canoe cautiously approached the damned shores. Without disembarking, without even drawing up alongside, someone threw some food and a can of water ashore. Then rowed off again at top speed. This went on for six years.

* * *

"The last time I saw her," this canoeist told me, "her feet couldn't support her any more; they'd been eaten away. I left her a little flour, but what could she do with it? Her fingers are so decayed that in kneading the dough she'd leave lumps of her flesh in it. . . . The dog has grown old. He was prowling surlily round her so-called bed."

There was a silence. The man looked away so that I wouldn't see the tears in his eyes.

Then suddenly he burst out with, "How's it going to finish, Monsieur? Shall I tell you?

"The day will come when she won't be able to get up at all. The dog will be hungry, very hungry. He'll sniff the dying woman. And as soon as she's dead – or before if he's hungry enough – he'll eat her.

"That's what'll happen, Monsieur. And there's nothing I can
do. Nothing. . . ."

And the man walked away, and I saw his shoulders shaking as
he disappeared into the night.

* * *

"It's true," the doctor told me. "I saw her too, when I was in
charge of the Tuamotus. As soon as my schooner drew near I
counted the eight coconut trees and the few stunted bushes on the
island. That's all it consists of. And a hovel made with anything
she could find. She came out of it – she could still just walk at that
time – and shouted to me: 'Don't come near! I've got leprosy!'
'What the hell does that matter to me? I'm a medico,' I said. Then
she smiled. Her first smile for years.

"She implored me to take her away with me, but I couldn't.
The crew refused. The crew said they'd leave the boat if she came
aboard."

I said I could imagine her anger and despair.

The doctor looked at me. Then, gently, "She wasn't angry,
Monsieur, not even bitter. She said, 'I understand'. And I wanted
to ask her forgiveness."

* * *

Naturally this isn't the first place where I've recounted this
terrible and heart-breaking story.

Response and help came quickly.

Five days later the excellent M. Ahnne, Administrator of the
Tuamotu Islands, accompanied by a nurse, set out for Taenga
on board the *Tamara*.

When I put down at San Francisco on my return journey I
received this telegram from Tony Bambridge:

"Taenga leper saved. Stop. Arrived Papeete. Very happy. It's
you who have done it all by your words and example. Thank
you."

CONDEMNED BY DIVINE RIGHT

I wanted to visit the outcasts, and it went beyond the limits of
horror. How can they go on living, how can they "last", how
can they hang on to life? They're piled up in hovels that they've
made with filth and covered up with old newspapers.

And how will they hang on in two months, when the monsoon

comes, and when it'll rain twenty days a month for three months, and sometimes so violently that the water comes half-way up the wheels of the cars on the roads?

They'll die. One fewer! Ten, a hundred, a thousand fewer! And all one can wish for them is to die quickly so as to suffer less.

But how about the others? There are thousands of them, hundreds of thousands, millions!

There are too many. . . .

* * *

I wanted to see them. I wanted to bring them help.

What happened? As soon as I got out of the car a horde of howling and threatening skeletons assailed me, besieged me, clung to my clothes, gripped my hands, paralysed me. . . . I had the awful feeling that I was going to be knocked down, trodden on, suffocated, before having been able to tell these wretches that I loved them.

Anyway they would certainly have laughed. It would have seemed to them a bad joke. Perhaps an insult. No one loves them, so why should I, who didn't even know them? And then what good could it do them? They don't ask to be loved. They're hungry, that's all. Too hungry.

I tried to free myself, reach my pocket. I had prepared for them . . . but it was no use. All those faces close to mine, sneering, howling. All those hands holding me fast. . . . I was their prisoner, and I wanted so much to be their friend.

And the police – yes, that's right, the police – had to come and set me free.

I had to be freed from this unhappiness, defended from those I wanted to help. They didn't understand. Why should they? They were hungry, too hungry.

My saviour, however, looked at me reprovingly. At the drop of a hat he would have issued me with a summons. For having to do with people under police supervision, I suppose. An offence quite unknown here.

I looked at his face which showed no sign of pity. For him, as for everyone here, want is a punishment from heaven. Hunger is chastisement that ratifies wrongs committed in a previous life. The poor are condemned by divine right.

They're paying their debt to God, like gaol-birds to Society. So . . . what of Charity?

It's a word that can't have any meaning. Because poverty is a punishment, and it "isn't done" to oppose the divine will. In this terrible country, Charity is the only thing that isn't infectious.

THE HOUSE OF HORROR

It was Holy Saturday. Holy Saturday is nearly Easter. It's a day when you don't expect visitors, so there's nothing ready – and nothing hidden either.

An American doctor was with me – a fine chap if ever there was one. He had left his star-spangled banner, his cottage and his ice-cream for this vain and squalid country. In the hope of doing good. Doing good is his reason for being. And he tries. He dedicates himself – with a simplicity that is not without grandeur – to looking after these people who make fun of him and cheat him. . . .

We arrived at the entrance to the leper-colony. The entrance was a guard-room. With guns and a radio set. Guns, indeed! So the guards hadn't had time to disguise themselves as nurses. I called to my friend. He had stopped in front of the radio, and I saw him shaking his head sadly.

The radio was an American present. For the lepers. Only in order to get to the lepers you have to pass the guards. And when a radio set is being delivered it's easy for the guards to imagine themselves lepers.

Along the walls of the passages – statistics. True ones. Two hundred and ninety-seven invalids. I heard the good doctor murmur, "But they told me six hundred. I always send money and provisions for six hundred."

Dear Doctor, what you don't realize is that there are guards. And the guards are hungry. Especially when it's the Americans or the French who are paying.

* * *

We went in. It was ghastly and unbelievable.

Idiots gaping vacuously, epileptics frightening the paralysed – good and proper ones, frothing at the mouth . . . and lepers too, of course. There had to be lepers because "this" was called a leper-colony. But it wasn't a leper-colony. It was a rubbish-heap, where all the jumbled refuse of humanity had been dumped. As society doesn't want to kill its refuse, it lets it rot. It makes it rot. I don't think I've ever seen anything quite so awful.

And we felt powerless, useless, bound hand and foot.

We would have liked to run away, we would have liked not to have come, not to have seen. We were cowardly in our turn.

And I didn't dare photograph that contorted creature with twisted hands and feet and eyes turned upwards, who was writhing about and filling the place with his howls.

I didn't dare photograph that dying man eaten up with gangrene whose closed eyes were already covered with white mushrooms. I refrained from crying out, "Can't you hurry up and die!" I held myself back so as not to cry out. . . .

I didn't dare take the children away from where they were mournfully playing beside this putrefaction, nor approach that breathing corpse from whose fissured skin seeped a ghastly yellowish liquid.

I didn't dare, I didn't dare. I was ashamed, I was ashamed.

And we looked at each other, the doctor and I. And, without saying a word, we took each other's hand, prompted by the need not to feel alone, not to be frightened.

For it was fear that had us in its grip.

*　　*　　*

Depressing return in the twilight. Probably the guards stood at the window watching the two strangers disappearing into the night, silently, holding hands. . . . Then, as a distraction, they listened to *La vie en rose*.

We returned. The canal was bathed in sweetness. Boats passed us with young couples singing, embracing. . . . And in my mind's eye I saw the man who'd been writhing about like some monstrous worm. And the man who was rotten through and through but who couldn't stop living; and the guns of the guards, and the blind old woman who was cutting the grass of that enclosure where the posts looked like crosses.

The doctor knew, and his hand pressed mine. We were friends, allies, because we love the people that no one else loves, over there in that communal grave. People who die as they were born and as they've lived: without hope.

A leper-colony without love is a graveyard.

THE DOCTOR TOLD ME . . .

"How many lepers are there in this country?" I asked a doctor friend.

"Perhaps twenty or thirty thousand."

"And how many do you look after?"

"About seven hundred and fifty."

I said nothing, and this excellent man, so dedicated to his art, went on:

"You're surprised, perhaps even shocked. But you have to know something about it before judging us. Here leprosy is a fetish illness, an honour that it shares with smallpox and tuberculosis. Leprosy is a punishment inflicted by the fetish. Because you've transgressed its law, because you haven't respected the 'interdict' that forbids you – you, especially – to kill and eat such-and-such an animal, for instance, because it's part of your ancestors.

"Don't laugh. And as leprosy is the fetish's punishment the leper belongs to the fetish-man. He has to pay, and dearly, if the man is to try and purify him, while the neighbours will pay dearly too so as to be protected from 'punishment'.

"When a leper dies without the hoped-for cure, it's the fetish-man who inherits his possessions. Better, he inherits his body. And he sells it – still more dearly – to the family which sometimes incurs endless debts so as to buy it back. . . ."

"But this is appalling."

"That's how it is. And no one would dare so much as to raise a murmur, because the fetish-man holds the secret of poisons. And he makes use of it. And that's why such-and-such a person whom you see in a smart green felt hat, or looking posh in his new car, who thinks himself evolved, civilized, all ready to give us a lesson in civilization, trembles before the sorcerer, pays his tribute, and is 'fetishist' like everyone else."

"How about the Christians?"

"There we must make a distinction. There are Christians, and plenty of them, who make an extraordinary and sometimes horrifying mixture of their Christian religion and their ancient beliefs. And it's not so very uncommon to find the fetish Atigali – the rage at the moment – enthroned in the same house as the Sacred Heart. Fetishists, you know, are in the habit of burying their dead in their houses. Go to any Mission church and you'll find it crowded out. Then go to the Christian cemetery and you'll observe that there's a mere scattering of graves. You'd think the Church's faithful were immortal. . . . But the truth is that they haven't really abandoned their old practices."

"It's disheartening."

"Not really. Not when you remember the centuries of superstition weighing on them, the terror that still reigns, and the influence of the family. The Christians who are really Christians deserve praise. But they're sowing for the future."

"And the lepers?"

"Yes, the lepers, we'd forgotten them, like everyone else. Well, the lepers are very difficult to reach and in certain tribes they're absolutely inaccessible because they mustn't be tended. They're the domain of the fetish-man, they're his preserve. And that brings him money."

"It's the most disgusting commerce I've ever heard of."

"Here, it's just life. The Blacks don't believe it any more but they go on behaving as if they do. Because they're frightened."

There was a heavy silence.

Then the old doctor continued in a far-away voice: "In Normandy, the apple-trees will soon be in blossom."

EVERY DAY FOR THE LAST FORTY YEARS . . .

She's not a sports champion or a film-star. Her name isn't associated with any scandal; she's never been divorced or broken a record or lost a pearl necklace.

She's called . . . what is she called? No one has ever known. For the other missionaries, her sisters, and for the lepers, her children, she's just Anne-Marie. Sister Anne-Marie.

When she arrived in the leper-colony hidden on the high plateaux of Madagascar she was twenty-five years old. She was young, lively, pretty.

That was forty years ago. For forty years she has never left her post. Not for one day. Not for Christmas nor for Easter. Not when her Superior told her that her father, in France, had died. Then her mother. Nor has she ever rested. Bending over her lepers, she has never raised her eyes except to look at heaven.

The fine young girl who dedicated herself to the most rewarding and most distressing apostolate has now become a little old woman, her face baked and baked again by the tropical sun. But her eyes . . . they contain the whole sky.

She goes with small steps, trotting like a mouse, through the huge house. But as she passes she arouses a wave of fervour. And all the lepers, trying so hard to bring a smile to their corroded lips, greet her with the simple words: "Good morning, mother!"

THE FUNERAL

While I was visiting the leper-colony, the bell began to toll. Slowly. Sorrowfully. The knell.

But in this centre of tragedy, one is surprised not to hear the knell all the time.

This morning a leper stopped suffering. He'd be put under the earth almost immediately. You have to do it quickly here.

He was at rest in his open coffin. Perhaps he was at rest for the first time. His eyes were shut, his face very gentle. They had put a garland of flowers round his neck, a cross on his breast.

Two candles were burning, and all around the sick were slowly and silently circulating. And as I passed, each one smiled at me sadly. And each held out his hand to condole with me. For we were his family. Because his family wasn't there.

He was a leper, you see, and even dead a leper's a leper. And in the depths of their squalid hearts, "they" were mighty relieved to hear the sad news. A leper in the family; people might get to know. . . .

Much better for him to be in the grave. After all it's easier to forget him.

* * *

Forget him, do. You're not worthy of his suffering or his death.

He's no need of you so as to sleep. His friends are here, the ones who've brought him flowers.

And the white mothers, the missionaries who have nursed him, loved him, and who, kneeling on the bare earth, are praying for him. He's no need of anyone. He's cured.

Cured, you understand? While you, you'll go on rotting in your foul selfishness and your prejudices.

And because he's with God, he knows now who are the real lepers. . . .

Extracts from *Des hommes comme les autres*
(Men like other Men), 1956 (out of print).

CONDEMNED TO DEATH

HE HAD SAID, "I don't want to stay here."

But the law is absolute: lepers must be isolated, shut up. And it's the police who take charge of it. We can guess how.

He escaped. He was recaptured. He was brought back handcuffed.

He said, "I'll do it again."

And he did. And once again he had the police on his tracks. He was caught, handcuffed, brought back.

He said, "If they catch me this time, I'll kill myself."

And he escaped a third time. And he hid. But he was found and caught.

He killed himself.

FOR ALWAYS

A hospital with a hundred beds, "colonial" style. Too big, thank God, for in this country people aren't often ill.

The lepers' wing was separated from the rest by a wire fence, no more; a far cry from the electrified barbed wire that I've sometimes seen.

There were twelve patients there, excellently cared for and content with their lot. Well and good. But what was this little girl doing there, a little girl of twelve? There was nothing wrong with her: an absolutely clean bill of health. But, you see, she was born at the Désirade. Where the lepers are; and of leper parents. So she had to go on living with lepers. Where else could she go? Who would want her?

"Where do you come from?"

"From where the lepers are."

"And your parents?"

"They're dead. They were lepers."

That's all. But it's enough.

It's enough for a healthy little girl, an innocent and pretty little girl, to be condemned to live with lepers for ever. . . . By people who go to Mass and are convinced that God is pleased with them.

NO LEPERS HERE

"There are no lepers here," said the Minister for Foreign Affairs of this country.

Shall I send him some addresses?

A few kilometres from the capital, there's the desert. In the desert there are some huts made of earth. That's all. No vegetation. No water. Here a hundred and fifty victims are waiting for death. They do nothing. And nothing is done to them. The Archbishop and I took them some provisions. They accepted them, resigned, without smiling. Just one old man whose red eyes were streaming with tears all the time beneath the cruel sun, clasped his hands to thank me when I gave him my glasses. What can one say to them? What can one promise them?

I can do nothing. There are no lepers here. So what?

As we went away we came on some filthy ponds full of enormous crocodiles. Night was falling on this sad, depressed and pallid landscape. The vultures were making huge circles above the Tower of Silence where the Parsees throw the corpses of their kinsfolk after having broken the bones.

It's really only the vultures who are happy here.

LEPER IN PERPETUITY

At his birth he'd been handed over to the missionaries. He was a fine child, robust, cheerful, and thriving well.

At twenty, the recruiting board; passed fit for service. Soldier, corporal, sergeant. Exemplary conduct. Good and brave. Daring in battle.

To tell the truth, it wasn't difficult for him to risk death; what frightened him was getting back to barracks.

Everyone drew away from him, shunned him. During time off his comrades-at-arms became strangers. A bit ashamed, perhaps, of being such cowards. . . .

But just put yourself in their place: on his service certificate were the words, "Born in the leper-colony of. . ."

So you see, to die is nothing. But to approach a leper, touch the hand of a leper. . . .

* * *

But this man isn't a leper.

No, I know. That's what they say. But all the same. . . .

Of course doctors have seen him, examined him, analysed him, sounded him.

But they always might be wrong. . . .

Of course he's a good companion, brave and loyal. We'd like so much to be his friend. . . .

But you see, he's a leper.

*   *   *

One day he found my address and wrote to me. Such a sad world-weary letter. "Can't my service certificate be altered, so that that line is deleted? Or how can I go on living since no one wants me to live?"

I made various moves. Oh, I was very well received. But change someone's civil status? What are you dreaming of? It's a great injustice, there's a man who can't go on. . . . But, Monsieur, you can't go against the regulations.

So I had to go to the President of the Republic himself to obtain the suppression of the "defamatory" line that some imbecile clerk had inserted . . . and to ensure that a healthy, good and brave man should cease to be condemned to leprosy in perpetuity.

HAPPINESS BOUGHT IN A SHOP

A leper-colony. No more or less horrible than many others. The lepers are given what they need so as not to die. But as for living. . . .

There's a little boy of seven or eight there who has a small mark on his forehead, no more. The beginnings of leprosy that a short sulphone cure would dispel for ever.

But the trouble is that he is in the leper-colony, and no one leaves a leper-colony. Not even when dead, because the graveyard, "their graveyard," is also surrounded by barbed wire.

The doctor is a weak man with frightened eyes. I said to him, "But, Doctor, you know perfectly well that this child isn't infectious. His illness could disappear in a few weeks. And if he stays here among all these sick people, all these creatures rotten with syphilis as well as leprosy, he'll be lost. He'll rot like the others. Look, he's so young, and he can still smile. Open the gates."

And as he said nothing, I went on, "At his age, children need their mother. He must have a mother somewhere. He must go and find his mother."

The man looked at me, shocked. "But he's very happy here, Monsieur," he said; "we've bought him a bicycle."

What could I say? I was in a strange country. I was a foreigner. And how could I make this wretched man see that a "civilization" that thinks it can replace a mother by a bicycle is sad, bad and barbarous?

GOTEMBA-SHI

As you go out of the village there's a little road. A signpost points to the Hospital of the Resurrection. It's the oldest leper centre in Japan, founded in 1889 by a French missionary, Father Testevide. This charming and sunny name suggests better than anything the charity that radiates from the place.

We were received by three French Canadian missionary nuns and two Fathers from the Foreign Missions. One of these was young and came from Lorraine; the other was Basque, Father Anchen, who has been in Japan for fifty-two years.

A quiet and smiling nurse was standing by a table. She was introduced to me and I greeted her without paying much attention. This was my mistake, for which I could kick myself, for this woman is a heroine – Mademoiselle Hori.

When she came here many years ago she didn't come as a nurse. In fact she didn't *come* at all, she was dumped. She was an orphan, and on the pretext of some kind of skin rash some distant relatives put her in the nearest leper-colony so as to be rid of her. And in those days once you were in a leper-colony you were a leper.

Many years later it was perceived that the little girl who had been dumped there sobbing had not got, and never had had, leprosy. But by now the little girl had become a young woman. She refused the freedom that was offered her and was her right. She thought without bitterness of her relations, those torturers with so much leprosy in their hearts. For their vile and cowardly action had enabled her to find her vocation.

She then graduated in the Order of Leprosy by becoming a nurse and a Christian. And for the past twenty-five years she has nursed her companions and made them her brothers through love.

Paradise is loving each other.

THE CANNIBAL

"Come and shake hands with our cannibal," said the young missionary nun who was showing me over the leper-colony.

Somewhat curious, I followed her.

The man was tall, appallingly thin, and greeted me politely.

He must have come from Nigeria, for he spoke English. We made small talk for a while, then I couldn't restrain myself any longer.

"Is it true, what Sister tells me?" He bowed smiling, as if flattered. "You really have eaten . . . ?" He gave a really big smile now, and I noticed what fine teeth he had.

Then I asked him the silliest possible question. "And was it . . . good?"

I shall never forget his eyes. Greedy eyes, filled with longing. And he said in English, "Very good, Sir."

I didn't press for further details.

On the way back I said to the Sister: "But why on earth is he so thin?"

She eyed me sadly. "It's because his taste is spoilt for any other meat . . . so you see . . ."

I did.

WITH THE LITTLE PEOPLE

They live by themselves. Savage, but not aggressive. Prodigiously brave and skilful huntsmen. They live in huts in groups of thirty to fifty, not more – huts made of three tree branches stuck in the earth and joined at the top, then covered over with leaves. They drink mineral water, or rather vegetable water. The water that flows from liana once it's been separated, that sweet clear water. If it gets turbid, they don't drink it.

Their hearts, too, are gentle and clear. But they get angry if you approach their wife, their one wife, or if some danger threatens their children.

Savage? I'm not sure. Is it really savage to refuse the "civilization" offered to them?

If they trade with other men, they avoid all contact with them. At night they go to the entrance of the village with the game they are selling. The following night they go back to the same place to fetch the payment – millet.

Ignorance, indifference, contempt?
Who can say?

* * *

The Babinga pygmies are very much the same. Their huts are round, very low, and made entirely with leaves. Each contains several "rooms", which are really no more than partitions.

Like their brothers in the Congo, they hunt. But they seem less tough than the Batswa. They don't attack head on, but lay traps. Their favourite weapon is the cross-bow. They throw minute arrows poisoned with strophantus.

They don't seem to be much affected by the so-called social diseases. They live so near nature. They live on nature. However, leprosy has not spared them. But the terrible scourge for them is the yaws. In some of the Babinga tribes 80% are affected.

People try to emancipate them, wrest them from the often tyrannical tutelage of the "songha-songhas" whom they call with respect "real men", but their gentle and resigned nature always wins the day.

. . . Until such time as, tired of being misused and exploited, they move off. One morning their huts are found to be empty. The forest has closed around them. Beneath its protection they have gone off to pursue their peaceful if miniature destiny.

I CAN SEE. . . .

For I don't know how many years he'd been living at the back of his dark hovel. He'd been crouching there, enclosed in his double night. He was blind. His leprosy had made him blind, and there was nothing to do but rot in this tomb.

Oh yes, he was taking the sulphone drugs that the missionary Sister brought every day. Just to please her – because, though he couldn't see, he knew she was smiling.

"He won't come out," she told me one day when I visited him. "He hasn't come out for months, perhaps years. Do try to make him listen to reason."

So I tried, and I backed up my words with gestures. "You're going to come out. With me. Now, at once. I shall lead you." And meanwhile I had taken him by the arm. Together we stumbled forward as far as the sun-lit doorway.

And then something happened that I shall never forget as long as I live. Having reached full day-light, the man let out a loud cry: "I can see!"

For the first time since leprosy had filled him with night, surrounded him with night, light had pierced the darkness. And he shouted to everything, to the trees, the stones, the sky: "I can see! I can see!"

But he couldn't yet see well enough to notice that our eyes were full of tears.

I SHALL GO BACK

This morning at 7 o'clock there was a knock at the door of my room in the Pacific Hotel at Numea. Two workmen were there on their way to work bringing a hundred francs each for the lepers. By midday seventy-two people had called on me, each with his modest but so moving offering. . . .

The largest of these offerings was a thousand and twenty-five francs, the collection made among the sick and the staff (native and European) of the hospital's tuberculosis department. Tubercular victims to the rescue of leprosy victims. . . . What more touching symbol of the Charity that must save the world?

In the afternoon I went to visit these kind benefactors.

In a little bed there was a Sister, as white as her white sheets, who was dying. She was attached to the leprosy service at Ducos, and by a cruel stroke of fate it was tuberculosis that was killing her.

Fever possessed her and in her delirium she was saying softly: "I shall go back . . . I shall go back." She turned her wandering eyes towards us and suddenly there was anguish in them. "I shall go back."

Those were her last words.

STRONGER THAN DEATH

A leper-colony. In the most harrowing, most odious sense of the word. Men who do nothing, to whom nothing is done, and who endlessly roam round their courtyard, their cage.

Lonely men. Worse, abandoned men. For whom everything is already silence and night.

But one of them, just one, still has bright eyes. He can still smile and, when he is offered something, say thank you.

Just one of them, one, has remained a man.

The nun wanted to know the cause of this miracle, wanted to know what held him to life. She watched him.

And she saw that every day a face appeared over the high, rough wall. A small face, a woman's face, and it smiled at him. And the man was there, waiting to receive the smile, the nourishment of his hope and strength. He smiled in his turn and the face disappeared again. Then he started waiting for tomorrow.

When he saw that the nun had been watching, he said simply, "It's my wife."

And after a silence: "Before I came here, she looked after me in secret. With whatever she could get hold of. A fetish-man gave her an ointment which she smeared on my face every day – except in one small corner, where she kissed me. But it was no good. Then I was found, hauled in. But she followed me. And when I see her every day, I know through her that I am alive."

Extracts from *Trente fois le tour du monde* (Thirty Times round the World), 1961.

THE CAGE

IN A SMALL TOWN there was a well-known and respected man.

He fell ill. The doctor was summoned. Leprosy.

And then everything started.

He was no longer to be seen in the street, no longer to be seen in his house.

His family shut him up in his room. And not only in his room, but under the mosquito net that surrounded his bed and from which he was forbidden to emerge "so as not to contaminate the atmosphere of the house". In spite of which they consented to slip in a little nourishment under the bed, and then leave him.

His mosquito-net became his world. He saw no one except through his net-prison. His cage.

Then one day he managed to escape, get free. And so as really to get free, he killed himself.

He was a well-known and respected man, and his suicide caused a stir. His body was found, examined. There had been some error; someone had made a mistake: the dead man hadn't got, and never had had, leprosy.

Only he was dead . . . dead from having been a "leper".

But who killed him?

R

THE PHANTOM LEPER-COLONY

Fifteen kilometres from a large town, a large town full of cars, cars which on Saturdays take to the roads. . . . Fifteen kilometres from this large town there are twenty-two lepers, hidden, gone to earth. When we went to visit them we weren't expected, naturally. It's a long time since they've expected anyone.

The chief had a ravaged face and two extinguished eyes. Stumbling, he showed us round. It didn't take long; there was nothing to see. All was ruin and desolation. In the "dispensary" there were exactly three field-dressing outfits – three. They must be kept there as curiosities, for the lepers' sores were bare and bleeding. The astonishing thing is that there should be a "dispensary" at all. For this "centre" isn't marked on the Health Service map. A phantom leper-colony, fifteen kilometres from a large town.

We questioned our blind guide. "How about food?" we asked.

"We get a hundred kilos of rice every three months – I don't know who from."

According to my calculations, that made fifty grams of rice per person per day. But I may have been wrong; I realized I was extremely agitated as if trying to shake off a nightmare.

I said to the chief: "Your miseries are at an end. We shall undertake to feed you and tend you. Immediately." But he wanted to say something. What was it? He hesitated. I tried to help. "Tell me what you want to say. It doesn't matter what it is. Say it. Don't be frightened." Then in a strangely soft voice the blind man said, "Could you send us a pick and shovel?" Then, more softly still, and almost with shame, "It's so as to be able to bury our dead. Because, you see, our hands being as they are. . . ."

We wanted to cry.

At that moment an almost limbless woman came wriggling over the ground like a huge worm and offered my wife an egg. An egg: her whole wealth. She had seen us arriving in our good car, seen us alighting in our clean clothes, seen the imbecile smile on our faces. She knew nothing about us except that we had all the things that she lacked. And yet she didn't want to throw stones. No, she had come to greet us, to give something to us. We had no option but to accept, though our hearts were rent. We had to give her the joy of being the one to give first.

. . . We were about to leave. I hardly dared hold out my hand.

And yet it was that gesture, and not all the things I'd promised, that brought the first smile to their faces.

We set off very slowly in the car, very slowly, so as not to let ourselves think we were fleeing.

THIRTY FRANCS FOR A MURDERER, EIGHT FRANCS FOR A LEPER

You stare and rub your eyes and wonder if it's all a bad dream. No, it isn't possible!

Perhaps it isn't possible, but it happens to be *true*. Yes, it's true.

In one of the provinces of a country I've visited recently, the Administration (with a capital A) allocates thirty francs a day for food for prisoners and eight francs a day for food for lepers.

They told me *they* didn't know that this was the case. For when the Administration is confronted with a monstrosity of this kind, it loses its capital A. It disintegrates, gets diluted, fades away. It becomes "they". All right then, let's find this "they", grab hold of it by the collar, force it to its knees and make it cry for mercy!

And then the traveller goes away, the vagabond wanders off, the dust settles, and as soon as the tiresome intruder has disappeared into the aeroplane, "they" become the Administration again, capital A and all.

But not this time! No, this time they must come clean and say who's responsible. And those who say nothing, whatever their rank, will be regarded as accomplices. And denounced as such.

Thirty francs to feed a murderer, eight francs to feed a leper.

While awaiting developments, *I asked the Government of this country, from the Administrative point of view, to put the victims of leprosy on the same footing as common prisoners.*

Because, after all, I can't advise lepers to kill their neighbour so as to be able to eat.

MILLIONAIRE LEPERS

The Minister told me, "We spend nearly a million a year on each hospitalized patient." Excellent.

To tell the truth it seemed too good to be true.

I've seen these "millionaire" lepers. There are four hundred of them living in rather wretched dormitories whose cleanliness leaves much to be desired. They are sad and badly clothed.

But there is a staff of two hundred and fifty to look after them (or rather, not to look after them), and they're well-fed, comfortably lodged, and have an unbelievable array of white overalls at their disposal.

Here, it's the staff that is looked after.

A BROKEN LEG

A woman got into a taxi. During the journey she looked at the driver who had some kind of a rash on his face. And suddenly panic seized her: suppose he was a leper? She had never seen a leper, but this man had little spots on his face, and spots could only mean leprosy!

So, wild with fright, she jumped from the taxi while it was going, rolled on to the road and broke her leg. Despite the pain she dragged herself to the house of some friends, took off all her clothes, burned them, borrowed some others, and arrived haggard and dishevelled at home.

There her children received her, her children who are now loyal friends and assiduous visitors to victims of leprosy in that little town.

Real leprosy is fear.

THE LEPER-COLONY AT THE END OF THE WORLD

To get to the town in question there are two possibilities. One way takes three hours, the other three weeks.

Three hours if the weather permits a flight across the Andes which, at the point in question, are not exactly inviting. Otherwise it's a matter of going by river as far as the Amazon. Three weeks.

I said to myself, "Let's do it in three hours".

The weather was an ally on that occasion. The aeroplane crossed the Cordilleras at good speed and arrived on the small air-field at more or less the right time.

"Where's the leper-colony?" I asked.

"The leper-colony? Oh, it's a little bit further on."

"Further on?"

"Yes, you must go down the Amazon."

"How far?"

"It'll take you a day and a half if all goes well. But for coming back you must allow a good three days because of the current, you see."

What I did see was that I couldn't spare four and a half days just looking at a river. What could I do? Near the town the army disposed of a small naval air base. Let's try our luck!

At dawn next day my wife and I embarked on a military seaplane. There were three places. Perfectly adequate (after all, it's preferable to have a pilot). We had to fly above the Amazon for seven hundred kilometres. We landed, somehow, on the river at a point where it was six kilometres wide and carrying down enormous tree trunks.

"Where's the leper-colony?" I asked the missionaries who came to greet us.

"It's a bit further on. . . ."

Thank God it wasn't too far. In fact it wouldn't have been possible to go much further. Finally our canoe reached "the leper-colony at the end of the world".

There were eight hundred victims. In his speech the village chief said to me quite simply, "Thank you. We were waiting for you. It's twenty years since anyone has held out a hand to us. . . ."

YOU GO TO THE PLACE DE LA CONCORDE

I'd been told that "they" wanted to make a leper-colony. But "they" haven't got many lepers, and most of them are non-infectious at that. But "they" are frightened. So "they" have bought a desert island: Aboukissa.

"Aboukissa?"

"Yes, near Santo."

"Santo?"

"Yes, the New Hebrides."

I'd got it. It was easy. You go to the Place de la Concorde and you dig a big hole. When you come out the other end you swim a few strokes and there you are.

All the same I went by another route. I reached Port-Vila, then Santo. I stayed two days in each island. I met the French resident and his English colleague (whom I'd known already in Mauritius), the French doctors and the English doctors. I boarded the cutter *Rossinante*, old Don Quixote of leprosy, and arrived at Aboukissa. It was a terrible place.

On my return I said to the two who were responsible: "It's out of the question." They answered: "We agree." Besides, in the English hospital at Port-Vila, and in the French one at Santo, I had found four lepers side by side with other patients, and the latter didn't seem to be showing any fear. I added: "Leper-colonies are being closed down everywhere in the world; surely you don't want to *open* one here!"

They repeated, "No, there won't be a leper-colony."

*   *   *

When we put in at Port-Vila on the return journey, two new friends came on board. "Thank you," they said, "for having opened our eyes; opened our hearts. But we know that your work is far from finished, and that you've got a long way to go before all the lepers of the world are 'men like other men'. We want to give you offerings for the sick that you'll be visiting on your way. Some are from Europeans, some from Vietnamese, and some from Chinese."

And this little land at the other end of the world, freed from its fear, handed over 415,000 francs to me, to help me free others from fear.

HIS TREASURE

In a stylish little hospital (yes, stylish is the word) there were twenty lepers. We visited them, conducted by the mayor.

There was an old man at the end of a ward who beckoned to me from his bed. I recognized him. I had first met him at the Désirade. The nightmare of that place came back to me.

He made me sit by his bed and said in a soft voice: "Listen. I'm near the end. I'm going to die. Don't try to lie to me or comfort me. My wife is going to die too. We've nothing left. Nothing but these ear-rings which I gave her a long time ago. Before, you understand? *Before*. Take them. They'll help you give a little joy to another victim who's not been so lucky as us here, who's not been cared for and loved."

I hardly dared hold out my hand. He placed his treasure in it and closed my fingers over it. Then – I couldn't speak, I was too near tears – I kissed him and went, like a thief, with his treasure.

IN ONE GENERATION

We were in Upper Volta. During the meal the doctor who was with me said:

"Twenty-five years ago, when I left college, I was assigned to an island in the Indian Ocean. One night there was a knock at my door. Two men came in. 'We've come to fetch you on a sick call,' they said; 'but you mustn't know where we're going. Not you, or anyone else. So I'm afraid we must blindfold you.' I was startled by this and wanted to protest. But I was also young, and mystery allured me. My two visitors couldn't have evil designs, they seemed so unhappy. So I consented. We followed the most improbable route. I realized that several times we were back in the same place. Finally we arrived. The bandage was taken from my eyes. A man was lying in bed. I saw at once that he was a leper. And I discovered later that he lived two houses away from me!"

We smiled, and silence fell between us.

Then a little girl came into the room, the daughter of the doctor who was our host. She was holding the hand of a superb Black, who seemed both proud and shy.

"Hullo," said our hostess, "here's one who might have been a patient of yours, doctor." We looked at her and she went on: "Yes, he's a cured leper. But the children are so attached to him that I kept him. He looks after them with such tender care. . . ."

Between these two anecdotes lies the "Fight against Leprosy", with its struggles and victories.

BUT THERE ARE THOSE WHO DIE OF HUNGER

A missionary nun, living in the heart of the African bush, told me:

"We can only dress the wounds of the worst sufferers, because we haven't enough compresses and bandages. But that's not the most serious problem. Our great worry is lack of food. These poor people eat only once a day, and not all of them at that. And their food doesn't contain the sustenance required by their condition. They never eat meat or fish or sugar or milk or eggs, but only millet and sauces made with water with pimento and the herbs that grow round about. And what about the children! Sometimes they go several days without eating. It's quite terrible in this poor country that no one bothers about.

"Many lepers die simply of hunger. . . ."

And now, look in your mirror, and draw your conclusions.

VICTORY

We saw them the moment the Paris plane touched down at Lamentin. And we saw nothing else but them. Twelve girls dressed in bright West Indian costume. Twelve girls – fresh, graceful, pretty – who were singing:

"Monsieur Follereau, gentle Martinique
again offers you welcome."

Twelve girls who were laughing at life, at the sun, at their joy.

Twelve lepers.

Doctor Montestruc was there, benign giant of friendship. It was he who had brought them. Only he could do a thing like that.

Ten years ago, and perhaps less, "they" wouldn't have allowed it. Just imagine – at an airport! "They" had said yes, and smiled.

Ten years ago, none of the girls would have dared to come. They would have been scared, ashamed. But they were there. Because they've become "girls like other girls".

Ten years ago the crowd would have drawn away in terror and disgust. On this day the crowd applauded, while the girls sang:

"Your presence alleviates our distress
because we know how much you love us."

And when I said to them, "Which of you will kiss me?" all twelve of them put their arms round my neck. With all their lipstick on my cheeks I must have looked like a much tattooed Indian!

The next day at the Pax cinema, "the young inmates of the Hansen sanatorium" were offering an evening's entertainment to the people. But would the people come? Just think, lepers! And in a cinema in town – in the middle of the town!

The Pax seats six hundred. There were more than a thousand people to acclaim (the word isn't too strong) our little invalids who danced with ravishing grace, accompanied by the excellent Folk Group of Martinique.

Our dancers and their friends gave the same performance again forty-eight hours later. But this time in their home, that is to say at the Clarac Hospital. The public had been to see them in a cinema in town. But would they dare go to the lepers' home ground?

The performance was due to start at 6. By 4.30 there wasn't a seat left. And the overflow crowded in as best it could. It was a real crowd, which had been making its way up to the Hansen Sanatorium all day.

It was 31 January 1960, Seventh World Leprosy Day.

In the morning pontifical high Mass had been celebrated by Mgr Varin de la Brunelière in the presence of the Prefect and all the authorities of the region. Then the crowd went to visit the various departments in the sanatorium. An exhibition of handwork and *objets d'art* made by the sick was invaded and ransacked. Who spoke of fear? Anyone who had done so, or had been frightened to touch a leper's hand, would have been laughed to scorn. Poor idiot! All day it was happiness, song and laughter at the sanatorium.

As night fell, everyone went away with regret, but with joy in their hearts.

And we left too. But we returned after dinner, for the celebrations weren't yet over. That night there was a dance. A dance for lepers? For lepers and non-lepers. To which were invited all who were ready to dance with lepers. They danced to an electrophone, a Seventh World Day present. There were certainly some eyes that closed, and the pace sometimes slowed down. To tell the truth, most of our friends were dropping with sleep after all the events of the day. One of the little singers of the aerodrome asked me to dance with her. For the first time in my life I chided myself for my idiocy at not having learnt to dance when I was young!

Extracts from *Une Bataille pas comme les autres* (A Fight that is different) (1964), and unpublished works.

TWO VILLAGES

THE VILLAGE wasn't marked on any map. If it had been swallowed up by an earthquake, there would certainly have been a *Te Deum* at the nearest cathedral. No road led there. When "decent people" found themselves in its neighbourhood they shut the windows of their cars so as not to inhale the fetid air. There was no church in the damned village, for how could anyone believe (short of sacrilege) that there could be a God for the sort of people who lived there?

Most of them were recorded as dead in the registers of their native places. It was easier like that. Others weren't recorded at all. Administratively, they had never been born. That made things easier still. They didn't exist. And that was the end of it.

Or rather that would have been the end of it if they had consented to die discreetly, without disturbing the happy people. But the trouble was that those lepers (for you will have guessed the nature of the people in question), whether "dead" or "unborn", were very much alive.

But as Society didn't recognize their existence, neither did the law. How can you arrest a corpse? Or put a ghost into gaol? With the result that they went in for all sorts of pastimes, of which the clandestine distillation of alcohol was the least immoral and the most harmless.

One naïve policeman wanted to do something about it – either he hadn't understood, or had understood too much. However, the matter was quickly dealt with – he was transferred to the other side of the country.

And the village continued not to be marked on men's maps, the village where drunken ghosts distilled the water of death.[1]

* * *

Ten years later. At the other end of the world the President of the Republic, on the occasion of World Leprosy Day, went to give his good wishes to the lepers.

Leading an imposing procession, he followed the new road which has replaced the shameful little track of days gone by. And by way of signposts – as if there was still a fear that people didn't know the way – great hoardings struck his eye.

He read: "We have planted a thousand palm-oil trees." And further on: "We have cleared twenty-five hectares of ground, and organized the cultivation of crops." And still further on: "We have created four artificial meadows."

Who were the "we"? The lepers.

Here the lepers have a name, an identity, a family, a future.

[1] In French "*eau de mort*", a play on words as "*eau de vie*" means brandy (Tr.).

They have reintegrated themselves into society by their work.
They work: so they are men.
They are men: so they sing.

*   *   *

Between the desperate lepers of the past, pursuing their
tragic industry, and the joyful peasants of nowadays, there lies
love, triumphant and unconquerable.

IT IS FORBIDDEN TO TOUCH LEPERS

The head of the leper-colony bore an astonishing resemblance
to General Durakin. He was a good man basically, and made touching attempts to interest himself in the sick – which showed, alas,
that it did not come easily to him.

A leper girl was introduced to me who spoke French and answered to the somewhat cruel name of Stella. A sad star indeed!
I held out my hand: she put hers behind her back. "It's forbidden," she said tonelessly. Durakin was embarrassed. As I was not
in the best of moods myself that morning I told him what I
thought of such infantile stupidity. And I added: "Does the rule
apply to kissing?" Victory! The regulations hadn't envisaged
such a contingency. So I put my arms round Stella's neck. . . .
Everyone now drew near. They argued, jostled each other to
get close to me, in the hope that I would pull their ear or tweak
their nose. . . .

And to think that it's so *easy* to give happiness . . . .

IT WAS SO SIMPLE

The doctor who discovered the wretched woman during a tour
of the bush took her off without a word. She consented. It didn't
matter to her whether she died here or there. . . .

She was hospitalized.

As for the child, it was so simple that it seemed perfectly normal. The doctor's wife had a baby of the same age, a fine baby
plump with its mother's milk who didn't, however, exhaust the
supply. So why shouldn't there be enough for two? There was
enough for two. The little boarder settled in. Shy at first, and
rather cautious, he finally sucked with a will, and that was the sign
that he was saved.

The leper woman was cured and went back to her village. But where are the doctor and his young wife? I haven't the faintest idea, and they would probably be amazed at my remembering all this. For him it was hardly so much as an incident. As for her, she did what she did because she had a kind heart and wanted to help. But without any idea of being a heroine or a saint. If you said to her, "You really were marvellous that time!" she wouldn't know what you were talking about.

It's people like that who've won the "Fight against Leprosy".

Let good well-meaning people meditate on this, those who think they intend to nurse lepers one day and so raise their eyes to heaven waiting for the halo that never comes. . . .

THANK YOU

When I visit lepers nothing exasperates me more than hearing a nurse padding along behind me with a flask of disinfectant and a napkin so as to "purify" me after I've shaken a patient's hand. I understand perfectly that doctors should disinfect their hands because they're always touching wounds and putting on and taking off dressings. It's valid for all wounds as for all illnesses, even non-contagious ones. It's a matter of hygiene, if not of simple cleanliness.

But having disinfectant ostentatiously poured over one's hands when one's visiting lepers is the same thing as proclaiming: "You're a danger for us healthy people. We must take our precautions. Not to put too fine a point upon it, we're afraid of you."

It's always absurd and often loathsome.

*   *   *

The nurse charged with that pitiable task on the day in question was a former leper who had been cured. He followed me with all the look of a beaten dog. He'd signed to me two or three times, but as I'd turned away my head he hadn't insisted. However, once my visit was over he took his courage in both hands and blocked my way, head down, flask and towel in hand.

I was tired and could stand it no longer.

"No," I said, "no. Haven't you understood yet?"

Then his face, which had been so morose, brightened. He looked at me with eyes full of joy and moist with tears.

"Oh," he said, "do you mean. . . ." The rest of the phrase

remained unsaid. There was a silence. Then in a low voice he said: "Thank you."

THE BEST LOVE STORY

Once upon a time there were a man and a woman who loved each other.

He had no fingers and his leprosy was now starting in on his feet. She was devoured by a cancer whose horrible and implacable advance was easy to follow. An accursed man and a woman from whom everyone fled in horror. No work, of course, for either of them. Poverty. But love.

With infinite patience and tenderness he set himself with his fingerless hands to renew the nauseous dressings that no one wanted to go near. The clumsy gestures of the sick man drew little cries of pain from the dying woman. Only then did his tears fall.

How long would it go on?

One morning, as I was visiting other lepers, I was told this story. Having made my way through a maze of unspeakable hovels, stinking with filth and mud, I reached the ill-fated hut.

The woman had died in the night. He had then dressed her, covering up the loathsome gaping wound. He had put a rosary between her long thin fingers, and he was there, beside her, saying nothing, looking at nothing. . . .

It was terrible, as you may imagine. But it was over.

But wait, because it was now that it began; it was from now that it was terrible.

It was 86°F in the hut. To bury the dead woman "they" were demanding 36,000 francs. Who were "they"? I don't know. Had they the right? I don't know. 36,000 francs were required. At once. He had nothing. For long now he had given his all to postpone this day. He was beside her, saying nothing, looking at nothing. The dead woman was there, with no coffin. It was 86°F in the hut. 36,000 francs were required. At once.

And you know why.

I handed him the money. He took it almost without speaking. Perhaps he was waiting for this miracle: he had certainly deserved it.

And we went away again, my wife, my friends and I, our hearts rent. And dazzled.

THE GENERAL AND THE SULTAN

Zinder. – The Sultan of Zinder was waiting at the air-field when our plane touched down. Golden robe, white coat, sword at his side, baton in hand. His court, ministers and dignitaries were around him, attentive to his least gesture. He was very impressive in full dress, his face more than half concealed beneath the veil. His eyes shone with life; we could see that he was smiling though we couldn't see the smile itself.

Greetings, respects and compliments were exchanged. Then suddenly the Sultan's face beamed with delight. Though he was standing still you felt he was ready to spring forward. He said nothing, but his eyes and heart were eloquent. I looked at the person he was looking at. By my side was my friend General-Doctor[1] Pierre Richet, and he, too, was motionless but beaming. . . .

* * *

Thirty years ago in a Niger laid low with the cruellest endemic diseases, a young lieutenant-doctor rode his horse day after day along its tracks. He was accompanied by an assistant, a smiling silent young man. Side by side on horseback they covered more than 40,000 kilometres in three years. A world tour. Not to break a record but to vaccinate and nurse, to bring hope, comfort and cure. For three long years they traversed all the paths of Niger, inspired by the same ideal and the same faith.

Then the lieutenant-doctor was assigned to another post. He became a captain. And then, and then . . .

As for his nurse-assistant . . .

* * *

Thirty years had passed. And here they were face to face. The young lieutenant of times gone by, still young, had become General Doctor Inspector – the highest grade in a career that he had honoured and served so well. The silent, reserved assistant – so reserved that he'd never said he belonged to the royal family – had been elected to succeed on his father's death. He was now the Chief, the Master, the Sultan.

We then repaired to the palace and, the official speeches having been made, they were able to talk together. In the language of the

[1] I.e. Doctor with the rank of General (Tr.).

country, naturally. The General knows it well. And the memories blossomed forth like flowers. We listened, entranced, knowing nothing about it all. The General reminisced, and the Sultan, who had recaptured the gestures and voice of the past, agreed with everything. "Yes, of course, General; perfectly true, General." Then, profiting by a silence, he said softly, "Do you remember when you were hunting that elephant, and how you bawled at me because I didn't arrive soon enough. . . ." And they laughed, a laugh half-strangled by emotion. The lieutenant and the nurse-assistant re-lived their exhilarating past. And I remembered in my turn. I remembered . . . and then I noticed the tall black Tuareg silently swinging the huge fly-swatter above His Majesty's head. And that was the end.

No, there was a magnificent moment as we were leaving. The adieux were made according to etiquette and protocol. It was General Richet's turn. Then in a low voice he murmured a name . . . the name of times gone by, not the complicated name of the Sultan, but his name as a nursing-assistant, his name as a man. And they fell into each other's arms. Now they dared not look at each other because both had tears in their eyes.

*   *   *

As he was walking by my side His Majesty broke the silence with, "Did you know that I have thirty-five children?" And as I made a gesture of surprise, he added modestly, "That's counting the girls, of course. . . ."

Yes, I feel at home with the Sultan of Zinder.

ESPIÈGLE

That's her name and I can do nothing about it. And even if I could, I wouldn't. For you only have to look at her to see how well it suits her[1]. Espiègle is no longer young – she's been twenty-five years in this leper-colony. To do honour to her civil status she had remained for half a century astoundingly young, dynamic and gay. But protocol . . . that's what gets her. . . .

That day I was surrounded by all the principal personalities of the country – but what did that matter? Espiègle didn't see them, didn't hear them, shoved them aside so as to throw her

---

[1] The word means "rogue", "monkey" (Tr.).

arms round my neck. She squeezed me, stifled me, crying, "Papa Raoul, Papa Raoul. . . ." Then suddenly, as if her heart was bursting: "My pet, my darling. . . ." Which was rather unexpected. Then she relinquished me to throw her arms round my wife. Then relinquished her to hug me again. . . .

Suddenly a noise spread through the crowd – the police were coming, the police!

The police? No, surely not. Anger rose within me, but while I was disentangling myself from Espiègle's embraces, I heard the sound of clapping from the lepers. I was totally bewildered. I looked . . . then clapped in my turn.

For the police, today, consisted of the police brass band. They were coming to give the lepers a concert, and each played with all his heart. And the sick clapped till they couldn't go on. And to my surprise I found myself shouting "Encore!"

I'd certainly never imagined that I would find myself applauding the arrival of the police in a leper-colony!

FROM ISOLATION TO POLLING-BOOTH[1]

"As they're men like other men, why shouldn't they join in?"

"Join in what?"

"Politics, of course. They're citizens, with the same rights as the others. They vote. . . ."

"Surely they can be spared that leprosy. . . ."

"Why? That leprosy – more contagious than the other, admittedly – is the sign of their reintegration into society. Then surely you've noticed how those abandoned and forgotten men have suddenly become interesting?"

"To whom?"

"But to the candidates, of course! Lepers never have so many champions as at election time."

"Yes, but after the elections?"

"The successful candidate will let them down again. But that only proves, doesn't it, that they're men like other men. Of course I don't like them to quarrel too much, less still that 'hitting' argumentation should develop; but election meetings that end up as wrestling matches – that doesn't only happen in leper-colonies."

[1] A play of words in the French, as polling-booth is *"isoloir"* (Tr.).

"All the same. . . ."

"Excuse me, but for me those scuffles are a sign of victory."

* * *

The other day at the leper-colony of Akata there were little cubicles set up in the recreation room, modestly draped with red muslin. I thought they were there for the sick to undress in before consultation. But my friends thought that a great joke. "But look, you have those in France too on election day. What do you call them? – I can't remember – polling-booths." And with sudden solemnity: "Out of respect for universal suffrage."

May universal suffrage forgive me, but I was seized with a terrible giggling-fit.

From isolation to the *isoloir*!

I don't know what was the result of the elections, but I know who were the winners.

THE FINEST CABBAGES IN THE WORLD

The oasis of Miria in the region of Zinder. The water leaps up, it's an Eden, a paradise in a purgatory of scorching rocks.

He broke through the crowd of the curious and the circle of friends and officials around me, and stood before me, tall and straight, holding in his arms a basket full of cabbages. In his arms, because of the condition of his hands. No fingers at all. Just a little stump of palm.

He looked into my face and said: "Father of lepers, listen to my story. Yes, I've had the disease. Yes, I was a fool, and when the nurse came to treat me, I fled. So, you see, I've lost my fingers and hands. When the disease started attacking my feet I realized my idiocy and came along. The doctor ordered the remedy and the nurse brought it every visit. My feet have been saved. But the doctor isn't Allah and through my stupidity I've lost my hands.

"Nevertheless, I kept up my courage. I didn't want to be a parasite, a bit of human refuse, but 'a man who works and sings,' as you told us. So I learnt to use my hands – without hands. It was hard. A hundred times my tool fell to the ground. A hundred times I knelt down to pick it up. And I started again. And I learnt to dig without hands, to sow seed without hands, to harvest my

S

crop without hands. I've just brought in my first vegetables.
You see – they're cabbages. They're good ones, aren't they?
I think they're the finest cabbages in the world; they come from
my garden. I give them to you because it's you who taught me
that I am a man. Now I'm sure of it, because I earn my living."

The crowd was silent. As for me I could say nothing, do nothing, except kiss him.

TWO MEMORIES

"For sick and hungry children," said the priest, holding out a
begging hand. The man was in a hurry, obviously; still, he had to
stop. He did so with bad grace but he had to, because it was a
street and people were looking. He rummaged in his pocket and
brought out 25 francs (West African, i.e. ·50 N.F.) and thrust
them into the missionary's hand. And before the latter could take
a breath, he went on: "Excuse me, but I'm on my way to the airport to fetch a dog, a pointer, that's been sent to me." Then,
retracing the step or two he'd taken: "They're asking 80,000
francs for its transport. Isn't it a scandal!"

Yes, Monsieur, it is a scandal.

But I'm not thinking of the dog.

* * *

Thérèse was my fiancée. This had been decided when I first
visited that leper-colony, and everyone was delighted about it.
And we had photographs taken with me with my arms round her.

I have just found her again. Thérèse is married now (not to me!).
She's cured and has found a job on the spot. She does the laundry.
It's hard work, certainly, but she's never been afraid of that.
And she earns her living.

And my "fiancée" said to me: "Papa Raoul, now I've pulled
through, and have enough to live on, and as I have no children
of my own, I'd like to adopt a sick child in some other country.
A little girl who would be mine though far away and to whom I'd
send part of my earnings every month so that she'd get better in
her turn, and work in her turn, and become in her turn 'a woman
like other women'."

There was a moment's silence, and she heard me murmur, "It's
a scandal."

"Why, Papa Raoul?" she asked, growing pale. "Isn't it a good idea?"

"I was thinking about a squalid, repulsive and hideous animal," I said. "Forgive me." And I kissed her.

... AND A TESTIMONY

The General Hospital on Reunion Island, Dermatology Department. Doctor Sarthre.

I was visiting.

"This is a leper," he said. "Not that one, this one."

"Haven't you a special room for them?" I asked. It was already so good to see them in a hospital for other patients too, like everyone else.

"A special room? Why? They're patients like everyone else. Same régime, same nursing, and, when their condition makes it necessary, the same isolation precautions. What do you want more?"

"Me? Oh, nothing. Absolutely nothing. Bravo!"

Later I said to him:

"Have you enough beds?"

"Not always. Some patients with other illnesses needn't really be here any more. But they're still weak. So as there's plenty of room now at the leper-hospital I've proposed that they should go there. They know that they'll be well looked after, well fed, free."

"And do they go? Do the non-lepers go in with the lepers?"

"Yes. My only fear is that there may be too many candidates. But as they're so comfortable there, what can you do about it?"

"Me? Oh, nothing. Absolutely nothing. It's victory."

AN IMPORTANT WEDDING

At the *Madeleine*? At *Saint-Honoré-d'Eylau*? No.

Who carried the bride's train? There wasn't a train. And there was no one who was anybody in the congregation. There was just a crowd vibrating with happiness; a crowd of people formerly despised, banished, spurned, and for whom this wedding was more than an important celebration: it was their own celebration.

The bridegroom was one of the "four musketeers" who, on my

first visit to Santa Barbara, had decided never to leave me as long
as I was in Greece. As you will have guessed, he was a leper.

He received regular treatment and was soon delivered of his
disease. Then everyone's intelligent friendship made him a man
like other men. He found work and lived in a small house with his
mother, loved by everyone.

Together we went to the theatre, to concerts, and dined in some
of the enchanting little restaurants in Athens. Finally I had the
feeling that being constantly in my company might be a risk for
him. . . .

Then came the crowning glory. He met a girl and was drawn to
her, and she was not exactly indifferent to him, so he dared one
day to ask her to marry him.

This is what he wrote me about it:

"Her parents have written to me as follows: we heard Raoul
Follereau when he spoke at the Parnassos. He convinced us and
we believe in him. So why should we refuse you our daughter,
since you are really a man like other men, and you love each
other?"

This happiness is our victory.

PRAYERS

LORD, teach us not to love ourselves any more,
not to be content with loving our dear ones,
with loving those whom we love.

Lord, teach us to think only of others,
to love those, first, who are not loved.

Lord, hurt us with the suffering of others.

Lord, give us the grace to realize
that at every minute of our lives,
of our happy lives, protected by you,
there are millions of human beings
who are your children,
who are our brothers,
and who are dying of hunger,
and who have not deserved to die of hunger,
and who are dying of cold,
and who have not deserved to die of cold. . . .

Lord, have pity on all the poor people in the world.

Have pity on the lepers
to whom you smiled so often in the past on this
    earth,
on the millions of lepers
who stretch out towards your mercy
their hands without fingers, their arms without
    hands. . . .

And forgive us for having for too long
and through shameful fear
abandoned them. . . .
Lord, do not allow us any more to be happy alone.

Grant us anguish in face of universal want,
and free us from ourselves
             . . . if such is your will.

PRAYER BEFORE JULIETTE'S TOMB

Beside the little innocent child
who died of wanting to love
those who didn't love each other,
grant us, Lord, the gift of love.

The gift of loving the whole earth,
of loving everything on the whole earth,
and especially men, our brothers,
who are often so unhappy.
Of loving, too, the happy people
who are often poor devils.

Grant us the strength to love
those, first, who don't love us,
those, first, who don't love anyone,
those for whom, when the hour strikes,
all is consummated
for ever.

Let our life be the reflection of your love.

*   *   *

To love the neighbour at the other end of the
      world,
to love the stranger who lives just near us,
to console, to forgive, to bless,
to stretch out our arms. . . .

To love those who wear themselves out in
      sterile activity
centred on themselves,
the selfish, the sceptical, the destructive,
to make a spring gush up
in the pale desert of their hearts.

To deliver those who are lonely,
to raise up those who are on their knees,
to free closed hearts

with a smile:
to love, to love. . . .

Then a huge Spring will convulse the world,
and everything will burst into bloom within us.

LORD, I WOULD SO LIKE . . .

Lord, I would so like to help others
   to live,
all others, my brothers,
who labour and suffer,
without knowing why,
while waiting for death to deliver them.

To work so as to eat,
to eat so as to work again,
with, at the end, old age and death;
no, that is not the Peace that you promised.

Lord, I would so like to help others
   to live . . .
without the insulting alms
of sterile compassion.
To stop the poor from dying, that's good.
But if it's so as to let them die of hunger
   all their life,
if it's to make their life an endless death,
I become an accomplice in this murder
because I have in excess what they need to live.

To share out the wealth of the world in
   friendship
is to play our part in your creation.

*   *   *

Lord, I would so like to help others,
all others, my brothers,
who fight and dispute
in the void.
To tear each other, to trample each other, so as
   to amass, greedily,

the heart bound, the conscience submissive,
a little of the needy money
that corrupts so many destinies;
or so as to win – as they say –
some minutes of non-existent time
from Paradise:
no, that is not the Peace that you promised.

*   *   *

Lord, I would so like to help others,
all others, my brothers,
who reel in their solitude. . . .

Permit me to spend my life
trying to deliver them
    from their speed, so that they may reach you,
    from their turmoil, so that they may hear you,
    from their wealth, so that they may understand
      you
    and from their petty vanity,
so that they may know the Peace that you promised,
                if such is your will.